Lincoln's Railroad Man:
Herman Haupt

Brigadier General Herman Haupt. (National Archives)

Lincoln's Railroad Man: Herman Haupt

Francis A. Lord

Rutherford . Madison . Teaneck
Fairleigh Dickinson University Press

Associated University Presses, Inc.
Cranbury, New Jersey 08512

SBN: 8386–7343–0
Printed in the United States of America

Brigadier General Herman Haupt. (National Archives)

SOURCES AND
ACKNOWLEDGMENTS

The main sources for this book are the Haupt, Stanton, and Lincoln papers in the Library of Congress and the National Archives. Haupt's *Reminiscences* and the *Official Records of the Union and Confederate Armies* have proved valuable for many details throughout the study. These details have been enriched and augmented by material from numerous personal reminiscences, regimental histories, and general works as listed in the bibliography at the end of the book.

Thanks are due to Dr. Robert S. Chamberlain and Professor William Culp Darrah for their many helpful suggestions on material used in this book. I am especially indebted to Mrs. Jean K. Haupt of Nazareth, Pennsylvania, for her assistance on details of the Haupt genealogy. Grateful acknowledgment is made for permission to quote from published works and authors as follows:

Professor Samuel RicheyKamm, Wheaton College.

Houghton Mifflin Company for *The Diary of Gideon Welles*.

Dodd, Mead and Company, Inc. for *Lincoln and the Civil War* by Tyler Dennett.

David S. Sparks, author of *Inside Lincoln's Army*.
The map, designed expressly for this work, was drawn
by Mr. Holly Byrne. His painstaking care and extensive
research to insure the accuracy of the map are sincerely
appreciated.

CONTENTS

CONTENTS

LIST OF ILLUSTRATIONS

INTRODUCTION

Herman Haupt, inventive genius and virtual founder of military railroading in the United States, has remained comparatively unknown to many Americans. This lack of recognition has been due in large part to Haupt's early retirement from active duty with the Federal armies and also to the pettiness of his fellow railroader, Daniel C. McCallum, who deliberately failed to even mention Haupt in the final report of United States Military Railroads at the end of the Civil War. Haupt's removal was effected by Edwin M. Stanton and thus the railroader joined an elite company of men whose brilliant services to the Republic were cut short by the Secretary of War. But from April 1862 until after Gettysburg, Haupt's superiors and fellow officers were very well aware of his amazing abilities in logistical support of the Army of the Potomac as well as his sound strategical concepts. Haupt developed a construction corps which served the railroads well right up to the end of the war. His energy and alertness kept Washington informed of the progress of the Battle of Second Bull Run after Pope's communications had been completely severed with Lincoln and the War Department. "For meritorious services in the most recent operations against the enemy near Manassas," Haupt was thanked in the presence of Lincoln and the Cabinet, and was commissioned brigadier general. His superlative efforts had not gone unnoticed. On September 1, 1862, as Pope's army retreated into the defenses of Washington, Lincoln's private secretary, John Hay, said of Haupt:

> It is due in great measure to his indomitable will, that Army movements have been characterized by such energy and celerity for the last few days. There is one man who seems thoroughly to reflect and satisfy . . . [Lincoln] in everything he undertakes . . . [Haupt] has, as Chase says, a Major General's head on his shoulders. The President is particularly struck with the business-like character of his despatch, telling in the fewest words the information most sought for, which contrasted so strongly with the weak, whiney, vague, and incorrect despatches of the Whilom General-in-Chief.

At Fredericksburg and Chancellorsville Haupt loyally and efficiently served the Union, while his services during the Gettysburg campaign were little short of incredible. Utilizing a rail line which normally ran only three or four trains daily, Haupt, by a well-regulated convoy system, forwarded daily 1,500 tons of essential supplies to Meade's army, with a return load of 2,000 to 4,000 wounded. After the battle, Haupt urged Meade to follow up and crush Lee. Moreover, he showed how the enemy could be intercepted by forwarding troops to Front Royal and cutting off the escape routes. But Meade refused, claiming his men were tired; and the war dragged on for nearly two more years.

Between periods of active campaigning Haupt contributed some of his most valuable inventions and innovations. He introduced the system of interchangeable parts in the reconstruction of bridges. His bridge trusses could be put together so quickly that a subordinate claimed to be able to build a bridge as fast as a dog could trot, while observers noted that "the Yankees can build bridges quicker than the Rebs can burn them down."

Haupt achieved results despite continued opposition from the Military. On one occasion General Samuel D. Sturgis informed Haupt that "I have just sent a guard to your office to put you under arrest for disobedience of my orders in failing to transport my command." Haupt *had* disobeyed this general's orders. In the midst of a crucial campaign, Sturgis had demanded special trains to move 10,000 men, plus horses and impedimenta, the ridiculously short distance of eighteen miles. This demand was refused; the railway was a single-track line with all too few locomotives and rolling stock. What little equipment was available was urgently needed to move up supplies; the men could march. Moreover, with the enemy only eighteen miles away and the area alive with guerrilla bands and cavalry patrols, the men in a troop train would have been helpless in case of attack. When Haupt telegraphed his superior for support he was informed that no military officer had the authority to interfere with the railroad. On showing this reply to Sturgis, who was insisting on his "rights," that worthy told Haupt to "take his damned railroad."

But the general stubbornly refused to cooperate, with the result that traffic on this one-track line was halted for a very critical twenty-four hour period, while 10,000 much-needed men were prevented from helping their hard-pressed comrades at Second Bull Run.

There were constant disputes between Haupt and the medical officers who detained trains for such long periods as to wreck Haupt's scheduled supplying of the front line troops. During one campaign Haupt was forced to telegraph the assistant Secretary of War:

I fear that I may be compelled tonight to do what may
appear inhuman—turn out the sick in the street. Doctors will
persist in sending sick, often without papers, to get them off
their hands, and we cannot send forward the troops if we
must run over trains to Washington with sick to stand for
hours unloaded. My first care is to send forward troops, next
forage and subsistence.

The refusal of line officers to cooperate with the Military Railroads, especially in promptly loading and unloading cars cost the Federals dearly. Even enemy saboteurs
and train wreckers did less damage than did those officers who constantly attempted to run the trains themselves. As late as Gettysburg, Haupt found confusion
everywhere. Roads were blocked and cars were not unloaded; supplies were left standing a long time. As a
result all rail traffic was prevented from moving. Many
of the cars were being sent back without being unloaded,
while the wounded were lying for hours with no facilities
for getting them back to the base hospitals in the North.
Fortunately, Haupt's superiors backed him up and by
strong measures, taken on the spot, Haupt was able to
overcome this confusion and get the trains running
smoothly.

Haupt's contributions to railroading were very significant, both before and after the war. However, except
when necessary for continuity and clarity of his military
status, this study is primarily concerned with Haupt's
service with the Army during 1862-1863. He did not
serve in any capacity after September 1863. But his
famous principles of military railroading, coupled with
his inspirational training of subordinates, went far in
assuring Federal commanders, East and West, of sound
dependence on their railroads during the 1864-1865
campaigns.

In analyzing the career of Haupt, one realizes that he is studying a controversial figure. Haupt was a scrupulously honest man. Much of the opposition he encountered was due to his brash honesty; he simply did not care who was hurt if truth was on his side. He suffered much from opponents, though Haupt himself was not without fault. Certainly one of these faults was a lack of flexibility in his relations with people of whom he did not approve; in fact one such instance involved his association with Cameron and eventually cost him an appointment as Assistant Secretary of War, a position he coveted.

Of all the commanders under whom he served, Haupt was only on really cordial terms with McDowell, yet he served all loyally, very quietly but efficiently. Moreover, his penetrating analysis of such divergent personalities as McClellan, Pope, Burnside, and Meade has been surprisingly well corroborated by the verdict of capable historians. An exception must be made in Haupt's appraisal of Gideon Welles; few contemporary historians can accept Haupt's lack of enthusiasm about Lincoln's Secretary of the Navy.

Haupt was very aware of his capabilities. In the construction and operation of railroads he believed he could render more valuable assistance than in any other field. Haupt maintained correctly that this was his specialty and while others could perhaps be more successful in command of a corps or army, he would "yield to none in experience, energy, resource and ability to organize so far as railroads were concerned." Moreover, one of the main sources of dissatisfaction in some quarters with Haupt was that he opposed speculation in the Government. Unfortunately typical of Haupt was his tactlessness in asserting his lack of confidence in high officials of the War and Navy Departments.

Although one regrets his lack of tact and his subjective analysis of several officials above him, his spirit is worthy of commendation. As he told Lincoln: "What others have *failed* to do in the management of the railroads, I have been willing to try to do . . ." (Haupt to Lincoln, January 16, 1864. Haupt Papers, Library of Congress.) While his patriotism was of a high order, he was continually antagonizing others by his readiness to offer suggestions in fields which were not his direct concern. To some he must have appeared as a "holier than thou" meddler who considered himself as omnipotent in every aspect of the war effort. He maintained that government contractors should pay back their profits into the Treasury. Men like Hooker would have winced had they known that Haupt believed that "officers in the field should dispense with the wines, liquors, luxuries, and superfluities which encumber trains and destroy the mobility of the army." Haupt went on to point out that "all who profess to be patriots should give some evidence by denying themselves . . . and making real sacrifices." He believed he had done this himself but considered it only his duty. (Haupt to Lincoln, December 22, 1862. Library of Congress.)

Unnecessary destruction of government property, even in wartime, disturbed Haupt greatly. Writing to Halleck after the evacuation of the base at Aquia Creek, he said that the burning of the wharf, buildings, and bridges was both unnecessary and "highly censorable." (*Official Records of the Union and Confederate Armies* [hereafter cited as *Official Records*], Series I, Vol. 12, part 3, p. 813.)

Although he was a graduate of West Point, Haupt did not strive for high military rank. He did believe that he could have risen high in the military service if he had so desired. In fact, he told Stanton that he could have obtained any position he wanted had he been so inclined, pointing out that his classmates and others who had graduated later had become general officers. But Haupt believed he could best serve his Country in his profession of a railroader. (Haupt to Stanton, May 28, 1862. Stanton Papers, Library of Congress.)

As a railroader, he preferred service in the field to any desk job. Early in his military service he informed Stanton that he wanted to have nothing to do with contracts, jobs, or money disbursements. When it was necessary to make purchases, he would do so through his administrative chief, Daniel C. McCallum.

Red tape irritated this man of action. One of his head-on collisions with Stanton was occasioned by the Secretary's absurd insistence on paper work involving receipts to be furnished by railroad personnel. (*Ibid.*) Even more illustrative of how Haupt could get things done with a minimum of regulations was his deft handling of an individual's request for a pass to travel on the railroad for the purpose of distributing much-needed medical supplies to Falmouth. Fully aware that he was not permitted to give the man (a clergyman of the Christian Commission) a pass, Haupt signed an order making him a brakeman on the railroad and forthwith ordered him to report to Falmouth!

Much of Haupt's success can be attributed to his enormous capacity for hard work. For example, in his testimony to the Committee on the Conduct of the War, Haupt described at some length how he worked. After discussing the destruction of transportation facilities between Aquia Creek and Falmouth, Haupt went on to report:

I commenced operations as soon as possible—within two or three days; I set men to work in the woods to cut cross-ties, transported rails from Alexandria; worked night and day, using lanterns at night, and in three days reconstructed the three miles of road, and in about two weeks completed the whole of the road and rebuilt the bridge from Aquia Creek to Falmouth. . . .

(*Report,* Committee on the Conduct of the War, Part III [1863], p. 427. This committee was composed originally of three senators—Benjamin F. Wade of Ohio, Zachariah Chandler of Michigan, Andrew Johnson of Tennessee—and four representatives—D. W. Gooch of Massachusetts, G. W. Julian of Indiana, John Covode of Pennsylvania, Moses F. Odell of New York.) Although civilians and strongly politically oriented, they were determined to "get on" with the war. Much of the testimony they elicited is valuable in analyzing military operations during the war.

Impatient with the dilatory tactics of a McClellan or with the playboy antics of a Hooker, the dedicated Haupt drove himself and his subordinates to accomplish miracles in military railroading during some of the most critical months of the Civil War. His accomplishments were a significant factor in Federal operations of 1862 and 1863, and inspired his subordinates who performed so brilliantly under Grant and Sherman during 1864 and 1865.

Lincoln's Railroad Man:
Herman Haupt

1

DEVELOPMENT OF THE RAILROADER

The name Haupt is of Teutonic origin and is found in old German and early American records in such varied spellings as *Haub, Haup, Haubt,* and *Haupt.* The latter spelling is the one in most common use in America. During the middle of the eighteenth Century several "Haupts" arrived in this Country. They came mainly from the Palatinate. Several settled in Pennsylvania and it is from one of these immigrants that Herman Haupt descended, although the complete line is obscure.

Herman Haupt was born in Philadelphia, March 26, 1817.[1] His father, Jacob Haupt, died in 1828, leaving a widow and six children. The family was in straitened circumstances and Haupt's appointment to West Point by Andrew Jackson must have been gratefully accepted. The original appointment, accomplished through the help of John B. Steriger, congressman from Pennsylvania, was made in 1830, but since Haupt was then only thirteen, the appointment was made effective for the entering class of 1831.[2] On graduation, Haupt was but eighteen years of age when commissioned brevet second lieutenant, 3rd Infantry, on July 1, 1835. At the Academy Haupt ranked 31 in a class of 56 and was the last surviving member of that class when he died. Of the 56 members, 13 reached the rank of general; 23 died before the outbreak of the Civil War; 9 did not serve on either side, while at least 5 joined the Confederate Army. Several served in the Seminole War and were killed in action. Among the more prominent of Haupt's classmates were: Montgomery Blair, Lincoln's Postmaster General; George G. Meade; Mansena R. Patrick, Provost Marshal of the Army of the Potomac; and Joseph Roberts, author of an excellent handbook of artillery which was widely used during the Civil War.[3]

Like many officers of his era, Haupt resigned from the army shortly after graduation to enter civilian life. In Haupt's case, his service in the Army was only three months; he resigned September 30th of the year he graduated. This became somewhat of a family tradition; his son, Lewis M. Haupt, who graduated from the Academy on June 17, 1867, resigned from the service September 20, 1869.[4]

On acceptance of his resignation, Herman Haupt became an assistant engineer and was employed in surveying a railroad from Norristown to Allentown in Pennsylvania and later in locating the Norristown and Valley Railroad. The next year (1836) Haupt, aged nineteen, was appointed principal assistant in Pennsylvania and worked in railroad construction on the Western Maryland Railroad.

Little is known of Haupt's family life. Haupt's *Reminiscences* contain only brief references to his home life or the individuals who made up the family circle. At the age of twenty-one he married Ann Cecelia Keller, daughter of his pastor, Reverend Benjamin Keller of Gettysburg. According to Haupt, she was a "lively, cheerful and accomplished woman,"[5] while Haupt's classmate Mansena R. Patrick noted that she was "wonderfully young" to be the mother of so many children.[6] She shared Haupt's fortunes for fifty-three years and bore him eleven children, of whom Lewis M. Haupt was the third son.[7]

In 1840 Haupt was hired to assist in building the York and Wrightsville Railroad, and while engaged in this work he became interested in the engineering theories and practical applications of bridge construction. A number of lattice bridges had been contracted for in connection with the York and Wrightsville Railroad, but Haupt believed them not sturdy enough for the duty they were to perform. Accordingly, this young engineer contacted prominent railroad engineers in the country to get their ideas as to the proper way to calculate the strength of a trussed bridge. He was amazed to discover that, generally speaking, not an engineer in the United States, or even in the world, had even attempted to calculate the strength of a truss, except for some simple triangulation, which did not give specific figures for the counter brace. Nor was it recognized that strains at different points of the same truss system varied greatly. Typically, Haupt believed that he could come up with a solution and searched intensively for laws governing the transmission of strains and for workable formulae by which such strains could be calculated, including the strength of all trusses. Lacking any reference books or scientific apparatus, he began a series of experiments and eventually discovered that strains could be represented by the ordinates of conic sections, which in turn led to an original but simple method of obtaining formulae and determining strains on beams in all variations of position. As a result of these findings, he was officially credited as the inventor of a method of "Representing strains of geometrical solids; deflections by parabolic areas; and the variable pressures at various parts of beams by the corresponding ordinates of plane curves."[8] This was in 1840, the same year in which he invented an improved lattice bridge truss.

Haupt continued his experiments with models which he designed and constructed, and observed strains of bridges during the passage of trains. He finally arrived at certain conclusions which he published anonymously in 1841 in a pamphlet entitled *Hints on Bridge Construction*. This work attracted much attention and led to some controversy.[9] In 1851, the pamphlet, in expanded form, was published under Haupt's name as *The General Theory of Bridge Construction,* and was a sound contribution to the advance of railroad engineering. This pioneer work became a standard textbook and was well received by such men as Robert Stephenson in England.

However, there were other pioneers in constructing truss bridges during this period. Among these was Squire Whipple (1804-1888), whose *Work on Bridge Building* appeared in 1847; it was a scientific analysis of computation of stresses and the designing of bridge parts.[10] The West Point-trained engineer, George W. Cullum, had published in 1849 his *Military Bridges with India-rubber Pontoons.* This study included an excellent discussion of the use of these bridges during the Mexican War.[11] Moreover, Haupt's future commander in the United States Military Railroads, Daniel Craig McCallum, also specialized in bridge construction, especially for railroads. In 1851, McCallum patented a form of bridge which was later (1859) described in printed form as *McCallum's Inflexible Arched Truss Bridge Explained and Illustrated.*

From 1844 to 1847 Haupt was professor of civil engineering and mathematics at Pennsylvania College. In 1848, the chief engineer of the Pennsylvania Railroad, John Edgar Thomson, visited Haupt, and, impressed with the young man's knowledge of bridges, took him on as his assistant. Soon Haupt was in Harrisburg, examining, criticizing, and making recommendations about the plans of location and construction from all parts of the Pennsylvania Railroad line. When the first division of the line was nearing completion, Haupt was selected as General Superintendent and directed to inspect the principal rail lines in New England for the purpose of examining their accounting systems, organization plans, equipment—in fact, everything connected with the operation of a railroad. On his return, he submitted a plan of organization and management for railroads, with forms and regulations for all branches of a railroad company, which was adopted without change and remained substantially in use for decades.

Moreover, Haupt, after careful analysis of local conditions along the line, demonstrated the wisdom of developing and using the local business of the line, especially in coal, lumber, iron and even agricultural products, by offering reduced seasonal rates. He showed that by increasing the volume of business for the Pennsylvania Railroad the freight business of the line could be very substantially increased. Eventually, this plan for encouraging local industries was adopted, along with the principle of low rates with moderate dividends. Soon after he became General Superintendent, his efforts to establish uniform rates culminated in a conference of trunk-line presidents in New York City, where Haupt took the initiative in effecting an organization and arriving at decisions.[12]

While Haupt was Superintendent of the Pennsylvania Railroad he met Thomas A. Scott, with whom he was to work so closely during the war. Convinced of Scott's abilities, Haupt recommended him for the position of agent and later was instrumental in Scott's appointment to the board of directors of the Pennsylvania line, which he was to serve for thirty years. Scott, in turn, secured Andrew Carnegie, a young telegraph operator, to serve as operator and instructor on the railroad's telegraph service.

In 1853 Haupt informed the Pennsylvania Railroad's Board of Directors that he had accepted the position of Chief Engineer of the Southern Railroad of Mississippi. Haupt recommended that Thomas A. Scott be appointed Assistant Superintendent of the Pennsylvania line, a recommendation which was accepted. Haupt remained with the Southern Railroad[13] for about six months during 1852-1853, and was then recalled to take the position of Chief Engineer of the Pennsylvania Railroad, which he retained until the whole line, including the Allegheny Mountain tunnel, was completed to Pittsburgh.

Three years later Haupt resigned his position as Chief Engineer with the Pennsylvania Railroad to become Chief Engineer and Contractor of the Troy and Greenfield Railroad and Hoosac Tunnel.[14] This change in positions, although difficult to foresee at the time, was for Haupt the most unfortunate decision he ever made. It brought him into direct opposition to powerful interests in a competing railroad and resulted eventually in his financial ruin, and an erosion of his well-earned reputation as a railroad executive. It finally terminated abruptly his service with military railroads and with the Federal service.

The Hoosac Tunnel controversy was extremely bitter and protracted. In 1852, a tunnel route had been surveyed, which would have involved piercing the Hoosac Mountains in northwestern Massachusetts. In 1855, while still Chief Engineer with the Pennsylvania Railroad, Haupt had been requested to make an examination of the proposed route and reported favorably on the feasibility of constructing the tunnel, which was to be nearly five miles in length. He was prevailed upon to assist in raising capital for the tunnel's construction; some of this capital came from Haupt's associates in the Pennsylvania Railroad. The contract, amounting to $4,-000,000, was signed in 1856, at which time Haupt resigned from the Pennsylvania Railroad and began a vigorous prosecution of the tunnel's construction. It soon became apparent that the tunnel construction would be successful whereupon a series of violent attacks was opened on the company by its chief rival, the Western Railroad. Leading newspapers carried articles written so as to arouse the public against the "tunnel scheme" which was described as "visionary and impracticable" with the contractors being denounced as swindlers. Subscribers to the stock were warned against liquidating their subscriptions and were told that the Company had no power to enforce payment. When the editors of those papers carrying attacks on the tunnel testified before investigating committees, their articles were invariably traced to parties close to the president of the line from Worcester to Albany, then known as the Western Railroad Company. Of course, the articles, despite the exposure of their origin, were very effective in seriously hampering the collection of subscriptions and State payments for further work on the tunnel. Obviously, these articles were designed to kill the tunnel project by ruining the contractors.

But Haupt was a fighter and these attacks only stimulated him to work harder. Unable to get any help from the Company of which the tunnel was a part, he mortgaged his own property in Pennsylvania, sold stocks, and even borrowed money from personal friends. Thus he kept his head above water until the financial crash and depression of 1857, at which time he was carrying a floating debt of some $200,000. He had managed to provide personally almost all the capital necessary to carry on the work. No help had been forthcoming from either the Company or the State of Massachusetts. Three of his partners had failed; the other one could render no assistance.

Fortunately a friend placed $30,000 to Haupt's credit and the work progressed until 1860. Meanwhile, Haupt had perfected (in 1858) the first automatic feed, reciprocating power drill, especially designed for work in the tunnel. This superior pneumatic drill was a definite advance over those previously used in tunneling. Incidentally, the construction of a tunnel through the Berkshire Hills between Boston and Albany was a great engineering feat in itself; although the work has since been overshadowed by greater tunnels, Haupt showed engineers how to build them.

In 1860 the Massachusetts legislature ordered an investigation which completely exonerated Haupt both of inefficiency and corruption. But when the State lent the tunnel project $2,000,000 John A. Andrew became interested. This was fatal for Haupt because Andrew permitted himself to be unduly influenced by the enemies of Haupt. However, the bill of 1860 became a law with the approval of Governor Nathaniel P. Banks. Had Banks remained in office just one more year, the tunnel would have been so far advanced that further attempts to prevent its completion would have been futile. Unfortunately for Haupt and the State of Massachusetts, in view of the fact that the tunnel eventually cost $20,000,000 to complete, Banks declined renomination, and upon leaving office in 1861 omitted by sheer accident to sign the order for the payment of the tunnel construction. His successor, Andrew, expressing lack of confidence in the State Engineer and the contractors, refused to sign the order. The State Engineer was forced to resign and his place was taken by an engineer favorable to the Western Railroad line.

The underlying reason for Andrew's action is to be found in Andrew's close personal friendships with influential men under the influence of Chester W. Chapin, President of the Western Railway Company. Chapin was desperately anxious to kill the Hoosac Tunnel project because, on its completion, it would open up the Troy and Greenfield Railway as a carrying line parallel and rival to his own. Moreover, Andrew had his own personal reasons for fighting Haupt. On leaving office, Governor N. P. Banks, had delivered such an elaborate valedictory on the coming rebellion that Andrew's inaugural effort, at the very last moment was stripped of its punch, and Andrew was greatly embarrassed and angered thereby. Banks neglected to sign the Company's order for $100,-000, money previously earned and formally allowed, and Andrew refused to sign the order. He thus slapped Banks whom he disliked and pleased his friend, Frank Bird, agent of Chapin's Western Railway Company.[15]

The controversy soon expanded to one between the Governor and a committee of the Executive Council, eventually resulting in Haupt's bringing suit in the Supreme Judicial Court. But the Attorney-General now denied the jurisdiction of the Court. After prolonged hearings and interviews, Haupt and the other stockholders received eight cents on the dollar for stock they had been compelled to accept at par. For some twenty years Haupt paid interest on debts contracted in connection with the tunnel project, but never was reimbursed —"absolutely not a cent"—and in consequence lost the fine coal properties in Pennsylvania which he had been forced to mortgage. At one time his financial condition was so serious that Haupt's wife pawned some of her jewels although Haupt was unaware of her act.[16]

During Haupt's absence at the front, construction of the tunnel was carried on by Thomas Doane who, as chief engineer of the tunnel project, introduced new methods of tunneling, including improved pneumatic drills and the use of nitroglycerine and electric blasting. The tunnel was finally completed in 1873 and open for rail traffic two years later.[17]

Haupt's role in the tunnel controversy was that of a single-handed effort, maintained with great courage and tenacity against powerful interests of a rival railroad company, supported to some extent at least, by a prejudiced and partial state governor. Haupt never lost a point in this struggle when his side of the case was presented before bodies in which integrity, intelligence, fairness and facts were permitted to control decisions.

With construction at a standstill on the tunnel and the North engaged in active military operations, Haupt applied for the position of Assistant Secretary of War authorized by a Congressional Act of August 3, 1861. At an early cabinet meeting several names were mentioned, including Colonel William T. Sherman and David Davis, one of Lincoln's campaign managers. But Simon Cameron, Secretary of War, pointed out that the War Department needed an experienced railroad man.

Secretary of the Treasury Salmon P. Chase, suggested Thomas A. Scott (Haupt's former protege), who received the appointment. However, Haupt himself had hoped to receive the appointment; he had been Chief Engineer for Cameron in the Southern Railroad in the 1850's. But Haupt had ruined his chances when he antagonized Cameron by criticizing the Secretary's suggestion to relax discipline at West Point. Haupt's bluntness was occasioned by Cameron's refusal to appoint Haupt's son to the Academy.[18] Although Scott got the appointment as Assistant Secretary of War, Haupt's attitude towards Scott was a friendly one and the two worked very well together during the war.

Haupt soon received his chance for war service. On April 22, 1862, while in the midst of the tunnel imbroglio, he received a telegram from Edwin M. Stanton, the recently[19] appointed Secretary of War, requesting his immediate presence in Washington. It is probable that

Thomas A. Scott had told Stanton of Haupt's special qualifications. However, it is equally probable that Stanton because of his railroad connections was already familiar with Haupt's background and experience.

About the same time that Stanton's telegram arrived, another arrived from Congressman John Covode of Pennsylvania, stating: "Come here immediately; Secretary Stanton wants you." Haupt showed both telegrams to several prominent members of the Massachusetts legislature who advised him to go, pledging themselves to protect his interests, which pledge was fully redeemed. Moreover, a special joint committee had rendered its report unanimously endorsing his management of the tunnel's construction; and had reported a bill to reinstate him in possession of work, of which he had been deprived by Governor Andrew, with compensation for damages sustained by the enforced suspension. But Andrew had announced that he would veto any bill which would permit Haupt to continue management of the tunnel project although the Governor did indicate his willingness to assume the partially completed tunnel as a State project. After a series of conferences Haupt agreed to surrender possession to the State on certain conditions and was promised that these conditions would be incorporated in a bill, but the bill had not been drafted when Haupt was called to Washington. Moreover, the action of Governor Andrew was by no means certain. The situation for Haupt was "critical," but nevertheless he immediately reported to Stanton in Washington. Haupt had not heard the last of the tunnel controversy; it plagued him constantly during his service at the front, and eventually was directly responsible for his leaving the military service.

Such in brief was the pre-war experience of the rail-road genuis who was to contribute so much, not only to the Federal military effort in the Civil War, but also to military railroading in warfare up to the present time.

Notes, Chapter 1

1. House *Report* No. 682, 62nd Congress, 2nd Session; p. 3.
2. Haupt, Herman, *Reminiscences,* p. XIII (Hereafter cited as *Haupt*).
3. Cullum, George W., *Biographical Register of the Officer and Graduates of the U. S. Military Academy,* Vol. I, pp. 462–493.
4. *Ibid.,* Vol. II, p. 635.
5. Haupt, p. XIV.
6. Sparks, David S., Editor, *Inside Lincoln's Army* (Diary of General M. R. Patrick, entry for June 11, 1863), p. 257.
7. Lewis M. Haupt is of special interest because of his protracted dueling with the Adjutant General of the Army over his father's military service. Lewis served at one time on the faculty of the University of Pennsylvania, and later as a member of the Isthmian canal commission.
8. House *Report* No. 682, 62nd Congress, 2nd Session, p. 3.
9. Haupt, p. XV.
10. In 1872 Whipple's elaboration of his theories of bridge building was published as *An Elementary and Practical Treatise on Bridge Building.* Later this book was republished in another edition.
11. Later editions appeared in 1863 and 1869. Cullum, 1809–1892, served during the war as Chief of Staff and Chief Engineer to General H. W. Halleck.
12. Haupt, pp. XV–XIX.
13. This line, organized in 1846, was originally designed to run from Brandon, Mississippi, eastward through Meridian to the Alabama line, and connect up with the Mississippi and Alabama Railroad leading to Montgomery. This did not materialize before the original charter ran out, but the company was reincorporated in 1850. In 1852 (the year Haupt joined it), the Company acquired the Jackson and Brandon Railroad.
14. House *Report* No. 682, 62nd Congress, 2nd Session, p. 3.
15. Haupt, p. XXXIII.
16. *Ibid.,* pp. XXVIII, XXXIII.
17. Doane, A. A., *The Doane Family,* pp. 444–447.
18. Kamm, Samuel Richey, *The Civil War Career of Thomas A. Scott,* pp. 46–48.
19. Stanton replaced Cameron as Secretary of War on January 15, 1862.

2

RAILROADING 1861–1862

At the time that Herman Haupt was called to Washington, there were some 30,000 miles of rail lines in active operation in the United States. About 9,500 miles of the Nation's mileage were in the southern states.[1] Although the use of railroads in warfare had been publicly discussed some thirty years before the outbreak of the Civil War[2] the only railroad in possession of the United States Government in 1861 was a seven-mile line from Washington to Alexandria, Virginia. This short line was in charge of a captain in the Quartermaster Department. Under the War Department order of January 10, 1862, the track for this line had been relaid with new T-rails, the entire roadbed repaired, and a track laid across Long Bridge* over the Potomac River. Previously, all passengers and freight had been transferred across the bridge by horse power. In Alexandria the tracks had been laid through the city to form a junction with the Orange and Alexandria Railroad.[3]

---

* This is the site of the present railroad bridge alongside the 14th Street bridge.

34

The Civil War was the first great conflict in which military railroads played a decisively conspicuous part. Haupt's contributions to military railroading and to Federal military successes can best be appreciated when examined against the background of the problems and advantages inherent in the status of military railroading at the time of his entry into service.

In the United States, due to the distances to be covered and the poor character of the roads, railways and rivers were to be of paramount importance in military operations. A line of railway was in many cases the only practicable means of communication and transport for moving an army, as well as supplying it with provisions, ammunition and reinforcements. In turn, the railway itself became a military goal—an object of attack. Expeditions were sent out to tear up rails, burn wooden ties and timber beams, capture and destroy locomotives and rolling stock, and render a railway temporarily (if not permanently) useless. Battles were to be fought for the possession of junctions, and those junctions for strategical reasons were of the first importance.

Due to the lack of rails for replacements, sufficient locomotives, and other rolling stock, the South functioned under serious disadvantages in providing adequate transport; and without railways the Confederates could not have carried on the war on a large scale successfully. But rail lines were their principal allies; they were the basis on which almost all their inland operations were conducted.

A British military expert[4] recognized the following principles as inherent in the military operations in "the American War." 1.) railways when available could often be used to great advantage in the theater of war as an auxiliary means of moving troops and as a principal means of supplying them. 2.) railways were more quickly and easily destroyed and more readily repaired in a temporary manner when the necessary materials were available than was the case with common roads or turnpikes. 3.) a single line of railway in good order, and laid out with a proper proportion of sidings, crossings, and rolling stock, was sufficient for the normal supply of an army in the field. 4.) railways constructed with a view to strategical purposes, and designed to transport troops, should be laid with a double-track arrangement. 5.) the commander should in no case rely upon a railway for communications with his base of operations in enemy territory, and should not rely unduly on a long line of railway which was subject to attack by the enemy. 6.) railways would be much better utilized in defensive than offiensive warfare, and railway junctions would then become strategical positions of the greatest importance.

Railroad communications in a country thickly covered with forests could not be irreparably destroyed unless the roadbed itself was effectively destroyed. For example, Lee had apparently destroyed the Orange and Alexandria Railroad during the winter of 1863, only to see it restored to running order in a few weeks by Federal working parties. Bridges of great length and elevation were rebuilt as quickly as the large but simple pontoon bridges in former wars. Experience demonstrated that there was no end to the purposes to which railroads and locomotives could be applied. For example, at Resaca, Sherman sent a locomotive and empty train at full speed to draw enemy fire and thereby reveal the existence of masked batteries; this unique use of a train was successful.

Criticism was directed at the short-sightedness of Federal military leaders who neglected to establish more than one regular communication, or at least one direct rail line between Washington and the immediate rail center of Pennsylvania. This strategical desideratum was pointed out early in the spring of 1861 at a time when the capital was cut off from the loyal North by the hostile action of the population along the single rail communication between Washington and Philadelphia. The dependence on this line and on the cooperation of civilian railroad executives demonstrated the necessity of a direct rail line under Government control which would unite Washington with the North. This was especially important not only because of the political importance of the capital in international affairs, but also because Washington, already a vast depot, was destined to become a much greater supply center, from which military supplies and troops were forwarded to the front.

Had these factors been appreciated and appropriate steps taken early in the war, immense difficulties and dangers might have been averted or provided for. Four times was the capital threatened, and twice it was actually surrounded by the enemy, whose partisan units threatened or prevented supplies from moving forward on the single track. The great civilian and military center of the Northern war effort was dependent on a single track for the supplies on which depended the safety not only of the city itself, but also of the great armies penetrating it! Prudent foresight and ordinary effort would have insured a quadruple flow of supplies and troops moving in by two or more military lines. For example, a railroad running east-southeast would have connected the Pennsylvania line with the Baltimore and Ohio Railroad, terminating at Baltimore. Thirty miles more of rail to the southeast would have permitted the cars to bring their invaluable freight to Washington. But these lines had not been connected when war broke out.

The construction of a few short connections or link roads would have enabled several main rail lines to unite in uninterruptible communication the nation's capital with the North. Not only would such a linking up have resulted in very substantial savings financially, it would have lessened or prevented the panics which occurred during enemy invasions of northern territory.

Nevertheless, the war greatly enriched the northern railroads. The press[5] pointed out that the railroads were being paid for every soldier and every pound of material transported, and the amount of transportation had increased enormously because of the war. The railroads should have rewarded the country by a better system, better cars, safer transit, quicker time, and greater excellence in every respect.

Haupt went even further. In his final report he discussed at some length the subject of damages claimed by railroad corporations, especially those damages inflicted by enemy raids or by suspension of ordinary business during the use of such roads for military purposes. Haupt maintained that "no payments should be made by the Government except for actual damages that could be proved to have been sustained, and no damages at all for the loss of prospective profits."[6]

Secretary of War Cameron, in his report at the end of 1861, pointed out that, due to lack of competition, railroad corporations, like individuals, "are liable to be governed by selfish motives." He sited as an example, the fee of $6.00 for transporting each soldier from New

York to Baltimore. By a new arrangement this fee had
been reduced to $4.00 for each soldier going from New
York to Baltimore via Harrisburg. The Secretary called
for the laying of a double track between Washington and
Annapolis Junction, with improved sidings and facilities.
He also pointed out that the damage to railroads arising
from "rebel authorities of Baltimore" attempting to
disrupt communications with the North and West via
Harrisburg, and with the East via Philadelphia, had been
repaired by the companies that owned the rail lines involved.[7]

Shortly after Bull Run, July 21, 1861, the Federal
Government attempted to secure the cooperation of military personnel in the successful operation of communications media, especially the telegraph and rail lines. The
War Department, on July 26, 1861, requested military
officers to "furnish, upon requisitions from A. Carnejie
(Carnegie) superintendent in charge of railways, such
facilities, rations, etc. as he may desire for the forces
under his charge."[8] However, although the North was
depending on the railroads to play their part in winning
the war, the Government permitted the railroads to go
their own way for a year after Fort Sumter. During that
period the railroads were under no supervision or control, and as a result the rail lines in the vicinity of Washington and to the south were in an almost hopeless state
of confusion.

First of all, rapid rail movements were greatly hampered by a wide variety in widths of track, varying from
4 feet 8½ inches up to as much as 6 feet. Often short
trips involved several changes of cars for freight and
passengers. If such a situation was annoying before the
war, one can readily appreciate what the many changes

meant to transfer of rolling stock. At the very time when unusually large freight shipments were essential for military operations, there was a serious shortage of cars. And Confederate raiding parties did not ameliorate the situation at all. For example, only a few months after the outbreak of war, *Harper's Weekly* pointed out that "no less than fifty of the finest locomotives of the Baltimore and Ohio had been destroyed in Virginia; they had been mutilated, some by burning, others by mere destruction with hammers and crowbars; and some by having been dumped into the Potomac."[9] The destruction of rolling stock continued, and by November 1862, D. C. McCallum estimated that at least 400 cars and 11 locomotives on Government-operated railroads had been destroyed, captured or wrecked east of the Blue Ridge alone. It was obvious that the Government would have to get additional rolling stock from the privately operated railroads, and this was done.[10] In addition the military railroads contracted for the manufacture of new equipment. On one occasion McCallum commandeered three locomotives which the Baldwin Locomotive Works was just finishing for the New York Central Railroad. Despite the protest of the company, Stanton would only say that he could not revoke the order.[11]

The whole atmosphere became remarkably similar to the World War periods of our day. When manufacturers threatened to garner large profits at the expense of the Government by setting their own high prices, the Government let it be known that it would construct factories and turn out rolling stock itself, unless the private railroads' prices were in line with their fees on civilian rail lines. And much weight was given to this threat by the fact that the military railroad was successfully operating a rail rolling mill of its own.[12] The private railroad companies saw the light and buckled down to supplying Government orders at the market price.[13] Altogether during the war, the United States Military Railroads purchased and built 312 locomotives, and captured 106 from the enemy. In addition, the Government purchased 5,111 cars, augmented by the construction of 55 and the capture of 409 more.[14]

During the initial months of delay and confusion following the fall of Sumter, the Federal Government had come to realize that railroads were to play a vital role in the prosecution of the war. In order to insure regular transportation of troops and supplies to the front, all railroads within the zone of active operations had to be under the absolute control of the Federal military authorities. Accordingly, Congress on January 31, 1862, authorized Lincoln, whenever in his judgment the public safety so dictated,

> to take possession of any or all the telegraph lines . . . (and) railroad lines in the United States, their rolling stock, their offices, shops, buildings, and all their appendages and appurtenances; to prescribe rules and regulations for the holding, using, and maintaining of the aforesaid telegraph and railroad lines . . . [and] to place under military control all the officers, agents, and employees belonging to the telegraph and railroad lines thus taken possession of by the President, so that they shall be considered as a post road and a part of the military establishment of the United States, subject to all the restrictions imposed by the rules and articles of war.[15]

The exigencies of the military situation in early 1862 certainly warranted this authority to support the Federal military effort, but probably only a few were able to see the implications inherent in this Congressional act. Actu-

ally, the seizure of the railroads was a step toward con-
scription. Total war as understood by later generations
of Americans was beginning to be apparent in such governmental assumption of power. Not only was property
seized but personnel of railroads, from president down,
were now declared to be a part of the military establishment of the United States, "subject to all the restrictions
imposed by the rules and articles of war." In fact, by
order of the War Department, "all engineers of locomotives on railroads" were declared to be exempt from
the draft of August 1862.[16]

The effect of the law providing for seizure of the railroads was a direct blow to States' Rights; it was directed
to the people and met with their approval. The railroad
executives wisely did not wait for the Federal Government to take possession, but patriotically met in conven-
tion at Washington where they submitted for governmental approval a tariff for the transportation of troops
and supplies. This tariff remained in force until the cessa-
tion of hostilities.

The unusual powers granted the Government by this
law can be readily appreciated in the following order,
issued by Lincoln on February 10, 1862:[17]

> War Department
> Washington D.C.
> February 11, 1862

Ordered: That D. C. McCallum be, and he is hereby, appointed Military Director and Superintendent of Railroads
in the United States, with authority to enter upon, take possession of, hold, and use all railroads, engines, cars, locomotives,
equipments, appendages, and appurtenances that may be required for the transport of troops, arms, ammunition, and military supplies of the United States, and to do and perform all

acts and things that may be necessary and proper to be done for the safe and speedy transport aforesaid.

By order of the President, Commander-in-Chief of the Army and Navy of the United States:

Edwin M. Stanton
Secretary of War

In his annual report for 1862, Stanton pointed out that there had been no need within the loyal states to exercise the power conferred upon the President by January 31, 1862. In his report for 1865 Stanton added that the 1862 agreement between the railroads had remained in force throughout the war and had been extended to include the railroads in Southern States.[18] However, throughout the early years of war there was much confusion on the railroads under military control as to the jurisdiction of railroad personnel and military officers. As events later showed, this conflict between the military and civilian was to be one of Haupt's major headaches throughout his service with the military railroads.

When Haupt was called to Washington in the spring of 1862, the logistical demands of Federal armies in Virginia had brought affairs to a critical stage. The commanders of the two Federal armies operating against Richmond—McClellan's Army of the Potomac and McDowell's army of the Department of the Rappahannock*—were agreed on the need for their mutual cooperation,

---

* The Department of the Rappahannock was constituted April 4, 1862. It included that part of Virginia which was west of the Potomac River and the Fredericksburg and Richmond Railroad, and east of the Blue Ridge. The limits and boundaries of this Department were not strictly adhered to. On June 26, 1862, the forces of the Department were merged with other forces to form the "Army of Virginia."

but both were obviously dependent on efficiently maintained lines of communications; and, especially in the case
of McDowell, these "communications" meant railroads.
The expected logistical support had been seriously hampered by the destruction of wharves and buildings at the
Aquia Creek base. Included in the destruction were vital
rail lines and bridge connections with Fredericksburg.
Moreover, the constant interference by individual military commanders and their staffs only served to increase
the general confusion.[19]

Nor was confusion by any means lacking in one of the
main functions of the railroads, that of transportation
of troops. There was general agreement, in all quarters,
that the soldiers should be transported as comfortably
as possible. This idea was good in theory but in practice
it just did not work out. An examination of the experiences of Federal units moving to the front is amply sufficient to show the overall situation during the Civil War.

Many soldiers had never been on a railroad until they
were transported to the "seat of war." Their first trip
was usually a long one, and very tedious. Usually the
initial stage of the trip was made in passenger cars and
was quick and pleasant, although the men ate all their
rations up in the early hours and were ravenously hungry
thereafter.[20]

Due to variations in the gauge of the rails, distances
travelled were short before it was necessary to change
trains. There were few regiments that were so fortunate
as some Indiana troops in April 1862, who went straight
from Indianapolis to Philadelphia without even chang-
ing trains.[21]

Normally, the movement of a regiment from its home
state to the theater of military operations was madden-

ingly slow, unless one of the periodic panics of "Washington threatened" pressed every railroad into exclusively military transportation, and sent every available unit flying pell-mell to "save the capital." It always seemed as though there were a siding for every half mile of main track, and at least one train had to be waited for at each siding.[22]

At one of the many changes of gauge, the troops were unceremoniously ousted from their commodious passenger coaches and hustled into another train made up of baggage or freight cars. "Are we cattle, to be used this way?" "Do they think, because we are so far from home, they can use us like hogs?" The mood and comments seemed silly to these same men later on, "for a clean boxcar was a luxury which any weary, foot-sore, sick, or sorely-wounded volunteer would thank God for!!" But the first essential in the discipline of a new regiment was a good shaking down process, and the first rail trip accomplished this. The very men who soon came to appreciate riding in freight cars, however, balked at riding in cars which were in a filthy condition because of their prior use in transporting cattle. The men heartily seconded their commander when he informed the quartermaster in charge of transportation, "Perhaps you did not fully comprehend my order. These are not cattle, but men, and must have transportation as such." The regiment was then provided with platform cars, and, as the night was warm, and the distance short, the ride was not uncomfortable.[23]

Sometimes the officers rode in passenger cars and the enlisted men in freight cars. This was the arrangement for the 40th New York when it left for the front. But the men were resigned to their lot. They climbed into the boxcars, forty or more per car, and sat on the benches or lay down on the floor, packed in very closely. "When our blankets were spread for sleep the floor was completely covered, with some reclining upon the bare benches, or sitting with the head resting against the side of the car. . . . Our first night on the train was one of great discomfort, and so also was the day that followed, for although grand spectacles were constantly presented to our view, we yet suffered from the intense heat of our confinement in unventilated cars, the two side doors of which alone admitted light and air."[24] However, some freight cars on other lines had windows or air holes cut in their sides.

The long trips took a toll of the troops. One diarist[25] tells of a trip of several hundred replacements who were "crowded in like sheep" and, after eventual arrival in Alexandria were "very tired and beat out." The reason was the long trip during which the men suffered from lack of sleep and were exposed to dampness and night air.

Often in cattle cars the regiments filled the cars so nicely that on one occasion a soldier in the 20th Iowa Infantry believed that the calculation must have been made after they had buried two of their comrades, "for there would have been no room for them had they been yet with us." The soldier thought it was essentially wise that cattle cars had been used instead of passenger coaches "For had there been such things as windows or doors we certainly should have sifted through before we reached our destination."[26]

In addition to the ever-present problem of overcrowding of troops in freight cars there was one which writers on the employment of rail transportation during the 1860's have scrupulously avoided: while sanitary con-

veniences were a part of the normal equipment of passenger cars, they were not available to the men "packed
in like sheep" in the freight cars. Since the men were
often refused permission to leave the cars, a real problem
existed during the long trips from State rendezvous
camps to the front. Late in 1862 Haupt was asked by
Quartermaster General Meigs for suggestions on the
problem. The reply[27] was characteristically prompt and
sensible. He said in part:

> I fully concur with you in the propriety of the arrangements
> you have suggested and have no doubt of their practicality. In
> this opinion Thos. A. Scott and other experienced railroad
> managers with whom I have consulted have concurred.
> The practical mode of affording the accommodations would be
> by preparing in advance a number of small square boxes which
> could be nailed over openings made in the corners of the cars.
> This with a curtain of some kind in front is all that decency
> and humanity would imperatively require.

Haupt went on to suggest that a circular be issued, requiring that freight cars be prepared as he had suggested, and that the circular be sent to all railroad companies involved in transporting military personnel.

The same day Haupt again wrote to Meigs on the
complaints of troops travelling in freight or boxcars.
"It is impossible," he said, "to provide at all times first
class accommodations for troops and the experience of
all railroad companies will establish the fact that good
cars when so used are usually ruined in a single trip."
Railroad companies were compelled to transport troops
in boxcars because of "deficiency of equipment and other
causes." Haupt pointed out that an investigation had
showed that the delays in travel were caused by "the
refractory conduct of the troops themselves."

Sometimes the crowded conditions of the trains resulted in tragedy for the troops involved. Such was the case of the 37th Massachusetts Infantry after it left Jersey City on its way to Washington. A participant described the incident as follows:

> About 9 o'clock we were again loaded into cars which did not get outside the boundary line of Jersey City until noon, and then the train loitered around on its way to Philadelphia all the afternoon, and arrived there about seven o'clock in the evening . . . At midnight we were loaded on freight cars, and started on our way southward, with most of the men asleep on the floor of the cars. A few miles out of Philadelphia, our train crashed into a passenger train mostly filled with soldiers returning to Washington from hospitals, on their way to rejoin their regiments . . . . We rescued out of the wreckage the mangled remains and corpses of more than thirty victims of the collision. A third train ran into the rear of our train while it was standing on the tracks."

Eventually this regiment arrived at its destination but "we had occupied four days and three nights in going from camp at Pittsfield [Massachusetts] to . . . Washington. This is a fair specimen of the way regiments travelled during the war."[28]

In addition to the inevitable exigencies of war, much of the extremely slow trips endured by troops was due to the fact that railroad companies used their poorest equipment for the military service. For example, when the 14th New Hampshire Infantry was on its way to Washington, the men made a day of it. All day long "that wheezy, most outrageous piece of mechanism that ever dazed the eye of man, a Baltimore and Ohio freight-engine, puffed, snorted, backed, filled, and stopped as the snail-train crawled toward the capital..."[29]

Occasionally, there were humorous incidents connected with the movement of a regiment to the "seat of war." In September 1861, the 63rd Pennsylvania Infantry[30] was marched aboard a train consisting of cattle cars, to be taken to Baltimore by the Northern Central Railroad. While entraining, Governor Andrew G. Curtin appeared on the scene to see the men after they were safely aboard the train. But the men were very indignant at being placed in cattle cars, and when they saw the Governor "they set up an excellent imitation of the voices of the usual occupants of these cars. Such a braying like mules, bellowing like cattle, bleating like sheep, and even squealing like swine probably never before greeted the ears of the old war governor." Curtin stopped, stared at the cars, then wheeled and strode away in a most indignant manner. It is small wonder the railroad used poor equipment, for the soldiers were often destructive. For example, as soon as the train was well under way, everyone who had a knife "began to get his work in one of the cars." It was not long before the cars presented a unique appearance; the sides were almost cut away because the men had cut so many windows in them. Officers tried to stop what they called vandalism, "but the boys had not yet learned to fear the officers" and paid little attention to their commanders' orders. By the time the 63rd had reached Baltimore, the cars presented the appearance of huge chicken coops. Of course the Government had to pay for the mutilation of the cars, but the soldiers did not let that trouble them at all.

Keeping supplies moving up to the front and the railroads in operation sometimes encountered the hostility of poorly disciplined soldiers whose experience with railroads had been anything but pleasant. Some of this hostility arose from experiences similar to that of the 125th New York Infantry. This regiment left Baltimore September 26, 1862, and went through to Chicago, non-stop, arriving about noon on September 29th. The regiment went by common freight cars, with no arrangements for sleeping, and with forty men in each car. They suffered considerably and were exhausted on arrival. It was almost impossible to rest "such was the tremble jolting and shaking up on the springless and uncomfortable vehicles." The men's rations consisted of hardtack and partially cooked fat pork. The men would have suffered even more if some citizens had not given them food along the way.[31]

Soldiers like those of the 125th Ohio Infantry resented being jammed into passenger cars and were especially impatient with being kept in the cars by guards placed at the doors.[32] Accordingly, the men often took out their frustrations on the railroads, and made themselves comfortable at the expense of rail facilities. When the 111th Pennsylvania Infantry went home on "veteran furlough" in January 1864, the weather was intensely cold. Fires were lighted on the car floors but fortunately did not set fire to the train.[33] Conditions were even worse in some units. When veterans went home in the winter of 1863-1864, some made the trip in unheated cattle cars which were still wet when the men were herded into them. The winter was an unusually cold one; often the wind blew a gale, while the men's feet were soaking wet from marching through snow to reach the trains. These troops suffered severely and not a few were forced to have fingers or toes amputated as a result of severe cases of frostbite.

Against the background of chaotic railroad administration, interference of military commanders, and gradual Governmental insistence on centralized control, Stanton summoned Haupt to Washington. McCallum, the
newly appointed superintendent of military railroads,
had been given arbitrary powers which certainly were
designed to expand Federal control over captured railroads as well as railroads hitherto under the control of
military commanders in the field. The Railroad Act of
1862 had brought all captured railroad lines under War
Department control, through its Military Railroads.

In theory the United States Military Railroads were
under the Quartermaster General of the Army, but
actually McCallum operated independently except for
fiscal matters. This resulted in ambiguity of responsibility for which Stanton was personally at fault. The
Secretary delighted in keeping the various elements of
the War Department under his own control. Stanton
even permitted McCallum to bypass Meigs and trans-
mit reports directly to the War Department without going through channels. Everybody's status became even
more uncertain when Stanton gave Haupt control of the
captured railroads in northeastern Virginia, an area
definitely within McCallum's province. And, typically,
Stanton's disregard for command channels resulted in
Haupt's finding still another individual, Daniel Stone,
operating independently of both Haupt and McCallum
in Haupt's territory! Naturally, this did not tend to further cordial relations between Haupt and his administrative chief.

NOTES: CHAPTER 2

1. Kennedy, Jos. C., *Preliminary Report of the Eighth Census* (1860) p. 234.
2. See *Appendix*.
3. McCallum's Final *Report,* May 26, 1866.
4. Tyler, H. W. (Captain, Royal Engineers) *United States Army and Navy Journal,* Vol. I, No. 42 (June 11, 1863), p. 693.
5. *United States Service Magazine,* Vol. 1, pp. 271–272.
6. Haupt, Report to Secretary of War, September 9, 1863.
7. Annual Report of the Secretary of War, December 1, 1861, pp. 12–13.
8. The order emanated from Thomas A. Scott, "General Manager, Government Railways and Telegraphs."
9. *Harper's Weekly,* July 20 and August 3, 1861.
10. McCallum, *Report,* May 26, 1866.
11. *Official Records,* Series III, Vol. 3, pp. 1083–1084.
12. McCallum, *Report,* May 26, 1866.
13. *Official Records of the Union and Confederate Armies,* Series III, Vol. 4, pp. 219–220, hereafter cited as *Official Records.*
14. McCallum, *Report,* May 26, 1866.
15. Callan, John F. *Military Laws of the United States,* p. 492.
16. U. S. War Department, *General Order No. 99,* August 9, 1862.
17. McCallum, *Report,* May 26, 1866.
18. Secretary of War, *Reports* for 1862 and 1865.
19. *Harper's Weekly,* May 24, 1862.
20. Buffum, Francis H., *History of the 14th New Hampshire Infantry,* p. 58.
21. *New York Tribune,* April 22, 1861.
22. Buffum, *op. cit.,* p. 59.
23. *Ibid.,* pp. 61–62, 122.
24. Floyd, Fred C., *History of the Fortieth (Mozart) Regiment New York Volunteers,* p. 52.
25. Peterson, B. F., Manuscript diary. Entry for January 15, 1864.
26. Barney, Chester, *Recollections of Field Service with the Twentieth Iowa Volunteers,* p. 31.
27. Haupt to Meigs, November 11, 1862. Haupt Order Book, Library of Congress.
28. Tyler, Mason W., *Recollections of the Civil War,* entry for September 8, 1862, pp. 34–36.
29. Buffum, *op. cit.,* pp. 62–63.
30. Hays, Gilbert Adams, *Under the Red Patch,* p. 18.
31. Simons, Ezra D., *The One Hundred and Twenty-Fifth New York State Volunteers,* p. 39.
32. Clark, Charles T., *Opdycke Tigers,* p. 17.
33. Boyle, John R., *Soldiers True,* p. 193.

3

HAUPT AND THE HIGH COMMAND

The Federal spring offensive of 1862 was already in a confused state, and the war had been going on about a year when Haupt decided to become a participant himself.[1] Although a West Point graduate he had served only three months on active military service. Essentially an engineer, he was never a military man either in the professional or colloquial sense of the term. Even his attempt to be appointed Assistant Secretary of War in July 1861 had been prompted primarily because of Cameron's need for a railroad man for the vacancy. Nevertheless, Haupt immediately reported in Washington to the Secretary of War, who told him that his services might be required for some three or four weeks. Stanton, moreover, added, "If the war is not finished in three months, I will resign."[2] At Haupt's request, Stanton put his orders in writing as follows:

Washington D.C. April 24, 1862

Herman Haupt, Esq.

Dear Sir: I desire you to proceed directly to the Headquarters of Major-General McDowell on the Rappahannock and receive his instructions respecting the engineering work which he desires to have executed for his advance. If, upon inspecting the operations, you can devote your time and abilities to the service of the Government in their completion, you will be regarded as rendering important and patriotic assistance to the country which will be cordially acknowledged by this Department.

Your obedient servant
Edwin M. Stanton
Secretary of War

To this communication Haupt returned the following reply:

Washington, April 25, 1862

Hon. E. M. Stanton, Secretary of War

I have considered your request and will go immediately to General McDowell to ascertain the position of affairs and the precise character of the duties to be performed. If they shall appear to be such as imperatively to require my personal attention, it will be given, although the sacrifices in other important interests will be great. If I can suggest arrangements to dispense with my personal services, this may be done. In any event, I would expect to continue only so long as public exigencies demanded it.

I have no military or political aspirations, and am particularly averse to wearing the uniform; would prefer to perform the duties required without military rank, if possible, but if rank is essential as a means to and in the performance of duty, I must acquiesce.

Pay I do not require or care about. If I take the position you have so kindly offered, it will be with the understanding that I can retire whenever, in my opinion, my services can be dispensed with and that I will perform no duties on the Sabbath unless necessity imperatively requires it, and of that necessity I must be the judge, so far as may be consistent with military subordination.

Yours with much respect,
H. Haupt

It appears that Haupt was the original "dollar a year man" as that type of patriotic individual was characterized in World War II. However, Stanton apparently did not so regard him. Haupt's pay account was questioned by the Secretary in mid-1863, and Haupt felt constrained to explain to H. W. Halleck the actual situation. In a letter to the General-in-Chief, shortly after Gettysburg, Haupt said in part:

> The Secretary of War hesitates to approve of my pay account; he desires a personal interview today, and after a full explanation, said he would postpone action until he had conferred with you . . . [When I consented to serve my country, I] declared that I would accept neither rank nor pay. It was represented by Secy. Stanton and also by Mr. Watson, that military rank was essential to enable me to exercise necessary authority, and a commission was made out which I regarded as a merely nominal appointment.[3]

Moreover, Haupt's conditions for acceptance of his appointment included stipulations that he would not be required to wear a uniform, would be allowed no salary or compensation beyond his expenses, and would be relieved when his services were no longer necessary. Stanton accepted these conditions, and on May 28, 1862, commissioned Haupt a colonel and appointed him Chief of Construction and Transportation in the Department of the Rappahannock, and on the following day (May 29) issued orders making him independent of all authority save that of the Secretary of War.[4]

So far as pay is concerned, vouchers on file in the Adjutant General's Office of the War Department as late as 1912 showed that on September 12, 1863, Haupt was paid for services as Superintendent of Military

Railroads from April 20, 1862, to September 12, 1863, the sum of $7,484.40, amounting to the pay and allowances of a brigadier general* of volunteers during the entire period.[5]

In his letter to Halleck, Haupt explained his attitude towards the implications inherent in his accepting a military commission. Haupt told Halleck that he could not accept any office or commission which would deprive him entirely of the control of his time, and that any acceptance of a commission "must be untrammelled with conditions." Haupt added:

> I considered the title merely nominal, but at the same time useful, to assist in exacting compliance, and preventing interference with my orders on the part of officers, whose shoulder straps are sometimes broader than their intellects, and who hold all citizens in a profound contempt.

Moreover, Haupt pointed out that he had never had a staff, nor employed the servants or kept the houses to which a commission entitled him, nor had he ever charged or received more than required to replace cash actually paid out in the public service, the whole averaging less than one-third the pay and commutations of a brigadier general. Haupt's reluctance to accept a commission was because he could foresee circumstances which would necessitate his absence for short periods of time in order to attend to his tunnel interests. If he could leave his military duties without injury to the public interest, he wanted to be able to do so without having to ask for a leave of absence. Haupt pointed out that if he could be the judge in such matters he would be willing to give his time and services without pay until the

* Haupt was promoted to brigadier general September 5, 1862.

suppression of the rebellion would permit him to return home or some individual capable of taking his place could be found. Since Peter H. Watson, Assistant Secretary of War, approved his quarterly accounts for cash expended "without hesitation," Haupt was at a loss to understand why so much explanation of his expense account was demanded by Stanton. In fact, Haupt pointed out, he would not even have asked for expenses but for the fact that the tunnel imbroglio had, temporarily at least, robbed him of everything. He still insisted that he did not want military rank and if his nominal rank of brigadier general could not be retained except by formal acceptance with the attendant restrictions, then he respectfully declined it.[6]

Eventually this refusal of Haupt to formally accept his commission was to cost him dearly, as Stanton used his refusal as an excuse to force his retirement from the service. From the viewpoint of the normal requirements of military service and the conventional relationship of an officer to his government, Haupt's attitude cannot be defended. There are few individuals, either military or civilian, who can see the logic or wisdom of having special privileges and obligations for some officers, while denying such favors to others. But there is more to Haupt's situation than can be appreciated by a casual glance at the facts. As will be shown later, Stanton deliberately forced the issue on Haupt's acceptance of his commission because of the Secretary's intention of restricting Haupt's freedom to visit Massachusetts to protect his tunnel interests. Moreover, as with other civilians who were making invaluable contributions to new elements in the Federal military forces, Stanton refused to adopt a flexible attitude towards Haupt or acknowledge his great value to the Army. Actually, Haupt should have been humored to a reasonable extent in his unique position. Haupt was a forerunner of the civilian consultant type which the Armed Services have utilized so effectively in recent years.

Haupt's quasi-military status was to plague him and his descendants for decades. When the West Point Committee desired to place Haupt's rank as brigadier general on a memorial tablet to its graduates, it was discovered that Haupt had in fact never actually held any military commission. For to "hold" a commission, an officer in the United States service must accept the commission and be sworn in. This Haupt had never done— neither for his commission as colonel, nor for his commission as brigadier general. Haupt himself made this clear in two letters[7] of September 27, 1862, to Lorenzo Thomas of the Adjutant General's Department. Haupt told Thomas that he could only accept a commission with the understanding that he would be free to attend to private affairs when not needed for duty with the military railroads. General Halleck endorsed one of these letters with the statement that Haupt's conditions for acceptance of a commission could not be met, but did recommend that Haupt be paid according to his *nominal* rank. Even George W. Cullum, aware of Haupt's service as a West Point graduate, recorded that Haupt was commissioned a brigadier general of volunteers but declined the appointment.[8]

Despite the written evidence in War Department files —some of it in Haupt's own handwriting—there ensued from 1911-1913 a long exchange of letters between Haupt's son, Lewis, and the Adjutant General of the Army. Bills "for proper recognition" of Haupt's Civil

War service were proposed in both Houses of Congress
to the effect that Haupt should "hereafter be held and
considered to have been in the military service of the
United States as . . . colonel . . . and [also] as a
brigadier general of volunteers . . . ."[9] However, the
report was adverse, due mainly to the report of the Adjutant General and the Judge Advocate General of the
Army. These men agreed[10] that "no such thing as a
conditional acceptance of an appointment to an office is
known in the military service of the United States . . .
the acceptance of a military office necessarily involves
the unqualified acceptance with it of all of the duties,
liabilities, and restrictions upon personal liberty that per-
tain to the office." And the Adjutant General was correct in pointing out that Haupt preferred to perform the
duties of superintendent of military railroads in the
capacity of a civilian and not as an officer of the Army.
This was Haupt's choice, made for reasons with which
we must be sympathetic. But his refusal to be mustered
in as colonel, and later as brigadier general, means that
actually he held the nominal rank for enforcing decisions
but never was legally a member of the military establishment of the United States.

Serenely unaware of the complications which were to
characterize much of his war service, Haupt left Washington, April 25, 1862, and reported to the headquarters
of the Department of the Rappahannock, General Irwin
McDowell commanding. McDowell had been the unfortunate commander of the defeated Federal forces
at Bull Run the previous summer. He remembered
Haupt as one who had befriended him at West Point
nearly thirty years ago; soon their relations were "most
cordial," and Haupt respected the General both as a

gentleman and a soldier. After consultation with Mc-
Dowell, Haupt returned to Washington, April 27, and
was appointed aide-de-camp on McDowell's staff with
the rank of colonel. Two days later, Haupt landed at
Aquia Creek with men and material for construction of
the road to Fredericksburg. In May, Haupt was appointed Chief of Construction and Transportation in
the Department of the Rappahannock.[11]

The problem of conflicting jurisdiction in control of
the railroads arose at once. Stanton had authorized still
another man to construct a bridge over the Rappahannock
and thereby open the Fredericksburg Railroad to the
south. More serious was the problem of Haupt's relations with McCallum whom Stanton had appointed "military director and superintendent of railroads in the
United States" on February 11, 1862.[12] This position
soon conflicted with Haupt's assignment as Chief of
Construction and Transportation in the same department. Yet both appointments emanated from Stanton,
himself. McCallum had been for many years the General
Superintendent of the Erie Railroad and was one of the
most experienced railroad managers in the Country. "He
could sit in his New York office and move his trains by
telegraph with the utmost precision, but the conditions
were widely different on the military railroads."[13] Haupt
considered McCallum a splendid office man, thoroughly
familiar with every detail of requisitions, accounts and
red tape. Because Haupt had no liking for such things,
he and McCallum agreed on a division of work. "Mc-
Callum took the office and I took the field . . . ."[14]

But Haupt erred if he thought that McCallum was
enthusiastic over Haupt's recognition by Lincoln and
the promotion to brigadier general over McCallum's

head in late 1862. Evidence of McCallum's hidden resentment at Haupt's laurels—and incidentally of Mc-
Callum's craven subservience to Stanton's denial of
credit to Haupt—can be seen in McCallum's final report
at the end of the war. In this report, which described in
detail the entire history of the United States Military
Railroads during the war, McCallum never even mentioned Haupt! The correspondence between Haupt and
McCallum indicates very strongly that their relations
were strained at times and that Haupt felt constrained
to explain his position and reassure McCallum from
time to time. For example, when Haupt was recalled by
Pope in August 1862, Haupt wrote McCallum in part
as follows:[15]

I found that . . . [Pope] wanted some one on his staff who
could be personally present and direct the practical operations
of the railroads under his command. Your duties in Washington in the purchase of cars and engines, the supply of materials, the settlement of accounts, and the various other duties
which occupy your time would prevent you from devoting your
whole personal attention to operations in the field. I supposed, therefore that I could comply with the urgent requests
of the Sec. of War and of Genl. Pope without crossing your
path or interfering with your duties. I propose to confine myself entirely to the reconstruction of roads and the management of transportation, leaving to you, as heretofore, all
purchases of rolling stock, material and supplies, and all
settlements of accounts.
I hope this division of duties will be satisfactory and that I
will be able to relieve you of part of your labors without giving
you offense. I do not feel at liberty to decline the position
which I have been so urgently solicited to take and yet I have
no idea of holding it permanently. I hope that I may be permitted soon to return to Massachusetts and stay there. In the
management of the road I propose to conform to your wishes
as far as practicable and make no unnecessary changes in your
arrangements or employees.

Apparently McCallum, in turn, reassured Haupt, because four days later Haupt again wrote McCallum, commending him on his good spirit and attitude.[16] However, the entire tone and terms of address in the Haupt-McCallum correspondence is most formal.

Much of the success of the Federal armies in the war was due to the logistical support rendered by the United States Military Railroads under experienced railroaders like Haupt and McCallum. These men were essentially civilians serving under the over-all control of the Quartermaster-General's Department, headed by Montgomery C. Meigs. This professional soldier, extremely competent, richly deserves his fame as head of the Federal supply services; but some of his subordinate officers were not efficient or capable administrators of railroads, about which they often knew little. Meigs supervised the shipments of troops and supplies by Northern railroads under contract with the Federal Government. Although the Quartermaster-General's Department, under orders of the field commanders, determined what supplies would be moved to front line areas, the railroad managers controlled the actual operation of the railroads.

Haupt's relations with the Federal high command, especially Lincoln and Halleck, were good, but exceptions must be noted in the case of Stanton and Welles. The President greatly appreciated Haupt's precise and informative reporting. Lincoln's secretary, John Hay, was not far off when he compared "Little Mac" with Haupt, pointing out that "if heads or shoulder straps could be exchanged, it would be a good thing . . . A good railroader would be spoiled but the General gained would compensate."[17] During the days of anxiety and near panic of the Second Bull Run campaign, one man satisfied Lincoln above all others. This was Haupt, who took on himself many responsibilities beyond his immediate assignment. He pushed men and supplies forward, rebuilt bridges, and kept in constant telegraphic communication with the President, working night and day, with little food and practically no sleep. During these critical days Lincoln's generals gave him little information, but Haupt's businesslike dispatches greatly impressed the President by their brevity and valuable, on-the-spot combat reporting. Halleck, who also was consistently a supporter of Haupt and one who saw clearly the railroader's worth, worked as hard as Haupt and also earned the President's gratitude. "Halleck," said Lincoln, "is wholly for the service. He does not care who succeeds or who fails so the service is benefited."[18]

However, the man who called Haupt to Washington in the first place—and a man whom Haupt had to please if he was to be successful—was the Secretary of War. Stanton's fifteen years of professional experience with both rail and water transportation certainly made him a competent judge of the possibilities of such media of logistical support. But since none of his military commanders had seemed equal to the task of repairing and managing the railroads they were capturing, Stanton called Haupt for this purpose.[19]

On the surface a man with a background such as that possessed by Stanton should have been especially responsive to the needs and problems of the railroad men under him. This unfortunately was not the case. Stanton's character was such as to make it very difficult for anyone except a few favorites to work under him for any period of time. Because of the Secretary's relationship with Haupt, and his role in forcing the railroader out of the service, it is essential that we analyze Stanton's character and actions in some detail.

Historians have too often passed over two very essential points about Stanton. In the first place, Stanton by personal dislike and vindictiveness towards important Federal leaders, both civilian and military, impaired their morale and effectiveness so as to reduce or eliminate their contributions to the Northern war effort. It is well known, for instance, that Secretary Welles did not hold him in especially high esteem. But Stanton had troubles with Adjutant General Lorenzo Thomas, Meigs, General Joseph G. Totten, and according to Lincoln, the Secretary and General Francis Blair were not on speaking terms. In April 1862, it was urged that General Ethan Allen Hitchcock be appointed to Stanton's place, but because of trouble with the Secretary, Hitchcock had handed in his resignation as major general of volunteers, although he later was regarded as the "military adviser" to Stanton.[20]

Stanton's Assistant Secretary of War, Thomas A. Scott, whom Cameron had chosen because of his railroading ability, finally resigned because of Stanton's caustic criticism and lack of enthusiasm for his work. However, Scott did serve on special missions later in the war.

As Grant tells us in his *Memoirs,* there were two occasions when he and Stanton clashed. One occasion was when Grant ordered a cipher operator to turn over the cipher key to one of his staff; the other involved Grant's rightful position of General-in-Chief of the Army. According to Grant, this second incident arose out of Stanton's "natural disposition to assume all power and control in all matters that he had anything whatever to do with . . ." Moreover, as Grant expressed it, Stanton "cared nothing for the feelings of others. In fact, it seemed to be pleasanter to him to disappoint than to gratify. He felt no hesitation in assuming the functions of the executive, or in acting without advising with him. . . . The Secretary was very timid [Welles believed him to be a physical coward]. The enemy would not have been in danger if Mr. Stanton had been in the field."[21] Nor was Grant alone in this opinion. Sherman considered Stanton "notoriously vindictive in his prejudices."[22]

Stanton's vindictiveness accorded such department chiefs as Albert Myer (Chief Signal officer), George D. Ramsay (Chief of Ordnance) and William A. Hammond (Surgeon General), was also to be directed against Haupt. Any individual who possessed an independent spirit and who was willing to stand up for his ideas was certain to incur the War Secretary's disfavor if their paths crossed. Therefore it was probably inevitable that a man of Haupt's temperament would be destined for trouble. The significance of all this is that incurring Stanton's displeasure was not merely a question of "clash of personalities"; the frictions engendered, morale lowered, and service of capable officers lost, all detracted from efficiency and early victory by Federal forces.

Stanton's role as Secretary of War has yet to receive the thorough analysis which is definitely called for in view of his position of authority and his official and unofficial acts from 1862 to 1865. It is entirely possible that the man was not mentally well at times. As early as February 1862, some people were saying that his brain was affected and that he acted "strangely."[23]

When Haupt reported for active war service he probably was completely unaware of Stanton's methods or eccentricities. Haupt had had some acquaintance with him at the time Stanton was practicing law in Pittsburgh prior to the war, but they had never been intimate. Haupt considered Stanton to be honest, patriotic, and fearless, but, in time, came to realize that the War Secretary was "impulsive and headstrong." Haupt tells us that, in general, he was well treated by the Secretary who was either lavish in compliments or irritated at Haupt's refusal to obey orders which were impracticable or unreasonable." "On the whole," wrote Haupt, in later years, "our relations were satisfactory until he was compelled to choose between Governor Andrew and myself, and, of course, chose the former."[24]

NOTES: CHAPTER 3

1. Haupt, p. 43.
2. *Ibid*. p. 44.
3. Haupt to Halleck, July 17, 1863. National Archives.
4. Haupt, pp. 54–55.
5. Adjutant General, U. S. Army to Lewis M. Haupt, January 30, 1912, National Archives.
6. Haupt to Halleck, July 17, 1863. National Archives.
7. Haupt to L. Thomas, September 27, 1862. National Archives.
8. Cullum, George W., *Biographical Register of the Officers and Graduates of the United States Military Academy,* Vol. 1, p. 479.
9. Senate Bill S. 5433, 62nd Congress, 2nd Session. February 21, 1912; House Bill H.R. 5868, June 3, 1913, National Archives.
10. Adjutant General, U. S. Army to Lewis Haupt, September 27, 1911, National Archives.
11. Haupt, pp. 45, 47. For chronology of Haupt's service see *Appendix G.*
12. Flower, p. 223.
13. Haupt, p. 312.
14. *Ibid.,* p. 313.
15. Haupt to McCallum, August 19, 1862, National Archives.
16. *Ibid.,* August 23, 1862, National Archives.
17. Dennett, Tyler (editor), *Lincoln and the Civil War in the Diaries and Letters of John Hay,* pp. 47–48.

18. Nicolay and Hay, *Lincoln,* I, p. XII.
19. But men like McClellan had had railroad experience and should have been helpful at this time.
20. Croffut, W. A., (editor), *Fifty Years in Camp and Field,* pp. 441, 443, (Stanton was appointed Secretary of War on January 20, 1862. See *Appendix.*)
21. Grant, U. S., *Personal Memoirs,* Vol. II, pp. 103–104, 536–537.
22. Sherman, W. T., *Personal Memoirs,* Vol. II, p. 7.
23. Sparks, David S., *Inside Lincoln's Army,* p. 45. See also *Ibid.,* p. 361.
24. Haupt, p. 301.

4

AT THE FRONT

Haupt left Washington for the front on April 25, 1862, making the trip down the Potomac in a small steamer which had been placed at his disposal to expedite his speedy arrival at the headquarters of his first assignment, the Department of the Rappahannock.[1] These forces were resting near the Potomac, unable to move until the Fredericksburg Railroad was put into shape for the transportation of supplies and troops. Troops of this Department had been ordered to cooperate with McClellan's Army of the Potomac which was now in front of Yorktown, in the early stages of the famous Peninsular Campaign against Richmond. But neither army could move without the cooperation of the other, and such cooperation was impossible without the use of the railroad as a means of communication with the depots on the base of the Potomac.[2] Stanton had called on Haupt to rebuild the destroyed bridge and track which served the Aquia Creek depot and the Fredericksburg Railroad. This reconstruction was essential to insure adequate supply of the troops of the

Rappahannock in their projected cooperation with Mc-
Clellan's operation against Richmond.[3]

The newly created Department of the Rappahannock
had been organized on April 4, 1862. This army, destined to retain its identity until June 26, 1862, was
actually McDowell's old 1st Corps, with some organizational changes. In the preparation of the Army of the
Potomac's advance on Richmond the 1st Corps had been
organized on March 13th and the next day its commander, Irvin McDowell, was promoted to major general of volunteers. He had been commanding a division
since October 3rd of the previous year.

After arrival at McDowell's headquarters, Haupt was
appointed as special aide on the General's staff. At first
all went well. Haupt's working arrangement with the
Administration functioned smoothly, and his superiors
in the army and War Department were satisfied. Haupt
considered himself to be a "temporary attache" to the
War Department—a sort of appendage. He sought to
be useful rather than ornamental and to render service
in any way in which he could. And he intended to retire
when the necessity for continuance ceased to exist.[4]

However, retirement was not to be thought of for
some weeks; there was too much of a challenge in the
new assignment.

Although McDowell's mission was to protect Washington during McClellan's advance towards Richmond,
Little Mac's advance on the Peninsula began to bog
down and the Administration decided that McDowell
could help relieve the pressure by a diversionary advance. Accordingly, on May 17th, he was ordered to
move down the Richmond and Fredericksburg Railroad
and cooperate with the army under McClellan, then

threatening Richmond from the line of the Pamunkey and York Rivers. Actually, McDowell's force was not a reinforcing but rather a cooperating army. His "primary duty" was still to protect Washington and was therefore not to be placed completely under McClellan's control.

McDowell's orders to cooperate with McClellan on the Peninsula could not be implemented until major repairs and construction had been made. Haupt's first job was to rebuild the rail line between Aquia Creek and Fredericksburg. All the bridges on this line had been burned, three miles of track had been torn up and the rails taken south of Fredericksburg. The cross-ties had been placed together in piles and burned, and the wharf and buildings at Aquia Creek burned to the water's edge.[5] After a careful appraisal of the damage, Haupt decided that he could get the line to Fredericksburg in running order within three or four weeks.[6]

Although Haupt agreed to repair the rail line, he believed that water transportation would need to be used in support of McDowell's operations. Unfortunately, most of the available shipping was already in use elsewhere; McClellan's army was being supplied with transports and supply craft on the James and York Rivers. Although water transportation on the Potomac River was in no way subject to Haupt's supervision, he did believe that a great saving of expense and an increase of efficiency could have been achieved by loading the railroad cars at the permanent Alexandria and Washington depots, running them on floats, towing them to Aquia Creek, and sending them to their destination without change of bulk. "This plan is entirely practicable," insisted Haupt, "there cannot be a valid objection to it, and if introduced at an earlier period it would have saved the necessity of the large warehouses at Aquia Creek, the services of hundreds of employees to load and unload, and would have permitted most of the transports to be dispensed with."[7] However, this novel method of moving men and equipment had to wait until later.

From the very outset, Haupt realized that he would have to depend on his own efforts to get things accomplished. Colonel Daniel C. McCallum, his immediate supervisor, outranked Haupt. McCallum had received his appointment as "Military Director and Superintendent of Railroads" back on February 11th. He was in charge of U. S. Military Railroads in all theaters of war, including those in McDowell's Army of the Rappahannock. It was soon apparent to Haupt that McCallum was an office man, not a field soldier. This was at least partially demonstrated during one of Haupt's rare absences from the field; the railroads stopped running, "scarcely a wheel in motion." Although Haupt ascribed this situation as perhaps due to the interference of officers with the management of the railroads, he admitted he was not sure if that was the real cause of the difficulty. Haupt told the Committee on the Conduct of the War that McCallum was in charge of the roads during his absence but that no censure should be attached to him: "He is one of the most able railway managers in the United States, and I consider his integrity and fidelity beyond question; but being confined by office duties in Washington he could not possibly give any attention in the field." Haupt then went on to inform the Committee that he was an opposite type completely. Quite frankly, the railroader informed the Committee that he consistently "declined to have anything to do with routine business or office details." This enabled him to be free to use his own abilities where they were most needed. "To this fact," maintained Haupt, "and not to any superior skill or experience, is any apparent efficiency under my administration to be attributed."[8]

Haupt's analysis of his contribution, although apparently couched in terms of false modesty, is actually an accurate estimate of how he got things done. His commanding officer, McDowell, was emphatic in his commendation of Haupt's achievements. For example, when reports reached Meigs that McDowell's men were suffering from lack of food, the Quartermaster General blamed the situation on poor railroad management and told McCallum that the Quartermaster Department would regulate the dispatch of stores by rail. McDowell replied at once with a letter to Stanton, requesting that the order be revoked. McDowell pointed out to Stanton that the failure to move supplies was not Haupt's fault. "He is, as you know, one of the best railroad managers in the United States, and I beg to assure you he is doing more than any other man can do. With the broken-down road, and weak, worn-out old locomotives, bridges going down with the freshet, and insufficient assistance, he has difficulty enough without adding to them by placing him under an officer [of the Quartermaster Department] who has had no experience of railroad management, of which Haupt is the head." The General concluded his letter with the urgent request that Haupt not be lost by being placed under a man inexperienced in railroad matters.[9]

In addition to the "broken-down road" and "weak, worn-out old locomotives," Haupt soon found an even more serious deficiency—that of trained and highly motivated construction crews. The only laborers available were soldiers detailed from regiments in the vicinity of the rail line. Many of these men were entirely unaccustomed to work of the type required, others were unwilling, and what is worst of all, the details were changed daily, so that after spending a great part of a day in organizing the labor force, the next day would witness the appearance of new details, and the process repeated itself. T. S. C. Lowe was having a similar experience in his futile efforts to get well-trained crews to handle his balloons on the Peninsula. Most regiments were merely marking time until they would be sent to the front and, very typically, they were averse to manual labor of *any* sort. With some outstanding exceptions, discipline in Federal regiments at this early stage of the war was poor, and some officers withheld support from the railroad managers by not insisting that the men work hard while on construction detail.

Symptomatic of the attitude of some Federal troops is the situation revealed in a telegram from McDowell to Haupt, dated May 4th. The General informed his railroader that "the 95th New York refused to work today, alleging that they were promised to be paid their extra pay by Saturday, and that they have no longer any faith in Government promises." This was mutiny and McDowell ordered all men who refused to work to be disarmed and sent to the rear.[10]

Obviously the utilization of untrained and poorly disciplined soldiers was not the answer to Haupt's construction problems. The railroader, pressed for time, had to reconstruct wharves and buildings at Aquia Creek, about three miles of completely destroyed railroad line, and bridges across the Accokeek and Rappahannock

Rivers and Potomac Creek. In addition, there were the additional projects of reconstructing seven bridges on the Manassas Gap road, relaying a portion of the track on that road, and forwarding supplies to the army by both roads. Accordingly, Haupt decided to use Negro laborers in so far as he was able to get them. These Negroes, mostly fugitive slaves, were used to the extent that they could be induced to stay on the job. Most of them, according to Haupt, "were all bound for Washington, as they said, to see 'Massa Lincoln.'"[11]

Although the Negro laborer was to make a very substantial contribution to Haupt's "Construction Corps" later on in the war, Haupt early realized that his laborers must be permanently organized to insure a well-trained construction unit to service the army. Accordingly he submitted his ideas to McDowell, hoping that they would aid the General in getting a permanent and efficient organization for his forces.[12] The railroader pointed out that the bridges to be built would probably be similar to the type he had built at Potomac Creek. Trestles would be used and built in the shortest possible time, to be replaced later by permanent structures if required. Bridges would be built of round stick cut on the spot.

Although Haupt's excellent plans were not immediately implemented, they clearly demonstrate his practical, common-sense approach to construction problems, an approach completely unknown to such theorists as McCallum. The eventual adoption of Haupt's ideas laid the groundwork for much of the later Federal success in military railroading.

However, with the materials at hand and such reluctant soldiery or contrabands as he could procure,

Haupt set to work. The reconstruction of the roads and wharves at Aquia Creek Landing, McDowell's main supply base, demanded immediate attention. The extensive wharf, covering more than an acre (about 50,000 square feet) with all the buildings, had been destroyed by fire. For a distance of three miles the rail line leading to this wharf had been destroyed, the rails removed and the ties burned. All the bridges were gone and in several cases even the abutments had been blown up.

Haupt began by laying track but cavalry had cut up the road bed while the wet weather had converted the clay surface into tenacious mud. The cross ties were of all conceivable sizes. Although the laborers were soldiers with no experience in and little enthusiasm for laying track, and although the weather was rainy, Haupt kept things moving. He did this mainly by taking the most intelligent young officers of the details assigned to him and using them as assistant engineers. They made levelling instruments from sticks, and by working all night in the rain, spiking rails by lantern light, they succeeded in laying the three miles of track in three days. Engines could now pass over the stretch and could transport construction material for the work yet to be done. More than 3,000 cross ties were cut by soldiers during these three days and delivered to the rail line.

During the work on the road, McDowell came out almost daily to watch the progress and encourage the men by his presence. He told Haupt that he had never heard sweeter music than the click of the hammers when the men were working all night near his headquarters, spiking the rails by the aid of lanterns, the men soaked with rain and the ties being laid in the mud. It was a rather sorry looking track when first laid, and when the

General went out to inspect it the next morning, he expressed doubts that any engine could run over it. Haupt requested him to suspend judgment until the following morning and to look at the road then. McDowell came as promised and was surprised to find the track well lined up, well surfaced and ballasted with earth. However, since the ties had been cut by soldiers and varied in thickness from four inches to a foot, the task of surfacing was not an easy one.

Haupt now turned to the construction of a bridge over Accokeek River. On the morning of May 3rd the first load of bridge lumber was brought up from the landing. At noon the working party was visited by Stanton, Seward, Chase and various officers who witnessed the commencement of the bridge framing. Although the project called for a structure 150 feet long and 30 feet high, McDowell himself rode across the completed bridge the next day on a locomotive. The time occupied in erecting it was about 15 working hours.[13]

The next and most formidable obstacle of all was the deep chasm of Potomac Creek nearly 400 feet wide which had been crossed by a deck bridge approximately 80 feet above the water. This bridge, like the others spanning creeks and rivers on the rail line, had been completely destroyed by the enemy. Haupt began work on this bridge at the same time he was working on the Accokeek bridge. On May 3rd some logs were laid for crib foundations, but work was held up three days until some kind of a construction crew could be assembled. Three companies of the 6th and 7th Wisconsin and the 19th Indiana regiments had been detailed as the construction force. Work dragged because many of the men were sick while others were absent on guard duty. It was seldom that more than 100-120 men could be found fit for service. Moreover, very few were able or willing to climb about on ropes and poles at an elevation of 80 feet. And yet, these men were from the "Iron Brigade," which was soon to achieve great fame for valor in combat!

Nevertheless, with soldiers unaccustomed to such work, with an insufficient supply of tools, with occasional scarcity of food, and with several days of wet weather, the work was pushed so rapidly that in nine days the bridge was crossed on foot. In less than two weeks the first engine passed over, to the great delight of the soldiers whose labors had constructed it. On May 19th trains were running to Fredericksburg.

It was not only the soldiers who were delighted with Haupt's Potomac Creek Bridge; their Commander-in-Chief was also impressed. After Lincoln had first seen the structure he remarked: "I have seen the most remarkable structure that human eyes ever rested upon. That man, Haupt, has built a bridge across Potomac Creek, about four hundred feet long and nearly a hundred feet high, over which loaded trains are running every hour, and upon my word . . . there is nothing in it but bean-poles and cornstalks."[14]

Professional engineers were impressed, too. Among the civil engineers of the day, one A. W. Hoyt noted that the bridge utilized 34,760 linear feet of timber, which, if placed in a straight line, would have reached nearly seven miles. The equivalent in board measure was about 2½ million.[15]

One of the most prominent military engineers cited Haupt's bridging of Potomac Creek and Daniel Stone's bridging of the Rappahannock in a textbook on military bridges which appeared the following year. Stone, an assistant of Haupt, constructed a bridge over the Rappahannock River in about the same length of time as that for Potomac Creek. This bridge was about 600 feet long and 43 feet above the water. Stone's bridge was part of the Fredericksburg rail line. The military engineer, General George W. Cullum, characterized Haupt's Potomac Creek bridge as "one of the simplest, boldest, and most remarkable bridge structures ever built." Cullum was impressed by the fact that the soldiers who assisted in the bridge construction never lost their discipline or their instruction as soldiers. "The work they did excited, to a high degree, the wonder and admiration of several distinguished foreign officers, who have never imagined such construction possible by such means, and in such a way, in the time in which [it was] done."[16]

And McDowell himself, in his testimony before the Committee on the Conduct of the War, was very complimentary of Haupt's feat:[17] McDowell pointed out that the bridge carried . . .

> daily from 10 to 20 heavy railway trains in both directions, and has withstood several severe freshets and storms without injury. This bridge was built . . . in *nine* working days, during which time the greater part of the material was cut and hauled.

Certainly the most remarkable feature about the bridge was that it was built by common soldiers, not by trained men. After a permanent construction corps had been organized and the men properly drilled, much larger bridges were built in half the time.[18]

After completing the road to Fredericksburg, Haupt set up his headquarters in the city. When the city was evacuated by the Confederates they had placed torpedoes with percussion fuses under the tracks about the depot grounds to blow up trains that might be coming in. However, friendly Negroes pointed out the location of these "infernal machines" and the soldiers removed quite a number and placed them in a small brick building detached from the railroad station which had been used as a powder magazine by the railroad company. A sentinel on duty one day apparently handled one of these torpedoes carelessly and set off an explosion which wrecked the building and shook the city. Nothing was ever seen of the sentinel except a piece of his gun at a considerable distance away. Since some torpedoes were probably under the track, a train was made up with the engine behind and a car very heavily laden with scrap iron in front, so as to explode any torpedoes before the engine reached them, but no torpedoes were found.

McDowell maintained good order in the city, aided by the very efficient Provost Marshal General of the Army of the Potomac, General Marsena R. Patrick. Private property was protected and depredations were punished. McDowell had fifteen to twenty soldiers at a time wearing such signs as "I stole a ham" or "I broke into a private house." When a Federal general dispossessed a widow of her house, McDowell reprimanded him, compelled him to vacate the house, and reinstated the former occupants.[19]

On Friday, May 23rd, Haupt sat in on a council of war at General McDowell's headquarters. Present were Lincoln, Stanton, and probably Chase. McDowell informed the President that Shields's division had joined him in bad shape, lacking shoes, clothing, and ammunition. The General went on to explain that he would like very much to move on the following day, but that he could not possibly be ready by that time, while Monday would be too late. He wished very much to move on Sunday, but knowing Lincoln's objections to these Sunday movements he would prefer to clear a Sunday movement with the President. Lincoln responded by telling McDowell to make "a good ready" and start on Monday morning. Every preparation was made for a rapid movement towards Richmond on Monday, May 26th. Haupt had a profile of the line to Richmond, knew the size of every bridge, and was prepared for prompt reconstruction operations.

On Saturday night the bridge across the Massaponax River, six miles below Fredericksburg, which had been prepared for burning by the enemy for about two weeks, was set on fire, the Confederates being apparently informed of the Federals' intended movements; and the enemy retreated, as was understood, to a distance of about twenty-five miles below Fredericksburg. Anticipating this movement, Haupt had prepared a bridge ready to be loaded on cars, which would be thrown across a stream in a single day or less, by means of which he expected to advance to a distance of twenty-five miles. Then, by forced marches the whole of the Corps of General McDowell was to be taken to Richmond, where he would be able to act in concert with General McClellan.

Briefly, the Federal plan provided that after McClellan had arrived on the Chickahominy on May 26th, McDowell was to join the Army of the Potomac from Fredericksburg. But before this could be accomplished Jackson had successfully completed his brilliant raid in the Shenandoah Valley and aroused great alarm in

Washington for the safety of the capital. Despite strong opposition from McDowell the Administration gave up the plan for reinforcing McClellan on the Peninsula, by way of Fredericksburg, and McDowell was ordered to strike across country, and if possible to intercept Jackson.

The decision to go after Jackson greatly depressed McDowell, who informed Lincoln that it would be impossible for him to accomplish the mission. In the futile attempt to nab the wily Confederate leader, McDowell would lose an exceedingly favorable opportunity of securing the early fall of Richmond. Nevertheless, he would of course obey orders, unless those orders were countermanded. But the orders remained unchanged, and the movement to intercept Jackson was commenced immediately.

McDowell was strongly opposed to the change in plans. He asserted that Washington was in no danger, that the forces under Banks and Fremont were sufficient for its protection, that Jackson had only one-third the distance to retreat which he (McDowell) had to advance, that before the Federals could reach Front Royal the enemy would be out of reach. McDowell deemed the move to be merely a diversion to break up the plan of the campaign, and that if he were allowed to advance Richmond would fall and the war would be substantially at an end. If the orders which he received were insisted upon, maintained McDowell, the war would be prolonged indefinitely. As it turned out, the orders were insisted upon, the war did drag out for three more years, and, since the public demanded a victim for Jackson's escape, McDowell was that victim. McDowell, Haupt noted, was seldom permitted to execute any movement which he recommended, but was compelled to act against his better judgment.[20]

The General requested Haupt to remain with him at all times in the advance to Front Royal. Haupt replied that he could not do so at once without leaving the transportation in great confusion. It was necessary, first of all, to regulate the transportation, which would require a day or two, and then Haupt could join him.

Haupt joined McDowell at Manassas and learned from the General that a bridge had been burned, and a portion of the track torn up on the Manassas Gap Railroad. Haupt sent for the construction corps, started the same night for Rectortown, constructed two bridges the next day, Friday, five more on Saturday, and reached Front Royal about Sunday noon, having reconstructed the track over the mountains on Sunday morning.

During this time, General McDowell had been using every exertion to forward his troops by forced marches, and succeeded in reaching Front Royal one hour before the time fixed by the President for him to be there. When Haupt reached Front Royal there appeared to be an engagement going on; frequent discharges of artillery were heard, and General McDowell was moving his troops into position, expecting a major battle. The General expected Haupt to hurry up the supplies and reinforcements. Haupt returned at once on a locomotive and on the same afternoon he put 5,000 troops into Front Royal. These troops were not needed; Jackson had already escaped.[21]

Shortly after the campaign, Haupt was quizzed as to what he believed would have resulted from McDowell's advance on Richmond in view of the general's preparations for that advance. Haupt replied as follows:

I have no doubts that Richmond would have been taken within a very few days. General McClellan's army at that time was probably 50,000 stronger than it is at present, being now wasted by casualty and disease. General McDowell's force was 40,000 strong, and in a very few days, probably in three or four days, he could have been in front of Richmond; and the two armies, acting in concert with each other, would have either caused Richmond to capitulate, or the rebels would have retreated, as on other occasions. We would have obtained possession of the city in either case.[22]

Although Haupt indicated to Stanton that he wished to return to Massachusetts after completing reconstruction of the line to Fredericksburg, he assured the Secretary he would stay on if McDowell really needed him for the advance to Front Royal.[23] On May 28th Haupt received his appointment as chief of construction and transportation in McDowell's Department of the Rappahannock, and was authorized to do whatever he deemed expedient to open for use all military railroads in the Department. Of more significance for Haupt's future operations, however, was his authorization to establish rules and regulations, appoint assistants and define their duties, and make requisitions with the approval of the commanding general. Thus, he was given sweeping powers to get the railroads in operation and keep them that way. Moreover, he was authorized to form a permanent corps of artificers "organized, officered, and equipped" in such manner as Haupt himself would prescribe. He could hire civilians as foremen and assistants to carry out his tasks.[24] Haupt's jurisdiction was later (August 18, 1862) extended to include "all railroads . . . within the limits of the Army of Virginia."[25]

During this brief campaign Haupt time and again demonstrated his abilities as a military engineer, and above all, as a man who was at his best when confronted with sudden and difficult problems to solve. On May 30th, a great storm washed away several of his bridges. McDowell soon was reporting that "the indefatigable Colonel Haupt" had already rebuilt two bridges destroyed by the enemy and in spite of the storm would have the road open by morning.[26] The next day an engineer officer informed McDowell that there was a bad break in the railroad, track torn up, with rails and ties thrown down the mountainside. McDowell got off a hurried note to Haupt, some distance away. However, the railroader replied by the same messenger that the General need feel no uneasiness, because, if the rails were within reach, the break could be repaired in a few hours. On June 1st, soon after daylight, the men reached the scene and got down to work. All broken cars were tumbled over the bank in short order. The track gang was divided into two working parties who worked toward each other from the opposite ends of the break. Rails and ties were hauled up from the side of the mountain below, and by 10 A.M. an engine passed over and was sent on to McDowell.[27]

The following day, Haupt, in his official capacity as superintendent of construction and transportation, USMRR, Department of the Rappahannock, issued a general order providing that all orders and instructions regarding train movements must be given by Haupt himself or his deputy on the spot, or by authorized train dispatchers. The order provided that no other orders would be allowed to interfere with these instructions, unless emanating from the Commanding General or the Chief of Transportation.[28] Despite this order, the mili-

tary railroads continued to have their schedules interfered with by line officers. As if this interference in the
midst of active campaigning were not enough, Haupt
was plagued by unreasonable demands from the Quartermaster Department, especially in respect to bureaucratic
insistence on filling out forms. On June 9th, Haupt received a letter from McCallum, with an enclosure from
the Adjutant General of the Army, ordering that receipts be given for all supplies transported by rail. As
Haupt correctly pointed out to McCallum, this red tape
was "seriously objectionable." The railroad cars were
loaded and unloaded by the Quartermaster Department.
Transportation personnel were not supposed to know
the contents of the cars, and if required to give receipts,
they would have to inspect every individual car, "without
the slightest advantage that I can perceive." Haupt went
on to state that if receipts were insisted on, the only
form which he would approve would be "cars numbered
such and such, said to contain commissary stores" etc.
If the Quartermaster Department so wished, it could
send a representative who could accompany each train,
but the transportation department should only be
responsible for transport and delivering the cars. Any
other method would only result in confusion.[29] Haupt
was right, and both Assistant Secretary Watson and
Quartermaster General Meigs agreed with him. But
Stanton, who had issued the order in the first place, was
furious. "To rescind this order," he said, "will make
me ridiculous. I issued a peremptory order, and will not
take it back, but if you [Watson] and Meigs say that
it cannot be enforced, go to Haupt and tell him to consider it a dead letter."[30] The lack of moral courage exhibited here was typical of the Secretary of War.

When it was obvious that Jackson had escaped, the

Army of the Rappahannock returned from the Shenandoah Valley and regrouped. McDowell set his headquarters up at Manassas and began to drill and reequip his demoralized troops. During this lull in active operations, Haupt directed his attention toward improving the organization of his construction corps, which was still composed chiefly of soldiers. Since the campaign was at an end, and believing he had accomplished the purposes for which he had been originally summoned to Washington, Haupt wrote a rather lengthy letter to Stanton, pointing out that he wished to return to Massachusetts in order to give some attention to his financial affairs, which were in "much confusion" because of his absence. To this letter no answer was returned.[31]

While awaiting a reply to his request, Haupt drew up regulations for transport of supplies over military railroads.[32] These regulations are a good example of Haupt's ability to state in clear sensible language exactly what a situation called for in terms of actual needs and in language every individual could easily understand. Briefly, the regulations as laid down by Haupt called on Quartermaster personnel, sutlers, and officers to send by rail only legitimate goods and supplies properly labelled and subject to inspection by the transportation department. Sutlers' goods were to be carried only at the convenience of the transportation department, while articles intended for the private use of military personnel could be sent by the Adams Express Company; but all such articles were subject to examination by the Provost Marshal. Strict enforcement of these regulations was certain to cause considerable grumbling, even among some officers of high rank, but no student of the logistical problems confronting the Federal forces in 1862 can doubt that such rules were long overdue.

The day after these regulations were published, Mc-Dowell was relieved of command. The entire campaign had been a bad one: rain, mud, and lack of shelter had resulted in a demoralized army. The public and press demanded a victim.

McDowell deserved a better fate. Of all the commanders in the East under whom Haupt was to serve, he considered McDowell to have been the most able, but also the most unfortunate and unpopular. While allowance must be made of the fact that Haupt was a personal friend of the hapless General, and had served with him at West Point, the analysis of his commander by Haupt is valuable, especially because it supplies details on McDowell's qualities which have not been sufficiently recognized.

Haupt was especially impressed by the exceptionally firm discipline maintained by McDowell, and his insistence on dispensing with unnecessary transportation.[33] This included regimental bands and intoxicating beverages, although the latter provision annoyed the German regiments. He commandeered anything whatsoever which was necessary for the use of the army, but always by proper requisition. McDowell claimed the privilege of being the "only plunderer in the Army of the Rappahannock." Orders were to leave sufficient subsistence to keep families from starvation. Obviously Haupt felt the same way about "living off the country." He took lumber wherever it could be found; in a short time, practically all the timber suitable for bridging was exhausted in the vicinity of Potomac Creek, and timber in the vicinity of Fredericksburg itself even disappeared. A large machine shop and foundry in the city, "with all the machinery and tools pertaining thereto" were appropriated for the use of the road in Fredericksburg.[34]

Haupt was also convinced that McDowell wanted to cooperate closely with McClellan in a joint advance on Richmond. In fact, he was willing to act in any capacity whatever, if only something could be accomplished.[35] The attention which McDowell paid to details of the construction work was very gratifying to Haupt. The General was almost constantly upon the road, and sometimes anticipated wants even before Haupt had thought of them himself.[36]

However, McDowell was predestined to failure. Naturally, his failure at First Bull Run made him unpopular with the public, while his strict discipline made him unpopular with the troops. He regarded newspaper reporters as a nuisance and they retaliated by writing him down. Thus, their papers, circulating in the camps, built up opposition to him among the rank and file. He was continually being hampered by instructions from Washington, and according to Haupt was not permitted the freedom of movement which his adversary Jackson had, nor which was accorded future Federal commanders."[37]

NOTES: CHAPTER 4

1. Haupt, p. 44.
2. Haupt's Report to Stanton, September 9, 1863.
3. Haupt, p. 43.
4. *Report,* Committee on the Conduct of the War, Part I, (1863), pp. 370–372. Haupt's initial assignment was a fortunate one in terms of personal relations. As Haupt was about to retire after reporting to McDowell the General said: "Why, Haupt, you don't seem to know me." Haupt replied that he did not recall ever having met him before. "Well," said McDowell, "that hurts my feelings. Don't you remember when I came to West Point as a plebe in 1834, that you took me into your tent during my first encampment and extended to me your protection as an older cadet?" Haupt did remember that "a fat boy from Ohio" had been quartered in his tent, but had no idea

that this boy was the General in command of the Army of the Rappahannock. (Haupt, pp. 44–45.)

5. *Ibid.,* Part III, p. 427.
6. Haupt's Final Report to Stanton, September 9, 1863.
7. *Report,* Committee on the Conduct of the War, Part I, pp. 370–372.
8. *Ibid.*
9. *Official Records,* Series I, Vol. 12, Part 3, p. 333.
10. McDowell to Haupt, telegram dated May 4, 1862. Manuscript in author's possession.
11. *Official Records,* Series I, Vol. 12, Part 1, p. 77.
12. *Ibid.,* Part 3, pp. 177–180.
13. Haupt, p. 46.
14. *Photographic History,* Vol. 5, p. 280.
15. Haupt. p. 46.
16. Cullum, George W., *Military Bridges,* pp. 222–226. This was the Cullum who was a classmate of Haupt at West Point.
17. *Official Records,* Series I, Vol. 12, Part I, p. 281.
18. Haupt. p. 48.
19. *Ibid.* p. 49.
20. *Ibid.* p. 50.
21. *Report,* Committee on Conduct of the War, Part III, p. 429.
22. *Ibid.*
23. Haupt to Stanton, May 28, 1862. Haupt *Letter Book,* Library of Congress.
24. *Official Records,* Series I, Vol. 12, Part 3, pp. 274–275.
25. *Ibid.* p. 598, 602.
26. *Ibid.* Vol. 15, p. 649.
27. *Photographic History,* Vol. 5, p. 284.
28. General Order dated June 2, 1862. Haupt *Order Book,* Library of Congress.
29. Haupt to McCallum, June 9, 1862, National Archives.
30. Haupt, p. 165.
31. Haupt, pp. 66–67, Letter sent June 20, 1862.
32. General Orders No. 7, June 25, 1862, Haupt, pp. 67–68.
33. *Ibid.,* p. 303.
34. *Official Records,* Series I, Vol. 12, Part 1, pp. 76–80.
35. Haupt's testimony to Committee on the Conduct of the War, *Report,* Part 3, p. 427.
36. *Official Records,* Series I, Vol. 12, Part 1, pp. 76–80.
37. Haupt, p. 304.

5

THE CONSTRUCTION CORPS

Despite the Federals' failure to catch up with Jackson, their railroad personnel gained invaluable experience in military railroad operations at the front. Haupt's genius for adaptability turned this experience into principles of organization and operational methods which were to be invaluable to him and the Federal cause throughout the war. It was during the campaign just ended that Haupt brought into being a construction corps, one of his major contributions to military railroading. Obvious from the very first day that Haupt reported for duty was the lack of a trained, dependable construction unit, well officered and manned by a full complement of permanently assigned well-disciplined personnel.

If Federal military operations were to be successful, these operations needed constant logistical support from a smoothly functioning railroad system. But in addition to a terrain unfavorable to construction of rail lines because of thick woods and numerous streams, the Federals were constantly harassed by hostile military and sabotage attacks on their attenuated line of communications. When the enemy forces retreated, they tore up and destroyed roadbeds while removing every item of rolling stock available. Illustrative of this was the destruction (June 23, 1861) of the railroad in the Martinsburg, Virginia, area by Stonewall Jackson. There were 56 locomotives and more than 300 cars in this area. Jackson burned 42 of the engines and destroyed what was left so thoroughly that a newspaper reporter observed:

> All along the railroad were scattered coal cars in long lines with the coal still burning, having been set on fire . . . [Jackson's men] had kindled huge fires around them, burning all the woodwork and a great deal of the iron. These cars held about twenty tons each . . . . Some small bridges had been burned with the cars on them and giving way, the cars were left piled one on another in the small streams below, all battered and bent.[1]

Enemy action and saboteur raids were only the beginning. Much more serious were the activities of guerrillas who placed obstructions on tracks, loosened rails, burned bridges, and then vanished to the woods or their homes where they posed as innocent farmers. Destruction of the many bridges along the rail lines was probably the most serious of the enemy depredations; certainly such destruction resulted in great loss of time for advancing Federal forces.

Train crews ran their trains under conditions of real danger. Train dispatchers and operators were entitled to great credit; they occupied positions near the enemy to report movements and held positions after line units had retired until nearly surrounded, then escaped through the bushes. One of Haupt's most efficient subordinates,

M. J. McCrickett, was killed by guerrillas. The engine on which he was riding was switched off the track on a high embankment by means of a telegraph wire attached to a rail and pulled by men concealed in a thicket. Several other men were killed at the same time. Engineers and firemen were fired on so often that it was necessary to armor plate their cabs.[2]

Unfortunately for the Federals, the construction, repair, and defense of rail lines had not been emphasized by American military engineers prior to the Civil War. Although a few engineers had written manuals on various aspects of military engineering, these officers tended to be theoretical and unduly emphasized siege operations at the expense of operations of movement. Their manuals were of little use to Federal commanders and military railroaders in 1861 and 1862. Moreover, some of the military engineers had not kept abreast of the military potentialities of the railroad. Some of the engineers (e.g. Captain J. C. Duane) adapted their earlier training to the new conditions of the war.

In the earlier months of the war great dependence was placed on the engineer units, regular and volunteer, that were regularly incorporated in the field armies. Prominent among these professional military engineers were such men as George W. Cullum, John G. Barnard, and J. C. Duane. Each of these men wrote manuals on military engineering, and in many instances their observations were reflections of their solutions to problems peculiar to the American scene. They were well acquainted with European writings, especially French and British, of campaigns from Waterloo to Sevastopol. But many foreign books on such subjects as military bridges were either nonexistent or so obsolete as to be of little use. For example, Sir Howard Douglas's treatment of the subject of military bridges and river crossings appeared in 1853 as the third edition of a work begun in 1808 during the Napoleonic Wars. This book of 430 pages and 14 plates was revised, but even in the 1853 edition the plates depicted pontoon bridges built on floating casks! The work contained much on British experience in bridging but the methods of laying bridges were both slow and cumbersome.[3]

Of some improvement was a work by Haupt's old classmate, Cullum, who had served as "superintending engineer for devising and constructing . . . ponton* trains for our Armies" in the Mexican War. A year after that war ended (1849) Cullum's experiences appeared in his *Military Bridges with India-Rubber Pontons*. During the Civil War he served in the West under Halleck as a member of a "ponton board" to examine all designs for military bridges presented to the War Department, January 22, 1863, to September 5, 1864. Cullum's *Systems of Military Bridges*, which appeared in 1863, was an elaboration of his 1849 work. A third edition appeared after the war.

Another classmate of Cullum and Haupt was John G. Barnard, a prominent officer, especially in 1862 under McClellan. Barnard, author of *Dangers and Defenses of New York* (1859), *Notes on Seacoast Defense* (1861), *The C.S.A. and the Battle of Bull Run* (1862), in conjunction with General W. F. Barry, summed up tactical employment of engineer and artillery units under "Little Mac" on the Peninsula.[4]

To the professional literature of these regular army engineers was added in 1864 an excellent manual on the

* During this period, *ponton* was the usual spelling.

tactical employment of engineers by Captain Duane, whom Barnard believed "possessed a more extensive and thorough practical and experimental knowledge of military bridges than any other man in this country."[5]

While Duane's work certainly merits high praise, it must be emphasized that his contribution was primarily in tactical employment of engineer troops. It remained for Haupt to write the most thorough and imaginative treatise on military engineering to appear during the war. In his work, *Military Bridges,* which appeared the year following his retirement, Haupt incorporated the valuable experience he had acquired during his tour of active service. The book includes detailed discussions of types of bridges, blanket boats, floating docks, suggestions for protection of military railroads and bridges, use of army telegraph, and the utilization of buried shells as mines. This book is especially interesting because it includes data on such innovations as "torpedoes" used in destroying bridges and various methods of destroying locomotives.[6]

Although there was no need for friction, it is now clear that the engineer units of the Army and the rough-and-ready construction and transportation personnel of the United States Military Railroads did not always see eye to eye. General Halleck, who consistently supported Haupt in 1862 and 1863, never did favor Haupt's idea of forming for railroad work a separate "construction and transportation corps" of civilians. The General believed that the engineer units of the line, who had been enlisted and received double pay for their work, should attend to all the engineering duties of the military forces. Haupt pointed out that if one of the engineer regiments were placed under *his* control on a permanent basis, he would get such a regiment well organized, drilled and made efficient for bridge construction duty, provided he could select the officers and men. However, Haupt preferred civilians to soldiers for such work.[7]

Although regular engineer officers like General Barnard spoke highly of the regular engineer companies, and especially such volunteer organizations as the 15th and 50th New York Engineers, they were too conservative in many cases to realize the potentialities of such innovations as canvas pontoon[8] bridges, one of the developments successfully demonstrated during the war.

It is a matter of record, though often overlooked because of the subsequent blood bath in front of the stone wall at Fredericksburg, that regular engineer officers like General Daniel Woodbury and Major Ira Spaulding failed Burnside miserably. As early as November 14th (a month before the battle) Burnside was desperately trying to get these officers to start the pontoon train toward the front. Apparently much of the trouble lay with the authorities in Washington, but even Halleck admitted that Burnside should have sent up some of his own staff to push matters. But General Woodbury, who had promised Burnside the pontoons on the 17th of November, did not even start them for the front until the 19th. On that day it commenced raining, which due to the bad roads delayed the pontoons so much that they eventually were transported by steamer and did not arrive until the 22nd or 23rd of November. According to Burnside, the non-arrival of the pontoons permitted the enemy to concentrate his forces and ultimately to defeat the Federals.[9] Woodbury was soon sent to an unimportant assignment where his dilatoriness would not hamper future Federal operations, but there remained some skepticism in regular army circles about the need for a new type of engineering task force for military railroads.

Shortly after his arrival at McDowell's headquarters, Haupt had begun to use soldiers for construction of rail lines and bridges. But poor organization had hampered his operations, especially in bridge construction. There were few men able or willing to climb about on the high trestles. In fact, out of twelve men selected to spike poles on top of bents in the Potomac Creek bridge, only one man even made his appearance! The Construction personnel were less than enthusiastic, "they were wet, dull and no life or activity in them."[10] However, the bridge was finished on May 13, 1862, and shortly thereafter Haupt drew up a projected organization for bridge construction.[11]

Due primarily to the surprising efficiency of Haupt's heterogeneous group of workmen in construction work during the first month of Haupt's active campaigning, Stanton included a special provision for forming a permanent construction force.[12] This authorization had appeared back on May 28, 1862, in confirming Haupt's original appointment of "Chief of Construction and Transportation" in the Department of the Rappahannock. In addition to sweeping powers in managing the military railroads in the Department, Haupt had been "authorized to form a permanent corps of artificers, organized, officered, and equipped in such manner as he might prescribe; to supply said corps with rations, transportation, tools and implements by requisitions upon the proper departments; to employ civilians and foremen and assistants, under such rules and rates of compensation as he deemed expedient; to make such additions to ordinary rations, when actually at work, as he deemed necessary."

With Stanton's authorization behind him, Haupt went to work to draw up the organization of his construction corps, aided by his experience of the past few weeks. The 300 workmen on the Potomac Creek bridge had been enlisted men, "the refuse of three [volunteer] regiments;" very few of them were mechanics; many of them could not even handle an axe. None were engineer troops; nor were any trained in the special duty to which they were assigned. Some were not able, and many not willing to work; and yet, by interrogating the men as to their previous occupations, it was possible to classify them and form them into squads. Thus was a degree of efficiency achieved which led to very satisfactory, and, considering the circumstances, very extraordinary results.[13]

These results were due largely to the rigid enforcement of a detailed and precise set of regulations issued June 11, 1862, for the nascent Construction Corps in the Department of the Rappahannock.[14]

Despite these regulations, Haupt continued to have difficulty in acquiring the type of workers he needed. Many of the soldiers were not used to hard manual labor; they were inexperienced and unskilled, "and much effort was required to infuse into them a proper emulation and induce efforts to hasten completion of the work."[15] Eventually, with the exception of the higher officers and foremen, the Construction Corps consisted almost entirely of contrabands, Negro slaves who had fled to Federal lines. Thousands of these refugees had flocked into Washington, and from them were selected several hundred healthy, able-bodied men familiar with the use of the axe. These contrabands worked with enthusiasm, and each gang vied with the others to excel in the specific tasks assigned them. Haupt constantly emphasized to the foremen that in the construction work, permanency was not considered. It was not a question of months or weeks, as in erecting permanent structures, but a question of hours.[16]

Although contrabands eventually made up the majority of Haupt's construction crews, he was compelled to use soldiers as workmen for several months. The work details from the regiments were composed of unwilling soldiers; they often resented their short tours with Haupt's construction work. Haupt soon realized that only permanently detailed men could be depended upon, but these never came from the army. Eventually civilian laborers proved to be the answer. Meanwhile, Haupt did the best he could with the detailed soldiery.

Occasionally, the soldiers would work well for a few days. This apparently was true for exceptionally fine units. For example, elements of the famous Iron Brigade assisted in the construction of the bridge over Potomac Creek. A participant[17] described how the men went to work with a vim although they had marched four miles to reach the construction site. Work squads, commanded by lieutenants, performed well. However, the men were impatiently aware that McClellan was pressing on Richmond and "a strong feeling possessed . . . [them] that we were to be a mere side show while others performed the real acts of war." This impatience was real, and it prevailed in this brigade which later was to lose more men in battle than any other brigade in the entire Federal Army.

Most troops likewise resented performing railroad guard duty. Such troops were very frequently brand-new regiments or short-term militia units. Although some excellent regiments were utilized as guard units on railroads, many units were so assigned for seasoning. All the troops found guarding rail lines or working on them to be dull and monotonous duty. Many of these men had enlisted to fight and such a "safe assignment" as guarding rail lines lowered morale. Discipline and esprit de corps were bound to suffer in such a situation. The situation did not improve as the months went by. As late as December 1862, at the very time a great battle was in progress, Haupt informed the army commander, Burnside, that he had been unsuccessfully trying to get a detail to load critically needed bridge timber, but was forced to give it up. Haupt told Burnside that he would try to get civilians to build the bridges beyond Fredericksburg, because soldiers could be used only on a temporary basis. Haupt even found that getting civilians for work on wharves and bridge construction was a slow task.[18]

The career of the Construction Corps was indeed a checkered one. It was inextricably tied up with the fortunes of the Federal forces which it served. The Construction Corps which Haupt had organized under McDowell was disbanded by Pope. Owing to differences of opinion over whether to use soldiers or civilians no effective reorganization was made under Pope. However, despite the disbandment of the Construction Corps, service of great value was rendered during Pope's August campaign by individual officers and employees of the military railroads, both in transportation and construction.

During the Antietam and Fredericksburg campaigns Haupt's construction crews functioned fairly well except for the hit-and-miss methods Haupt was forced to use in order to get laborers, whether military or civilian. A small core of trained railroad repair men and carpenters served loyally and efficiently; the laborers were often soldiers detailed for short periods of time for construction work. Many military men, including Halleck himself, believed that the engineers of the army should be used exclusively for construction work.[19]

Early in 1863 a small Construction Corps of some 300 men was formed. This Corps, deliberately separated from the Transportation Corps,[20] numbered some 10,000 men, East and West, by the end of the war. The Corps was so organized as to combine a body of skilled workmen in each department of railroad construction and repair, under competent engineers, supplied with abundant materials, tools and transportation.

Under Hooker, the Corps had been rapidly whipped into shape. At the request of Fighting Joe, preparations had been made well in advance. In the operations which preceded Chancellorsville, Haupt was all ready to reconstruct rail lines and bridges faster than ever before. The Construction Corps had its bridging material all ready for Hooker's advance. Ample materials were in readiness for the "on to Richmond" movement, "but the enemy was so unaccommodating as not to give us an opportunity of using them."[21]

This reconstituted Construction Corps performed excellently during the Gettysburg campaign. Impressed by their performance during the battle of July 1-3, Haupt, on July 7th, pointed out to Stanton that the men of the U. S. Military Railroads were not in a position to acquire military distinction or rewards. He therefore suggested that some recognition of their services would be a great encouragement to men who so richly deserved it.[22]

The concept and organization of the Construction Corps was a major contribution to solving the logistical problems of Federal armies in the field. It developed into well-organized task forces for constructing rail lines and bridges, both East and West. Haupt told Stanton as early as July 7, 1863, that "no department of the military service is of more importance than that which is charged with constructing, reopening, and maintaining communication and forwarding supplies."[23] In his *Reminiscences,* Haupt closed his last chapter with the statement that generals who fought the battles have been eulogized and costly statues erected to their memories, but the Construction Corps, through whose fidelity and efficiency victories were rendered possible, have found no historian to do them honor. He ended his book with high praise for the faithful contrabands; "no other class of men would have exhibited so much patience and endurance under days and nights of continued and sleepless labor."[24]

A foreign observer[25] who saw the war in the United States at first hand noted that railroad service improved steadily during the war. He was particularly impressed by the "veritable prodigies" accomplished under Sherman in the West. "Few soldiers in the field" said this professional soldier, "were exposed to as great danger and hardship as were the men of the railway service."

In addition to this hazardous work at the front, the Construction Corps participated enthusiastically in a long series of experiments which Haupt conducted on bridging, river crossings, floating dock construction, and many tests of railroad line construction, and destruction. These new and experimental elements in military railroading were described by Haupt in written text and visually portrayed by the photographic department of the U. S. Military Railroads under Captain A. J. Russell.[26] The descriptive text and the accompanying photographs were sent to Halleck who had them printed up and distributed among officers in command of military departments, posts, and expeditions, where they were very useful. This information was to be strictly confined to the officers' own official use for the duration of the war; since any publication of details previous to the war's termination would be improper. The artist was detailed from one of the regiments and received no compensation except his normal pay, while the expense of the photographs was "inconsiderable."[27]

There were about one hundred of these valuable photographs* made to illustrate the original innovations and inventions of Haupt to promote the military operations of the Federal war effort.

NOTES, CHAPTER 5

1. *National Intelligencer,* July 12, 1861.
2. Haupt, p. 318.
3. Douglas, Sir Howard, *An Essay on* . . . *Military Bridges,* 3rd edition, London, 1853.
4. Barnard, John G. and Barry, W. F., *Reports of the Engineer and Artillery Operations* . . . *to the Close of the Peninsular Campaign,* New York, 1863.
5. *Ibid.,* p. 57.
6. Haupt, Herman, *Military Bridges,* New York, 1864.
7. *Official Records,* Series I, Vol. 21, p. 855.
8. See Barnard, John G. and Barry, W. F., *op. cit.,* p. 59.
9. Burnside's testimony to Committee on the Conduct of the War, *Report,* Part 1 (1863) pp. 651–655.
10. Haupt, p. 48.
11. Haupt, *Military Bridges,* pp. 13–17. See Appendix.
12. Haupt, p. 55
13. Haupt, *Military Bridges,* p. IV.
14. Haupt, pp. 64–66.
15. *Ibid.,* p. 268.
16. *Ibid.,* p. 319.
   * See appendix C.

17. Dawes, Rufus R., *Service with the Sixth Wisconsin Volunteers*, pp. 42–44.
18. *Official Records*, Series I, Vol. 21, pp. 850–855.
19. Haupt, p. 178.
20. *Official Records*, Series III, Vol. 3, pp. 1–2.
21. Haupt's final report to Stanton, September 9, 1863.
22. *Official Records*, Series I, Vol. 27, Part 1, pp. 23–24.
23. *Ibid.*
24. Haupt, p. 319.
25. Chanal, de. V., *The American Army in the War of Secession*, p. 194.
26. Russell, an officer of the 141st New York Volunteers, was a photographer and artist. He was specially detailed for this work at Haupt's request.
27. Haupt, p. 279.

6

THE PROBLEM OF SUPPLY, DISCIPLINE AND MILITARY INTERFERENCE

The transportation of supplies to troops in the field was to be one of Haupt's main problems and responsibilities. Although the military railroads were used extensively to move supplies and troops, Haupt constantly called his superiors' attention to the advantages of water transportation. Haupt realized that this method would permit the army to dispense almost entirely with baggage trains that so constantly obstructed roads and retarded forward movements. The use of rivers and the sea, which led to greater mobility, was more efficient. An army's rear communications could not so easily be broken, supplies were not so easily cut off, and, in Haupt's words, in case of disaster the army could fall back to positions, flanked by navigable rivers, where naval cooperation could be secured.[1] As a result of repeated requests Haupt was finally able to use water transportation to augment his movement of supplies by rail

during the Fredericksburg campaign. From supply depots on the Orange and Alexandria railroad, carloads
of supplies were sent to Alexandria; the cars themselves
were then loaded on barges and floated to Aquia Creek
where the rail trip was resumed. As Haupt pointed out,
the entire trip, without break of bulk, was accomplished
in about the same time as was required by the army to
march overland.[2]

Supplying the military forces was the primary responsibility of the Quartermaster's Department under the
able leadership of General Montgomery C. Meigs.
There can be no doubt of Meigs's opinion of Haupt.
In a letter to Halleck on October 21, 1862, the Quartermaster General said bluntly of Haupt that a more capable man could not be found.[3] And Halleck himself, a
week later, commented on the excellent work of Haupt
in forwarding supplies, with delays "less frequent and
of shorter duration than was usual with freight trains."
Moreover, Halleck believed that armies in the East had
been better supplied than the Federal armies operating
in the West.

Supplying Federal forces in the field was complicated
by the substantial quantities of supplies sent by rail and
water by such civilian agencies as aid societies, the Sanitary and Christian Commissions, private agencies, rela-
tives, friends, and other non-military sources. A large
proportion of the supplies were handled by the Adams
Express Company. On February 20, 1862, this Company
was granted a permit "to follow the Armies of the
United States . . . subject to such regulations as the
commanding officer of each column of the Army may
deem expedient."[5] In time, the Adams Express Company

became a household word both at the front and in the North generally. Thousands of boxes of food and other supplies were shipped by the Company to troops in the field and the volume of such traffic greatly decreased the space available for essential military supplies on the railroads. Moreover, many of the boxes of foodstuffs sent from the home front were allowed to pile up at rail heads to the outspoken disgust of the ultimate recipients when they found the contents rifled or spoiled by the delay in forwarding them.

Further complicating the supply problem was the granting of special privileges to newspaper men who followed the army. These ubiquitous individuals, invaluable for their news reporting, were furnished transportation and, in some cases, allowed military secrets to become public information. Most commanders did not often dare to contend with the large and enterprising corps of newspaper correspondents. General McDowell was forced to station guards about the telegraph instruments so the reporters could not intercept telegrams.[6]

In addition to the non-military agencies which constantly harrassed military movements by rail and water, Haupt ran counter to Stanton in the expediting of supply movements. It was probably inevitable that the railroader and his superior would clash. Stanton's order of November 12, 1862, directed railroad personnel to give receipts for property delivered to the railroads for transportation. Haupt believed this a duty of the Quartermaster Department and the order was not implemented.[7]

Stanton's rigid control of the telegraph hampered Haupt in his attempts to keep the trains moving smoothly on schedule. At first the trains were regulated entirely by telegraph without depending on any schedule. However, this system was liable to collapse and during the Second Bull Run campaign, a serious stoppage of all rail traffic occurred just when supplies were most needed. Haupt pointed out that a system which was so uncertain lacked reliability. "To require trains to lie for hours, perhaps for days, upon sidings waiting for instructions when there is no possibility of communicating with them," was a situation Haupt could not recommend. He resolved this by having officers walk or ride horseback from one train to the other to direct operations. To solve the problem permanently it was necessary to adopt a new system whereby all trains ran by schedule. If telegraphic communications failed, Haupt kept the trains moving by sending runners ahead with flags and relieving the runners when they were too tired. Cumbersome as this system appears today, it functioned well, especially during the Gettysburg campaign when thirty trains a day were sent over a road that under normal conditions had a capacity of only three or four.[8]

Although Haupt was reasonably successful in solving the supply problem he never received the support of military personnel which he should have had. Line officers especially were reluctant to cooperate. Some corps commanders were able to accumulate an excess of supplies while others suffered from deficiencies. Fodder for horses required approximately twice the rail facilities as food for the troops. The entire transportation for men and animals in the Army of the Potomac was as much as would have been required for 500,000 men without animals. No subsistence could be garnered from the country; all supplies had to be transported, often on a single rail line.[9]

As if this were not enough to slow down rail movements, Haupt had to contend with officious Quartermaster and Subsistence officers who were unable or unwilling to unload promptly the trains which did manage to get through.

Military railroads were charged with transporting the supplies while the Quartermaster Department loaded and unloaded them. It was essential that the loading and unloading be done promptly so that schedules could be maintained. And Haupt insisted that there should be a definite priority in the shipping of supplies and men. The order of importance was as follows: subsistence for men, forage, ammunition, hospital stores, veteran troops and raw troops.[10]

The most persistent slow-down practices which confronted the military railroads were, according to Haupt, attributable to the carelessness of the Quartermaster Department. Two aspects of this carelessness were particularly important: the practice of ordering unduly large quantities of supplies taken up to the front, and inefficiency in unloading supply trains. Each quartermaster in the field acted independently, and each of them tended to stockpile for any contingency. As a result, every time the armies retreated carloads of supplies were returned unused to base supply depots or destroyed. These supplies were not only wasted, but they monopolized the limited amount of equipment at the disposal of the military railroads. Rapid movements of the army were thereby impeded. Lack of promptness in unloading and returning cars merely added to the confusion. Instead of unloading an entire train on its arrival, only one or two cars would be unloaded. The remaining cars would be run on a siding and often remained there for weeks.[11]

Throughout his service Haupt had difficulty in getting

the cooperation of quartermasters in loading and unloading his trains. This trouble arose from the antagon-
ism of the military men toward the railroad men (who
were civilians) and the awareness that Haupt was
actually under the command of the Quartermaster General and *not* a free lance agent. On occasion Haupt had
to appeal to the immediate field commander to get back-
ing in his differences with the quartermasters. At Piedmont, Haupt found a serious back-up of loaded cars. He
protested to McDowell, who ordered his Chief Quartermaster and Chief Commissary to the depot at night in
a pouring rain in order to superintend personally the unloading of the cars.[12]

Haupt had to emphasize the importance of prompt
movement of supplies to responsible quartermasters who
should have been equally aware of the need for haste.
In November 1862, he urged Captain James F. Rusling,
Assistant Quartermaster at Manassas, to remember that
immediate unloading and return of cars was the only
salvation of the army. "Retreat or starvation is the pen-
alty of delay." The captain was urged to compel his men
to unload and return cars without a moment's delay. On
this occasion Burnside supported the railroader.[13] However, on another occasion General Daniel Sickles took
over control of train movements thereby taking it out
of the hands of the quartermasters. Sickles changed the
orders for unloading the trains, claiming that engines
were not being used wisely, and that he had neither wagons nor soldiers to be used for conveying supplies to the
depot, when there were engines available for the purpose.[14] However, he later agreed to cooperate with the
railroad personnel.

From this welter of confusion Haupt gradually developed an efficient system of transporting supplies and men to the front by rail. By Special Order No. 248, September 18, 1862, Haupt was authorized to do whatever he might deem expedient to facilitate the transportation of troops and supplies to aid the armies in the field in Virginia and Maryland. Halleck signed the order.[15] This was followed up by a more explicit order[16] from Stanton ordering commanding officers to assist railroad officers and quartermasters in unloading cars so as to prevent delays. On arrival at depots, whether in the day or night, the cars were to be unloaded instantly. Any military officer who neglected his duty in this respect was to be reported by the quartermasters and railroad officers and his name would be stricken from the rolls of the army. No officer, whatever might be his rank, could interfere with the running of the cars as directed by the superintendent of the road. Anyone who so interfered was to be dismissed from the service for disobedience of orders.

As a result of his experiences, Haupt laid down three fundamental principles for military railroads in movement of supplies. These principles were to be observed by all subordinates. First, supplies were not to be sent forward to advanced rail terminals until these supplies were actually needed, and only then in such quantities as could be promptly removed. Second, railroad cars were to be promptly unloaded and returned. Third, no delays of trains should be permitted beyond the time fixed for starting, but when necessary and practicable, extra trains should be furnished if the rail load and schedule permitted.[17] Later in the war, McCallum added a fourth principle involving not "How much will it cost?" but rather "Can it be done at all at any cost?"

THE PROBLEM OF SUPPLY

Despite these principles, official orders, and numerous directives, local crises arose constantly with civilians, officers, and men asserting their independence of Haupt's "red tape." Haupt has given us some examples of the type of high-handed interference which so frequently upset his tight schedule of rail movements. When he arrived at Piedmont in late May 1862, he found that a paymaster had appropriated one of the boxcars standing on the main track and was using it as his office. This officer was "greatly impressed with the importance and dignity of his position" and positively refused to vacate the car. When Haupt pointed out to the officer that the army could not be supplied unless the track were kept open, the officer replied that payment of the men was just as important as supplying them with rations. Haupt then told the officer that he could set up his office in a house just as well as in a boxcar, but the officer refused to leave the car. Faced with this, Haupt went off, assembled a guard detail, went back to the car and had the guard remove the money, chest, table, chairs, and papers to a brick house near the track. The paymaster was directed to follow, which he did without further opposition.[18]

Occasionally the wives of officers would go up to the front to visit their husbands when the army was in a quiet sector. During McDowell's forced march to Front Royal, Haupt had ordered several trains of supplies, expected them to arrive during the night at Rectortown to move forward to Piedmont by daylight. Haupt waited for these supply trains at Piedmont but as they did not arrive he walked the four miles back to Rectortown to meet them. At that place Haupt found them, standing motionless on the track. He asked the conductor why he had not obeyed orders and was informed that the wife of a prominent officer had been a passenger on the train and had gone to a farmhouse to seek accommodations for the night. Haupt ordered the conductor to get his train under way at once, but just as he gave the order an elegantly dressed lady came tripping across the field to take her place in one of the cars. Haupt assures us that he did not display extra gallantry on the occasion nor even offer the lady any assistance. She had detained four trains for three hours during a period of real urgency and Haupt, rather understandably, was not in an amiable mood.[19]

Due to the poor discipline of many volunteer regiments, the very soldiers whose welfare depended on the railroads often seriously hampered even their routine operation. A direct result of this poor discipline was the soldiers' insistence on appropriating for their own personal use two essentials of railroading—wood and water.

Since the locomotives used were wood burners the supply of wood was vital to rail movements. At intervals along the tracks wood supplies for exclusive use of the railroads were piled. In testifying before the Committee on the Conduct of the War[20] Haupt pointed out that "though we may have hundreds of cords of wood for the road, every stick of it would probably be burned by the soldiers." Haupt's men were compelled to carry wood all the way from Alexandria for use of locomotives on the Fredericksburg railroad. "Although we employed several hundred contrabands for cutting wood, the wood would be taken from them by the soldiers as fast as it could be cut, and even before it could be corded."

Adequate supply of water for the locomotives was equally essential. When Haupt and General Rufus Ingalls, Quartermaster of the Army of the Potomac, left Manassas on one occasion, the water in their locomotive gave out. Fortunately they had two buckets on the train and were able to dip water from streams and puddles along the way. However, it became necessary to cut off one of the cars and leave part of the train guard; later the other car of the train was left and a few soldiers were taken on the tender of the locomotive.[21] One of the main reasons for such acute shortages of water was that the soldiers washed in the streams above the railroad water stations. In their washing the soldiers so fouled the water with soap and other impurities that it would cause the engines to foam, thereby disabling them. At times, Haupt's men had to send out special engines to tow disabled engines into the stations.[22]

Of course, poorly disciplined men were a reflection of inefficient or untrained officers. One of the main headaches for Haupt was the constant interference of military officials who would appropriate the telegraph facilities for their own use, sometimes when the railroaders had only one telegraph operator. Such was the situation described by John H. Devereux at Alexandria to Haupt in the field, June 3, 1862. Devereux reported that he had control neither of his trains nor his telegraph, nor did his men.[23]

Many army officers seemed determined to run the railways in their areas to suit themselves. This led to confusion and bewilderment for subordinates, military or railroad. Some of the military resented the Construction Corps raised by Haupt which he organized as a military unit, commanded by commissioned officers, drilled and functioning as line units in the field. Medical officers insisted on sending sick soldiers by rail, often without proper authorization, merely to get them off their hands. The railroads were thus unable to forward the troops because trains to Washington, loaded with the sick, would stand for hours unloaded. On one occasion, General Samuel D. Sturgis stopped the trains coming into Alexandria two and one-half miles from the city. These trains, with their cargo of sick soldiers, were prohibited from entering the city thus preventing other trains from coming out and blocking all traffic completely.[24] Haupt had difficulty with officers who often insisted on unloading the wounded on the main track despite the remonstrances of the train officials. Surgeons in charge of the wounded men would insist on unloading although the process was slow and could upset a tight schedule involving hundreds of cars in a few days.

However, some units cooperated well with the railroads. For example, the 149th New York Infantry enjoyed its service of picket and patrol duty on the railroad repaired by Haupt from Aquia Creek. The regiment furnished details patrolling up and down the railroad. Frequently, both day and night, officers of the regiment personally inspected the track, especially after the passage of trains.[25]

Haupt realized that the main cause of slow rail movements was the non-compliance of military officers with the orders of officials of military railroads in the various military departments. It was obvious that transportation for all the military railroads must be centralized and controlled in Washington.

There was, also, the interference which an advancing army must expect when operating in the enemy's country. So active and efficient were the enemy guerrilla bands which interfered with his train movements that Haupt asked for authority to issue a notice which seems more appropriate to later wars. Haupt wanted permission to warn the civilians that if any attempt was made to destroy the track, bridges, telegraph, or any rail lines used by the Army of the Potomac, residents in the vicinity for a distance of ten miles would be "held responsible in person and property. All able-bodied citizens would be arrested; if the offenders could be discovered their punishment would be death."[26]

The constant interference with the running of the military railroads by both friend and foe made it abundantly clear to Haupt that a bureau of military railroads was imperative. Stanton himself, when he called Haupt to Washington, partially realized the need for such a bureau. The War Secretary saw all too clearly that none of his military commanders was equal to the task of managing, repairing, or running the railroads that were affording them vital logistical support, including the ones they were seizing in enemy territory.

Haupt was in Washington but a short time before he realized that nothing approximating an efficient organization existed in so far as military railroads were concerned. Accordingly, he sought out Halleck and asked how he, as general in chief, could plan campaigns on a large scale, dependent for success on an efficient line of communications, when Halleck did not know which railroads were under military control. How, asked Haupt, could Halleck use railroads when he did not know their condition, equipment, their capacity for feeding large field forces, or the defense system necessary to keep them from damage by the enemy. Halleck admitted that there was no office in Washington where this information could be obtained and requested Haupt to draw up an organizational plan. Haupt later submitted such a plan to Halleck, who urged its adoption on Stanton; but it was not adopted. In the spring of 1863, Haupt had an officer conduct an inspection of railways in the western theater, who found there the worst possible state of affairs and the necessity for immediate remedial action. Haupt's recommendations, although repeated several times during his service, were not acted upon.

On September 11, 1863, he wrote[27] to Stanton outlining the conditions which had to be met if he were to accept a commission unconditionally. These conditions revolved mainly around Haupt's projected bureau of military railroads which included the following provisions:

1. A central railroad bureau would be established in Washington which would receive reports on railroad operations, direct rail operations, and inspect the construction and operation of all military railroads. The bureau would have authority to remedy defects and correct abuses.

2. Difficulties with commanding officers would be averted and all steps involving military railroads would be done with the bureau chief's i.e. Haupt's approval and cooperation.

3. The chief of the bureau would not be tied to his office but rather would be free to move wherever his personal presence was most necessary to inspect personally the condition and operation of railroads.

However, in his recommendations, Haupt included the provision that he, as bureau chief, would be free to attend to his private business affairs when his presence was not needed with the railroads. This stipulation Stanton was never willing to grant. One wonders what Stanton's decision would have been if Haupt's personal provision had not been included.

In his letter Haupt included a suggested order for a centralized organization of military railroads, with himself as chief. (See Appendix D.)

But nothing was done. As early as the spring of 1863, in a gradual disclosure of glaring deficiencies in the West, Haupt emphasized that there was no central organization of military railroads. No reports from the West were made to any bureau in Washington; there was no way of determining the condition of the roads, and bridges, the officers in charge, the amount of rolling stock, prices paid, salaries of employees, or any other such information. Haupt told the Committee on the Conduct of the War that Halleck apparently approved his suggestions for a railroad bureau, but had said Stanton was too busy to give Haupt's proposal his attention.[28]

Firmly convinced of the need for a bureau of military railroads, Haupt, even after he had severed all connections with military railroading, emphasized to Lincoln the role of the railroads in military operations. In a letter[29] of January 16, 1864, Haupt reviewed for the President the condition of military railroads in the West and stressed the importance of efficient construction and maintenance of railroads for the armies in the field. Haupt pointed out to Lincoln that in constructing and operating railroads he could render the most valuable assistance to the war effort. "It was my specialty," wrote Haupt, "and while others could perhaps be more successful in command of a corps or army, I would yield to none in experience, energy, resource and ability to organize so far as railroads were concerned. . ." Haupt, apparently, still hoped that a bureau of military railroads would be established and that he would be put in charge of it.

This was not to be, nor was such a bureau organized at all throughout the rest of the war. Because such a bureau did not exist, Haupt and other railroaders had to contend with the abuses affecting the forwarding of men and supplies by the railroads under military control. Many of these abuses could have been prevented, or at least corrected, if Haupt's suggestions for a railroad bureau had been followed.

NOTES, CHAPTER 6

1. *Report,* Committee on the Conduct of the War, Part I (1863), pp. 682–687.
2. Haupt, pp. 165–166. See Chapter 9 for details on use of these barges during the Fredericksburg campaign.
3. *Official Records,* Series I, Vol. 19, Part 1, p. 18.
4. *Ibid.,* p. 8.
5. P. H. Watson, Assistant Secretary of War to E. S. Sanford, Vice President, Adams Express Company, February 20, 1862. National Archives.
6. Flower, Frank A., *Edwin McMasters Stanton,* p. 209.
7. Haupt, pp. 160–165.
8. *Ibid.,* pp. 59–60.
9. *Report,* Committee on the Conduct of the War, Part I (1863), p. 384.
10. Haupt to Devereux, August 25, 1862, *Official Records,* Series I, Vol. 18, p. 663.
11. Haupt, pp. 143, 166–167.
12. *Ibid.,* p. 56.
13. *Official Records,* Series I, Vol. 19, Part 2, pp. 564–565.
14. *Ibid.,* pp. 566–567.
15. *Ibid.,* p. 326.
16. McCallum's Report of May 26, 1866, p. 33.
17. Haupt, p. 139.
18. *Ibid.,* p. 56.
19. *Ibid.,* p. 175.

20. *Report,* Part I (1863), pp. 682–687.
21. Haupt, p. 148.
22. *Report* of the Committee of the Conduct of the War, Part I (1863), pp. 682–687.
23. Haupt, p. 58.
24. *Official Records,* Series I, Vol. 12, part 3, p. 636–637.
25. Collins, Geo. K., *Memoirs of the 149th Reg't N.Y. Vol. Inft.,* pp. 91–92. But the Provost Marshal of the Army of the Potomac noted the difficulty in getting a system of guard duty for the railroads, "owing to the want of system at these headquarters . . . " Sparks, David S., *Inside Lincoln's Army,* p. 186.
26. Haupt, pp. 250–251.
27. Haupt to Stanton, September 11, 1863, Library of Congress.
28. *Report* of Committee on the Conduct of the War, Part I (1863), p. 385.
29. Haupt to Lincoln, January 16, 1864, Library of Congress.

7

SECOND BULL RUN

The Federal military situation in the East deteriorated steadily during the midsummer months of 1862. McClellan's Army of the Potomac, frustrated in its drive on Richmond, went back to Harrison's Landing to the transports which would return that army to the defense of Washington. Lee was now free to detail his "right arm," Stonewall Jackson, for operations in the Shenandoah Valley. In June Jackson had been successful in leaving McDowell in the Front Royal area. Accordingly, McDowell retreated out of the Shenandoah Valley until he arrived in the Manassas area where he set up his headquarters.

Haupt had expected to remain with McDowell for a few weeks at most, but after the railroader had opened the line to Fredericksburg, McDowell told him that the services he was rendering were indispensable and that he must also open up the Manassas Gap railroad. Haupt did this then and remained with the hapless general until McDowell was superseded by Pope, June 26, 1862. The new commander did not at first appreciate the services of

Haupt; he gave him no instructions, and apparently chose to regard him as a civilian interfering with military operations. Moreover, in addition to believing that military railroads were not essential to successful operations, Pope also believed they should not be independent but rather should be completely under the control of the Quartermaster's Department. Accordingly, he dispensed with the Construction Corps. McDowell, very loyally, did his level best to change Pope's mind, pointing out that prior to Haupt's appearance on the scene the army had never been properly supplied and that reliance had been placed completely on wagon trains. Due to the execrable condition of roads in Virginia in 1862, this definitely had not been the answer. Nevertheless, Pope's attitude did not change. Haupt then informed McDowell that he was returning to Massachusetts since his services were no longer needed. He went back to Washington, explained the situation to Assistant Secretary of War Peter H. Watson, and then went on to Massachusetts, after having asked Watson to keep him informed of developments.[1]

During the first few days after his departure, everything went well. Watson told Haupt that if other departments had been as well organized and managed as Haupt's "the war chariots would not have been so frequently off the track." However, affairs with Pope actually were not going well at all. For example, on July 15th Pope had occasion to complain to McCallum that he had received many reports on the "bad management and shameful neglect" of the personnel in charge of the rail line to Warrenton. In one letter Pope complained that twelve hours had been spent in coming from Warrenton to Alexandria; the train personnel had stopped

to pick blackberries along the track. Pope asked Mc-
Callum to give immediate attention to this matter since
the army's movements had already been greatly delayed
by this road.[2] It was not long before the railroads were
practically at a standstill; something had to be done. The
Confederate drive on the Capital was developing rapidly
and Jackson was extremely active in his diversionary
campaign in the Shenandoah Valley.

The morale was low as a result of Pope's own actions.
The new commander's words, especially, were not tact-
ful. In his address to the army Pope said in part: "I have
come to you from the West, where we have seen the
backs of our enemies—from an army whose business it
has been to seek the adversary and to beat him when
found. . . . Meantime I desire you to dismiss from your
minds certain phrases which I am sorry to find much in
vogue among you. I hear constantly of . . . lines of retreat and bases of supplies. Let us discard such ideas. . . .
Let us look before us and not behind." With such tactless
remarks and the announcement to his men that his headquarters would be in the saddle, Pope soon became an
object of derision to his men, many of whom were justly
sensitive to slights on their fighting ability—an ability
which had been amply demonstrated on the Peninsula.

The defeat at Cedar Mountain in August was disap-
pointing but not decisive. However, the condition of the
railroads had rapidly deteriorated to a point of paralysis.
Haupt had been in Massachusetts about ten days when
Watson at the War Department sent him the following
telegram:

Without your aid to organize and manage the railroads of
Virginia the army cannot be supplied. Please return immediately.

Putting aside his pressing professional and business commitments, Haupt went to Washington, reported to the War Department, and proceeded to the headquarters of Pope near Cedar Mountain. Pope welcomed Haupt and immediately placed him in charge of all railroads within the limits of the Army of Virginia. The General put teeth in this appointment by ordering that no officer, whatever his rank, should interfere with Haupt's management. Haupt was free to issue whatever orders were necessary to implement his directions. All orders involving troop movements and railroad construction were to go to Pope *through* Haupt.[3] Stanton backed up Pope with the following order, promulgated August 19th:

Ordered: that the Department of Colonel Herman Haupt, formerly Aide-de-Camp to Major-General McDowell, and Chief of Construction and Transportation in the Army of the Rappahannock, is hereby extended to embrace all the railroads which are or may hereafter be included within the lines of operation of the Army of Virginia; and the instructions of May 28, 1862, are continued in full force.[4]

Haupt's return was resented by a few railroaders whose loyalty to McCallum apparently was stronger than to Haupt. A letter marked "Private," dated August 19th, was sent to McCallum by J. H. Devereux in which he said in part:

Col. Haupt is back, and has a special order from General Pope, constituting, dubbing, and creating him the Head of the Railroads of the Army of Virginia, and that all persons shall report to him forthwith, and that all things through and by him shall be carried on."

Other subordinates were less subtle in their resentment.

The same day a Lieutenant Franklin H. Barwell, Assistant Commissary of Subsistence, wrote to McCallum the following:

> In fact from my own personal observation and knowledge of the facts I would say that I do not believe it is in the power of any man to run these roads better than they have been run by Mr. J. H. Devereux. . ."

While there is no doubt that Devereux was an efficient railroader, this type of behind-the-scenes politics strongly suggests a McCallum clique hostile to Haupt. Moreover, Haupt was aware of McCallum's concern over the railroader's return to service. Accordingly, Haupt sent the following to McCallum from Alexandria on the 19th:[5]

> I supposed when I last left Washington that my connection with Rail Road operations in Va. was permanently ended but I was not permitted to remain long in Massachusetts before I was recalled by a dispatch from the Sec. of War. I arrived in Washington Saturday night and after ascertaining at the War Dept. what was desired of me, I went next morning to the Head Quarters of Genl. Pope. I found that he wanted some one on his staff who could be personally present and direct the practical operations of the railroads under his command. Your duties in Washington [are] in the purchase of cars and engines, the supply of materials, the settlement of accounts and the various other duties which occupy [your time]. In the management of the road I propose to conform to your wishes as far as practicable and make no unnecessary changes in your arrangements or employees.

Apparently McCallum replied to this with a letter friendly in tone. On the 23rd Haupt wrote a letter to McCallum, in which receipt of the letter was acknowledged, and went on to express Haupt's appreciation of the ex-

cellent "tone and spirit" of McCallum's letter, which
Haupt characterized as "very much like D. C. Mc-
Callum." Haupt urged McCallum to communicate his
wishes, and assured him that every attempt would be
made to conform to them. Haupt closed by stating that
he had had a hard week and for the past three days had
had no sleep at all.

Haupt was now responsible for the supplying by rail
of an army about to enter a short but active campaign
which was to end in one of the most sanguinary battles
of the war. The railroader's contribution to this campaign, hitherto comparatively unrecognized, was very
substantial and demonstrated the caliber of the man who
was as conspicuously efficient in the subsequent battles
culminating at Gettysburg. Haupt's services were limited
in the Second Bull Run campaign in that he was directly
under Pope's command rather than under War Department control directly. Haupt realized the need for freedom of action and during the ensuing campaign he
decided not to personally be present with Pope because
the railroader's duties rendered it necessary to move
about freely, especially at the supply base. He was frequently at the general office in Alexandria.[6]

Haupt reported to Pope on August 18th, the very day
Pope retreated behind the Rappahannock. The railroader was with the General when information was received of the enemy's approach. Haupt hastened back
to Culpeper where were located the reserve supplies for
Pope's army. Haupt had these supplies sent to the rear
for safety. It was typical of him that he saved them,
rather than having them destroyed, a custom which had
been so frequently indulged in by McClellan on the
Peninsula.

In the retreat from Culpeper, Haupt had one of the three or four interviews* with Pope as reported in the railroader's reminiscences.[7] The Confederates had begun their offensive which led to Second Bull Run. Jeb Stuart's raid on Pope's headquarters had destroyed the bridge across Cedar Creek, cut off a great deal of rolling stock, and caused substantial damage in general.

While Pope's army had remained in position behind the Rappahannock, the Confederates had turned his right flank. Haupt, who was with Pope on August 21st and 22nd, had sensed that something was wrong, and did not like the looks of things, especially the scouts' report that wagons in large numbers had been seen passing up the river. This strongly suggested that the enemy intended to cross the river. Accordingly, the railroader asked Pope how far Federal scouts had been sent up the river. Pope told him that they had been sent up for some fifteen to twenty miles; but Haupt, very realistically asked if that was far enough, to which question the General replied affirmatively. Haupt, not satisfied, then asked what was to prevent the enemy from going even as far as the Shenandoah Valley, crossing by Manassas or some other gap, and cutting the Federal rear communications. Pope confidently assured Haupt that there was no danger. The railroader, somewhat reassured, returned to Manassas. But that very evening the train which followed Haupt was fired into at Catlett's Station.[8]

This was the first definite information of the enemy's intentions. It was soon followed by an attempt to capture several trains at Bristoe. Unfortunately, Pope had ordered a large portion of the rolling stock to the front.

---

* These interviews were of little value. Pope was personally friendly to Haupt but not interested in his advice on the military situation.

This rolling stock could not be withdrawn from its exposed position. Rear communications had broken down. As a consequence, seven good locomotives were captured by the Confederates and nearly three hundred freight cars were destroyed.

Haupt made great exertions to keep the communications open. The ability and loyalty of the railroad personnel contributed greatly to the transportation of facilities and supplies; they remained at stations loading cars and removing stores long after the retreat of the Federal forces. This was especially hazardous because there was no military protection for them at a time when the enemy was pressing forward rapidly. As Haupt pointed out in his final report to Stanton, the railway personnel remained at their posts during this critical period, without rest or regular food. "From the superintendent to the lowest grade of operatives they are all entitled to much credit for the important services rendered on that occasion."[9] On several occasions during the campaign the railroad men showed conspicuous bravery. Volunteers were ready for any service, however dangerous. On one occasion General Philip Kearny asked Haupt to run a pilot engine over the road in advance of his troop trains because a train had been fired upon by a large enemy force. A sufficient number of railroad men volunteered for this service without hesitation.[10]

Haupt's most pressing problem was to remove Pope's supplies to the Washington-Alexandria area (or at least to the Manassas-Warrenton area) in order to prevent their capture by the rapidly advancing Confederate forces. Pope spelled out the army's plan for evacuation of supplies to Haupt. A train of twenty cars, for subsistence, was to be kept in constant readiness to supply the troops with rations. Pope urged Haupt to see that all trains ran according to schedule and that most of the rolling stock be switched off the tracks, either at Catlett's Station or Warrenton, so that, if necessary, all Pope's baggage and materiel of his army could be taken back at the shortest possible notice. Pope pointed out that he had no wagons for this purpose.[11] Haupt at once informed Halleck by telegraph that he was carrying out Pope's directive and all stores not immediately needed were being sent to Manassas. In addition, sixty empty cars were to be at Warrenton Junction in case they were needed. At the same time Haupt sent a similar message to Pope, and also pointed out that Pope's concentration of rolling stock would leave Alexandria short of cars and locomotives for the forwarding of troops. However, Haupt on the 22nd assured Pope that he would continue to forward troops to Manassas unless Pope should order otherwise. At the same time, Haupt informed the General that beyond doing this, he would hold trains to await Pope's orders or until further orders were received.[12]

Meanwhile, on August 22nd, troops began to arrive at Alexandria from the Army of the Potomac. Halleck estimated that they would total about 15,000 during the period, August 22nd-23rd, and so informed Haupt.[13] According to Haupt's testimony before the Committee on the Conduct of the War, the troops of the Army of the Potomac were in condition for service when landed at Alexandria and should have marched at once to join Pope. Not only could they have supported each other in case of attack, but the railroad was taxed to its capacity. If McClellan's men had marched at once to Manassas, Haupt maintained, there was no doubt that they could

Rail line over "Long Bridge," Washington, D.C. Over this bridge literally thousands of Federal Volunteers, eager but raw, passed on their way to the front. (National Archives)

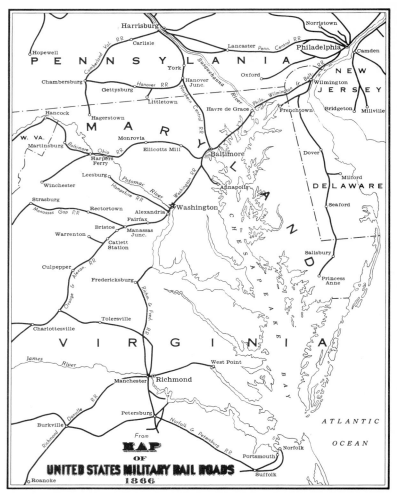

This map shows the main railroad lines involved in Haupt's military service. It is adapted from an official 1866 map. (Resketched by Holly Byrne, Falls Church, Va.)

Haupt's bridge over Potomac Creek. Constructed in May, 1862, this amazing structure was admiringly dubbed the "Beanpoles and Cornstalks Bridge" by Lincoln. (National Archives)

Haupt (in boots, right foreground) and his "Construction Corps." Notice that the locomotive, the "General Haupt," and the cars are on one of the few sidings then available on single-track lines in the South. (Library of Congress)

Bridge trusses prepared for Hooker's campaign. The span is sixty feet. (National Archives)

The essentials of war: Railroad rails at Alexandria, Virginia. (National Archives)

The stockade at Alexandria. (National Archives)

Haupt on float made of two small rubber cylinders. This float
was designed for use by one man on reconnaissance duty. (National Archives)

Infantry with full field equipment in Haupt's "Blanket Boat."
(National Archives)

A float of two canal boats transferring eight loaded railroad
cars from Alexandria to Aquia Creek. (National Archives)

Haupt observing the effect of Federal artillery fire—second
Fredericksburg, May 3, 1863. (National Archives)

Straightening slight bends in rails by use of a jack-screw.
(National Archives)

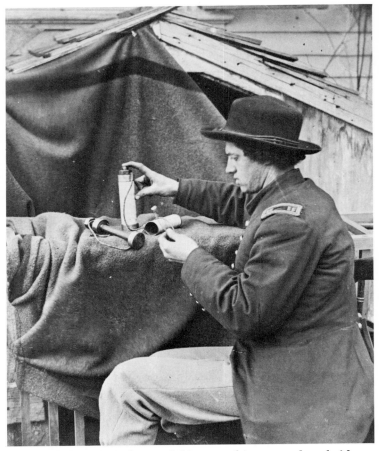

Haupt's "torpedo" for quickly wrecking wooden bridges. (National Archives)

Destroying track by corkscrew twist, using levers and steel hooks. (National Archives)

Haupt's successor—Brigadier General Daniel C. McCallum. (National Archives)

Steel hooks, and piece of rail twisted by their use. (National Archives)

Forerunner of the small boats used in World War II—Haupt's "blanket boat" assembled as a raft. (National Archives)

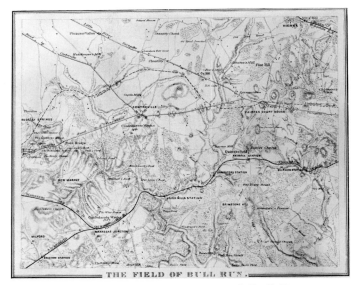

This map shows the area around Bull Run.

have rendered efficient support to Pope and would have contributed to a decisive victory.[14]

Eventually however, some 20,000 of the 91,000 men comprising the Army of the Potomac actually got through to Pope.[15] By the 23rd, some 6,600 troops were marching to the front, but trains were not being unloaded rapidly enough. Haupt had the tracks cleared, bridges in good order, and six engines ready for shuttle service back to Alexandria from the front. By these steps the number of reinforcements was shortly to be increased.[16]

However difficulties now arose which were to result in the most hectic days of Haupt's entire service with the Federal Army. A Confederate attack on a train which had left Catlett's Station was thwarted only by the conductor's opening the throttle and running through the attackers at full speed. The train personnel escaped by lying down to avoid the heavy small arms fire. Later at Manassas Junction enemy cavalry piled ties on the track and the train escaped only by the engineer's making a run of it, although the engine itself was well riddled with bullets.[17] Meanwhile, the enemy was cutting telegraph lines; Pope's communications were being disrupted at vital points.

The enemy was not the only contributor to Haupt's logistical problems. Serious delays and derangements of train movements resulted from orders given by military officers to railroad personnel. The situation got completely out of hand despite three orders from Halleck in the period, August 23rd-24th, emphasizing that the railroad was entirely under the direction of Haupt and that no military officer had any right to interfere wtih it. Rapid forwarding of troops was essential and Pope prepared for battle confident that he would be loyally supported by prompt arrival of supplies and reinforcements from Washington and Alexandria. He later stated flatly that he was completely aware of the enemy's movement on Manassas and notified Halleck, who replied that heavy reinforcements would begin to arrive at Warrenton Junction on the 24th. As Pope's orders still held him to the Rappahannock line he naturally supposed that these troops would be forwarded rapidly. Pope asked especially that Franklin's corps be moved rapidly to Gainesville. He telegraphed Haupt to direct one of the strongest divisions coming forward to be at Warrenton Junction on the 24th, where the men could be moved into the defensive works at Manassas Junction.[18]

Back at Alexandria Haupt had been working feverishly to ascertain what elements of the Army of the Potomac had arrived from the Peninsula and were in readiness to be moved out to join Pope at the front. On the 24th, Haupt telegraphed Pope that some 30,000 troops needed transportation from Alexandria but that the railroad could not handle that many. Haupt told Pope that he could manage 12,000 a day, with supplies, if no accident occurred. The new troops could march, the veteran troops go by rail, and horses could be driven. In this emergency, Haupt pointed out, essential supplies should take precedence over baggage and tents. The next day, the 25th, Haupt informed Pope that he expected to move out all the troops then in Alexandria, including the ones expected during the day.[19]

Difficulties arose at once from the unwillingness of the military to cooperate. During the pressing need for transportation to move such units as Cox and Heintzelman to the front, General Samuel D. Sturgis, commanding a brigade, decided that his men had priority even though they were not ready for a rail movement. On the 23rd Haupt had informed Watson that Sturgis had stopped the trains coming into Alexandria about 2½ miles from the city. These trains transported sick soldiers and Sturgis's high-handed action was blocking trains going both ways. Apparently Watson got in touch at once with Halleck who told Haupt that the railroad was entirely under Haupt's control. "No military officer has any right to interfere with [the railroad]. You will inform General Sturgis that your orders are supreme." However, still another day was lost because of the neglect of Sturgis's officers to load the cars furnished to them.[20] Sturgis's attitude was well illustrated when Haupt first arrived on the scene to straighten out the mess. Sturgis received the railroader with drunken gravity and the famous words: "I don't care for John Pope one pinch of owl dung."

On the 23rd, Hooker's division had arrived at Aquia Creek from the Peninsula. This division was supposed to march to Pope but orders were changed and the division went by boat to Alexandria where the men waited for rail transportation to join Pope. Haupt met Hooker and they agreed that the division would leave the evening of the 24th. But Hooker decided to spend the day in Washington. When Haupt had completed the arrangements for transporting Hooker's division, Hooker himself was nowhere to be found. Haupt got in touch with Watson at the War Department and was advised to see if Hooker was at Willard's Hotel. Watson also warned Haupt to "be as patient as possible with the generals. Some of them will trouble you more than they will the enemy." Hooker's division didn't get on the way until the 26th, because of the delay in finding the general.[21]

On that day, Haupt, still struggling to get cooperation from high-ranking officers of McClellan's army, asked Halleck's Chief of Staff, General George W. Cullum, to do something about settling questions of priority as to which units should go forward. Haupt urged that an officer be detailed to handle this problem and that the responsible unit commander be notified so that everything would be in readiness, thus preventing delays. As Haupt put it: "I neither know what regiments have arrived, where they are located, nor which are first to be transported."[22]

Much was rightfully expected from McClellan in the way of rendering assistance by forwarding elements from the Army of the Potomac to reinforce Pope. On the 27th Halleck informed McClellan that Franklin's corps should move to Pope's aid by forced marches, carrying three to four days' rations, and, if necessary, be supplied by rail. Halleck urged McClellan to see Haupt and assist him, not only in reinforcing Pope but also in guarding the line of rail communications. Since McClellan did not follow Halleck's suggestion, the railroader went to look for the General. On the morning of the 27th, Haupt went in a rowboat to look for McClellan among the fleet of transports which were anchored in the Potomac at Alexandria. Eventually Haupt found the "little Napoleon" surrounded by his staff. Haupt bluntly informed McClellan that with Pope out of forage and rations, Lee was harrassing his rear, cutting off communications, and Pope needed help at once. Haupt got McClellan to go ashore and pointed out that if the trains had protection, relief could be promptly sent to Pope. McClellan's reply was characteristic of the man "with the slows"—the undertaking was too risky. Little Mac refused to provide

protection, approve Haupt's plan, or make any suggestion himself. All he did was to take a drink of brandy
and ride away on his horse.[23]

At that moment there were 30,000 veteran troops in
the Alexandria area, only 16 miles from Pope. But as
McClellan's Own Story shows,[24] Little Mac was occupied
in writing his journal and penning a letter to his wife.
He had no time (nor inclination) to cooperate with
Haupt in the rescue of Pope. McClellan began his writing in the early morning and at 10:30, after Haupt had
finally stopped begging him for help, he complained to
his wife that he had *again* been interrupted by telegrams
which required replies. Haupt, completely frustrated by
McClellan's refusal to help and his obvious desire to see
Pope fail, looked elsewhere for help. He prepared a
relief train himself and asked McClellan for a convoy
of 200 sharpshooters. At 1 A.M. in the morning of the
28th, the request still was not being granted so Haupt
got a lantern and walked four miles to General Winfield
Scott Hancock's camp. On arrival he routed that excellent officer out of bed and promptly secured the required
escort. At 4 A.M. that morning Haupt was able to begin
dispatching the relief trains which were so desperately
needed.[25]

The escort Hancock sent out to protect the vital railroad bridge over Bull Run was the New Jersey brigade
under Brigadier General G. W. Taylor. Later, the 11th
and 12th Ohio Infantry under Colonel E. P. Scammon of
Cox's command were sent as reinforcements to Taylor's
brigade. But Taylor's men did not save the bridge. Instead of obeying orders and putting his brigade in a
strong defensive position to cover the bridge, Taylor
crossed it, and, with no artillery support, attacked a

strong enemy division. He was roughly handled and his four New Jersey regiments left the field, practically in a rout, leaving their equipment and rations behind. Taylor was mortally wounded in the action and the command fell on Colonel Scammon, who had arrived later. Scammon was highly disgusted at the New Jerseymen who, with the exception of two officers and ten men, refused to defend the bridge.[26] Scammon held on the best he could but finally had to withdraw his force and march back to Alexandria.[27]

At 4:20 P.M. Lincoln received a telegram from Haupt that the enemy was reported crossing Bull Run bridge at 4 P.M. Scammon had held them off until that time. The 11th Ohio Infantry covered the retreat.[28] By noon of the next day the situation was clear and Haupt was able to inform the anxious President that Scammon and his men were safe back in Alexandria. Haupt went out on an engine and brought in the Colonel who had much important information to communicate. Also Haupt informed Lincoln that he had sent out a reconnoitering party by rail to repair telegraph lines and to open up communications again.[29]

To implement this "railroad reconnaissance" Haupt wisely cautioned the train conductor that the advance or return of the train and its rate of speed was to be governed by the officer in command of the reconnaissance troops. This reconnaissance was to go to Burke's Station at the usual speed, but beyond that point it was to proceed with great caution, with skirmishers advanced on both sides of the track and in the woods. The commanding officer was to signal the conductor on the movements of the train. If an enemy was found to be in superior numbers, the force was to retire and telegraph the fact.

Apparently this reconnaissance was the answer because later on the same day Haupt informed Halleck that the railroad reconnaissance had worked "extremely well."[30]

Meanwhile the military situation was rapidly deteriorating. The enemy advance toward Pope's right flank forced him to abandon the line of the Rappahannock. He decided to retard as much as possible the drive of Lee's army on Washington until he was certain that the Army of the Potomac had reached Alexandria from the Peninsula. On the 27th Pope had abandoned the Rappahannock line and moved his troops toward Gainesville and Manassas Junction. But Jackson had already arrived at the latter place and had captured 8 pieces of artillery, 300 prisoners and 200 tents. Immense quantities of supplies fell into the enemy's hand. What could not be transported away was burned, including 50,000 pounds of bacon, 1,000 barrels of corned beef, 2,000 barrels of salt, and 2,000 barrels of flour and other property of great value.[31] After destruction of the supplies at Manassas Junction, Lee concentrated his army on the old battlefield of First Bull Run. Both armies were in position on the 30th and the two-day battle began.

Pope had lost most of his supplies, including reserve ammunition stores. Halleck realized this and on the 30th informed McClellan that ammunition, especially for artillery, should be immediately sent forward to Pope. Halleck said this must be done "with all possible despatch."[32] McClellan replied with the following amazing reply to Halleck's urgent order:

I know nothing of the calibers of Pope's artillery. All I can do is to direct my ordnance officer to load up all the wagons sent to him.[33]

But Halleck didn't give up. At 2:10 P.M. of the same day (August 30th) he told McClellan that Franklin's and Sumner's corps should be pushed forward to Pope's relief. "Old Brains" pointed out that the men should "use their legs," making forced marches, since "time now is everything." Halleck ordered McClellan to send sharpshooters with the trains to Bull Run as defense against enemy cavalry. "Give Colonel Haupt all the assistance you can," urged Halleck. The sharpshooters on top of cars could also assist in unloading the trains on arrival at Pope's army. McClellan's reply suggested that Sumner and Franklin were moving to Pope's assistance "as rapidly as possible," and that he had sent everything except a small camp guard to the front.[34]

But Little Mac's "assistance" to Pope was too little and too late. McClellan was intentionally dilatory, and, what was even more censurable, he communicated his lack of enthusiasm to his cronies in the Army of the Potomac, e.g. Sturgis and Fitz John Porter, and they too dragged their heels while Pope was fighting at Bull Run. Meanwhile Lincoln had become aware of McClellan's refusal to come to Pope's assistance.

While the fighting was in progress, reports and rumors kept the Washington-Alexandria area in high excitement. Troop ships were arriving in Alexandria from the Peninsula, and troops from McClellan's army were mingling with the new levies from the North. Carloads of forage stood on the sidings because no officer had the authority or interest to unload them. On the afternoon of the 30th crowds were aware of the great battle being fought on the old battlefield of Bull Run. A bulletin on the Treasury Building announced that thousands of Federals were lying on the battlefield and that surgeons and male nurses

were needed to help evacuate them. Pope had lost ambulances and medical supplies in his retreat. In response
to the need, some thousand male nurses got on freight
cars to go out to Pope's defeated army. Some of these
nurses took stimulants with them, ostensibly to be given
the wounded. However the tedious trip was too much for
many of the volunteers—who were actually motivated by
a morbid curiosity to see what a battlefield really looked
like—and the stimulants were consumed by the volunteer
nurses with damaging effects. By the time the train had
reached Alexandria about half of the "nurses" were
drunk. Haupt, in a white fury, contacted McCallum asking him to get an order from Stanton, preventing the
transport of any more people. Haupt told McCallum
that nearly a thousand had arrived in Alexandria during
the night of August 30th-31st, half of them drunk. "We
don't want one of them," Haupt informed McCallum.[35]

Haupt, working around the clock, continued to pour
supplies into Sangster Station and Fairfax, including 500
tons of ammunition with provision for eleven different
types of small arms ammunition.[36]

During all this, Haupt's great exertions were not lost
on Lincoln. During the protracted engagement, August
24th-September 2nd, the President was in a state of
extreme anxiety and slept but little. He was in constant
telegraphic communication, day and night, with Haupt,
asking for an up-to-the-minute account of all possible
events. Lincoln's intuitive perception of the practical requirements of his position as commander-in-chief enabled
him to support Pope effectively. During the campaign,
Lincoln and Halleck, and Stanton as well, actually depended on Haupt more than either Pope or McClellan
for accurate information on enemy movements. On Sep-

tember 1st, John Hay recorded in his diary[37] that "there is one man who seems thoroughly to reflect and satisfy ... [Lincoln] in everything he undertakes. This is Haupt, the railroad man at Alexandria." Lincoln was especially taken with the businesslike character of Haupt's dispatches, brief and extremely timely and informative.

Of much value to Lincoln during the campaign was Haupt's gathering of intelligence on Lee's forces. When a surgeon of Scammon's force returned to Federal lines after a brief period of detention by the Confederates, Haupt questioned him thoroughly on the enemy order of battle, notified the President and made sure that McClellan interviewed him as well.[38]

Haupt sent "operators" forward, who, equipped with field glasses, passed through the lines and maintained constant surveillance of enemy movements from such vantage points as tree tops. Whenever a person possessed with late and significant knowledge of enemy movements reached Haupt, he was rushed by special locomotive to Washington. In glaring contrast to McClellan's fatal propensity for overestimating the size of his opponent's forces, Haupt's reports were extremely accurate. For example, Haupt informed Lincoln and Halleck on the 29th that the enemy numbered 60,000, explaining that he had arrived at this figure on the basis of information supplied by two ambulance drivers. The best authority, using many sources not available in August 1862, gives the figure as 48,527.[39]

With the evacuation of Fairfax, the Army of Virginia was merged into the Army of the Potomac. McClellan was in command again and the hapless Pope was sent West to fight Indians.

Amid all the criticism and recrimination on the lost

battle, Haupt stood out as a shining exception. Actually, he, along with Halleck and the President, were the ones most responsible for salvaging anything at all from the disaster. The railroads functioned under great difficulties. Obstacles were overcome during the campaign; valuable experience was gained which stood in good stead in succeeding battles with Lee's army. Certainly one of the valuable results for Haupt was that his future commanders—McClellan, Burnside, Hooker, and Meade—appreciated the value of railroad communications. Direct interference by the military with rail operations was not often encountered again. And the Construction Corps, which Pope had foolishly disbanded, became an experienced force which functioned effectively, especially during the Gettysburg campaign.

In retrospect, the contrast between Haupt and McClellan is an object lesson in the importance of the *will* to do something against great odds. It is interesting to note that both Haupt and McClellan were possessed of high intelligence; both performed well in their respective classes at West Point, and prior to the war both had become successful engineers after leaving military service. But Haupt, in his civilian experience, had proved to be the type to make quick and decisive decisions. Against the advice of skeptics, for example, Haupt had said the Hoosac Tunnel could be built, and it was.

The President's anger at McClellan's inaction during the campaign was very strong but he felt compelled to hold on to him because there was no man available who commanded the loyalty of his men to the degree that McClellan did. Lincoln was aware of McClellan's very great ability at organizing and training the new troops who, in September and October, were pouring into

Washington from the various state rendezvous camps. There was still much to do with the untrained thousands who had volunteered in the late summer and early fall of 1862. No man excelled McClellan in this work and the President knew it.

On assuming command of the defense of Washington, McClellan had Haupt evacuate all supplies from Fairfax because of the close proximity of the enemy. Haupt sent out cars to pick up the wounded with orders to abandon whatever supplies couldn't be taken away. Units marched toward Washington for mutual defense rather than attempting to go by rail, the few stores left were set on fire by Haupt's telegraph operators, among the last Federals to leave the battlefield.

With active operations over, Haupt returned to Washington and called on the Secretary of War who received him very cordially, addressing him as "General" Haupt. Present at this meeting were Lincoln and most of the cabinet. Stanton warmly thanked the railroader for his services during the recent campaign.

It was Halleck who recommended Haupt's promotion. On September 5th, Halleck recommended to Stanton that Haupt be made a brigadier general for "meritorious services in the recent operations against the enemy near Manassas, Va."[40] On the 27th, Haupt received his commission as brigadier general of volunteers.[41]

Haupt expressed his appreciation for the promotion but accepted the appointment on the condition that when "no public duty required . . . [his] presence," he could take leave of absence to return to Massachusetts to protect his Hoosac Tunnel interest. Stanton "fully understood the situation" but pointed out to Haupt that he was not permitted to include conditions in the commission. Haupt expressed his willingness to rest on a single verbal promise without making a record that might establish a troublesome precedent. Stanton agreed to this[42] but, unknown to Haupt, was to use Haupt's conditional acceptance against the railroader at a future time.

NOTES, CHAPTER 7

1. Haupt, p. 69.
2. Pope to McCallum July 15, 1862, Library of Congress.
3. Haupt, *Order Book,* Library of Congress; *Report,* Committee on the Conduct of the War, Part I (1863), pp. 307–372.
4. Haupt, p. 70.
5. Haupt to McCallum, Haupt Letters, Library of Congress.
6. *Report,* Committee on Conduct of the War, Part I (1863), pp. 370–372.
7. Haupt, pp. 304–305.
8. *Report,* Committee on the Conduct of the War, Part I (1863), pp. 370–372.
9. Haupt's report to Stanton, September 9, 1863.
10. Haupt to Stanton, *Official Records,* Series I, Vol. 27, Part I, pp. 23–24.
11. Pope to Haupt, August 20, 1862, *Report,* Committee on Conduct of the War, Part I (1863).
12. *Official Records,* Series I, Vol. 12, Part 2, pp. 59–60.
13. *Report,* Committee on Conduct of the War, Part I (1863), pp. 372–384.
14. *Ibid.,* p. 384.
15. Haupt, p. 74.
16. *Report,* Committee on the Conduct of the War, Part I (1863), pp. 372–384.
17. *Ibid.*
18. Pope, John, in *Battles and Leaders,* Vol. 2, p. 461.
19. *Report,* Committee on the Conduct of the War (1866), Supplement, Vol. 2, p. 133.
20. *Official Records,* Series I, Vol. 12, Part 3, p. 638–648.
21. *Ibid.,* Part 2, pp. 438, 443; Part 3, p. 648, 650, 662.
22. *Ibid.,* Part 3, pp. 678–679.
23. Haupt, p. 98.
24. McClellan, George B., *McClellan's Own Story,* p. 529.
25. Flower, Frank A., *Edwin McMasters Stanton,* pp. 174–175.
26. *Official Records,* Series I, Vol. 16, pp. 405–406, 539–544.
27. *Ibid.,* Vol. 18, p. 699.

28. Haupt to Lincoln, August 27, 1862, Library of Congress.
29. Haupt to Lincoln, August 28, 1862, Library of Congress.
30. *Official Records,* Series I, Vol. 12, Part 3, pp. 718–719.
31. *Battles and Leaders,* Vol. 2, p. 511.
32. McClellan, *op. cit.,* p. 519.
33. *Ibid.,* p. 520.
34. *Official Records,* Series I, Vol. 12, Part 3, pp. 747–748.
35. *Ibid.,* p. 776.
36. *Ibid.,* Vol. 18, pp. 743–768.
37. Dennett, Tyler (editor), *Lincoln and the Civil War in the Diaries and Letters of John Hay,* pp. 46–47.
38. Haupt to Lincoln, August 28, 1862, Library of Congress.
39. Livermore, Thomas L., *Numbers and Losses in the Civil War in America, 1861–1865,* p. 89.
40. Halleck to Stanton, September 5, 1862, Library of Congress.
41. Haupt papers, Library of Congress.
42. Haupt, p. 135.

8

THE MARYLAND CAMPAIGN

A LULL FOR HAUPT WHO THEORIZES, INVENTS,
AND MEDDLES

On September 2, 1862, Pope was relieved of command and McClellan was assigned to command the defenses of Washington and the troops assigned thereto.
Soon Little Mac was leading the Army of the Potomac
northward into Maryland against the invading Army
of Northern Virginia.

Haupt's participation in the campaign was limited because of his involvement in preparing the rail lines in
the Alexandria and Fredericksburg areas for further
offensive operations by the Army of the Potomac. However, he was at Hagerstown two days after Antietam
where he conferred with military commanders and civilians on a projected withdrawal of militia before a
rumored enemy attack. Haupt opposed the withdrawal
which was finally suspended because it was learned that
Lee was doing all the retreating. On the 20th, Haupt

visited the battlefield, chatted with McClellan at head-quarters, and returned to Washington.[1] After Lee re-crossed the Potomac, no movement of pursuit was made by McClellan for some time. Haupt learned on October 7th that the enemy had reconstructed the bridge over the Rappahannock on the line of the Orange and Alexandria Railroad and were running trains to Bristoe, five miles south of Manassas, carrying off the disabled engines, car wheels, and axles left behind by Pope. Haupt formed a plan for capturing the enemy train, but when a member of the Federal force lying in ambush exposed himself the Confederate locomotive engineer reversed his engine and escaped.

Logistical support to McClellan during the Antietam campaign was supplied mainly by Haupt's well-trained subordinates who rendered good service in forwarding supplies and men to the Army of the Potomac, using civilian railroads. Haupt provided the guidance for his subordinates in their use of these non-military railroads during the campaign. In a letter to William W. Wright, one of his subordinates, Haupt laid down specific principles as follows:[2]

> In general, it is desirable that roads used wholly or partially for military purposes should be operated by and through the regular officers in charge of such roads, but when the management is characterized by incompetency, or inefficiency, it becomes necessary to assume military possession and place in charge agents and officers who will promptly forward troops and government supplies. When the amount of rolling stock is insufficient, requisitions must be made upon connecting roads . . .

It is interesting to note that the Quartermaster General of the Army accepted these principles as valid, and incorporated them in orders to his officers on October 1, 1862.³

During the operations in Maryland, railroad operations in Virginia were suspended but Haupt's Construction Corps assisted in rebuilding the bridge across the Potomac at Harpers Ferry. Haupt inspected the Federal base at Aquia Creek and later reported his findings to Halleck, pointing out the unnecessary destruction attendant on the evacuation of that installation. Haupt reported that the burning of the wharf, buildings, and bridges was "unnecessary and highly censurable."⁴

During the campaign Haupt was busy in insuring prompt supply of the old Army of Virginia, now merged with the Army of the Potomac under McClellan. By a special order issued September 18th by Halleck Haupt was authorized and directed to do whatever he deemed necessary to facilitate the transportation of troops and supplies to aid the armies in the field in Virginia and Maryland. (This order was reissued on June 27, 1863, during the Gettysburg campaign, expanded to include armies in the field in Virginia, Maryland, and Pennsylvania.⁵) Haupt was very active in keeping supplies moving, repairing the Virginia railroads in preparation for future operations, and clearing up the stoppage of cars and engines on sidings. When McClellan complained of delay in receiving supplies Halleck pointed out that Haupt was doing excellent work with the equipment he had, and moreover, that McClellan was being much better supplied than were the armies in the West. Halleck pointed out that McClellan had no cause for complaint.⁶ Much of the trouble was caused by the necessity of feeding 60,000 animals exclusively by rail, and McClellan's requirements for transportation were four or

five times as great as Haupt had experienced under Mc-
Dowell. Probably never before, pointed out Haupt, had
a single track with such limited capacity been so severely
taxed. This could only be overcome by exceptionally good
management and good luck. Complicating the situation
was the lack of an adequate number of sidings and inadequate stations and equipment. On November 7th
Haupt met with McClellan and Ingalls to discuss the
entire transportation problem. Apparently the conferees
agreed on what was to be done. Both the Chief Quartermaster of the Army of the Potomac and the Chief Commissary of the Army assured Haupt that there had been
no suffering or inconvenience from any deficiency of
supplies.[7]

Three days later (November 10th) the War Department issued a special order,[8] signed by Stanton, which
put teeth into the mandate for cooperation by military
officers with railroad operations. By this order, commanding officers of troops along the U.S. Military Railroads were enjoined to give all needed assistance to
officers of the railroads and quartermasters in loading
and unloading cars. In order to prevent delays the officers were ordered to have working parties organized
and ready to unload the cars, as well as guards for track,
sidings, wood supplies, and water tanks. The order,
moreover, prescribed that any military officer who neglected his duty in these respects would be reported and
his name stricken from the rolls of the Army. Any officer, whatever his rank, who interfered with the running
of the trains would be dismissed from the service for
disobedience of orders.

Haupt put the Orange and Alexandria Railroad in
running order, built up a substantial surplus of supplies

and then looked to the next area of operations. Antici-pating a change of operations to the Fredericksburg Railroad, Haupt, with Halleck's approval, ordered a million feet of lumber which soon arrived at Aquia Creek, where Haupt continued to repair rail lines and bridges in the Fredericksburg-Falmouth area.[9]

Haupt's last official contact with McClellan was on November 7th, the day on which Little Mac probably received notice that he was being relieved. Actually the order had been issued on the 5th. Haupt had been con-fidentially advised of the change of commanders by As-sistant Secretary of War Watson. On the evening of the 7th, Haupt had supper with McClellan, who seemed entirely ignorant of the fact that he was to be relieved within an hour. He discussed future operations with Haupt although the latter knew that if these operations were carried into effect it would be by a new commander of the Army of the Potomac.

Relations between McClellan and Haupt, although of short duration, were generally good; the commander heeded Haupt's suggestions regarding the best means of supplying the Army and selection of lines of com-munications. Haupt personally liked McClellan but found him too slow and possessed of excessive caution. Little Mac did not wish to move until he could strike with positive certainty. Indeed, when all the reinforce-ments and supplies asked for had been furnished, he would continue to ask for something more. Neverthe-less, Haupt was not prepared to state that McClellan could have intercepted Lee's retreat after Antietam.[10]

All during this campaign Haupt worked unceasingly to get his ideas on strategy and technical improvements before his superiors. He saw early the need for a centralized leadership of all Federal armies in the field, and throughout 1862, both in the field and back in Washington and Alexandria, he saw the lack of cohesive and effective leadership of the Federal forces. He noted the haphazard planning and the tendency of each individual Federal army in the field to fight its own war in its own fashion, with little attention paid to the other armies. Some of this was doubtless due to the lack of an effectively organized high command. The situation had become so serious that by the end of 1862 Haupt wrote Lincoln a lengthy letter on this subject[11] in which he stressed the imperative need for a supreme military council. This council would be composed of seven members, including Lincoln and Stanton. For the other members, Haupt suggested three: Halleck, McClellan and McDowell. Orders would emanate from the President in his capacity as Commander-in-Chief, but the public would understand that the responsibility of all campaign plans and important military measures would be the President's *and* the council's. This projected body would interest itself in "all measures for promoting the efficiency and economy of the service." The members of the council would concern themselves with the measures needed to improve the service, would study details of these measures carefully, and would then submit their conclusions at meetings of the council. When necessary, council members could be sent to the theaters of currently active operations to represent the President. On such occasions the members would be vested with discretionary powers, always with whatever limits the President or the council itself might prescribe.

Haupt was very hopeful that such a council would go

far to end much of the inept leadership which he believed was all too characteristic of the Federal High
Command. As he pointed out, his council plan would
involve no change in the current assignment of field
commanders; on the contrary, it would aid without em-
barrassing them. At the same time it would satisfy the
public clamor for a change of military administration.
As a result, there would be a "drawing the veil of ob-
livion over the past [and] we could address ourselves
anew to the task of saving the Union . . ."

The need for a military council was obviously directly
related to a well-planned over-all strategy. Accordingly,
as a result of his service with the Federal forces, Haupt
had gradually formulated certain principles of strategy
which he considered essential for Federal military success.

During this first year of his service, Haupt thought
not only of his own theater of war but also pondered
problems confronting the Federals in other theaters.
Much of what he predicted[12] as necessary to final military victory was extremely accurate. He believed that a
basic policy should involve opening and keeping open
the navigation of the Mississippi River, penetrating the
streams and rivers of the southern states by light-draught
ironclads, and preventing the construction of rams.
Moreover, Haupt believed that the North should capture and hold all the maritime cities and ports and
should select some easily defensible line between the Atlantic and the Mississippi which could be fortified and
held, "isolating the rebels," and preventing their advance
pending further developments. In the implementation
of this plan, advanced posts and strategic points would

be seized, and converted into bases for concentrating troops upon a threatened point and dispersing bodies of the enemy whenever they should attempt to concentrate.

This plan would naturally involve a standing army. Haupt maintained that if this plan of containment were followed it would be much easier to come to some arrangement with the South; certainly a suspension of active offensive operations for a time would be the best method of bringing such an arrangement about, as well as lessening the hatred towards the North.

Haupt believed firmly in this strategic plan. He, like many thinking men of the North, was seriously concerned about the danger of foreign intervention. Because of this danger, insisted Haupt, it was necessary to improve the Navy by adding rams of greater power and speed than the world had yet produced, so as to destroy any fleet that would attempt to raise the blockade or land troops upon the coast. If, in addition to this, the harbors were made invulnerable, the North could let foreign commerce go, "and with our energy, capital and resources, hold our position against the combined world."

McDowell, Haupt's first commander, had early noted that the railroader was constantly attempting to anticipate positions a year ahead and to provide for these situations. As Haupt put it, if this was a fault, it certainly was on the safe side. Haupt believed it was better to look too far ahead than not to be ready at all.[13]

Part of the problem of anticipating enemy intentions during the advance was the interference with military operations by hostile guerrilla bands. Haupt believed that every citizen of suitable age for military service in the South who was not in the military forces of the Confederate States should be regarded with suspicion and therefore closely watched. According to reports, many men who had been exempted from the Confederate draft had been so treated on condition they join Colonel John Mosby's band, who were farmers by day and guerrillas by night. As Haupt pointed out, the Federal trains were run as much as possible in daylight and with train guards, but in active campaigning it was necessary to run trains at night and the train guards afforded very little protection.[14]

Haupt believed that no single rule could be laid down for the force required to guard a projected line of railroad communications in the enemy's territory; the exceptions would be so numerous the rule would become inapplicable. If an army in its advance left any substantial force of the enemy in the rear, it was impossible to secure efficient protection for the communications. No matter how large the force assigned to protect those communications might be, it was always possible for the enemy to concentrate a large force on a single point and effect a temporary break in the line of communications. The only solution was rapid reconstruction of that portion of the line which had been broken. Haupt believed that the Federals were much more successful in quickly repairing damage to rail lines than were their adversaries.

Much of the damage to communication lines was done by small cavalry forces and by guerrillas who were constantly placing obstructions on the track, switching out rails as trains approached by means of wires running into the bushes, and burning bridges. Valuable lives were lost by these enemy tactics. It was impossible to prevent the disruption of communications but, according to Haupt, "they were restored with such celerity as to occasion the greatest surprise in Europe" where newspaper accounts regarded them as fabulous.[15]

When Haupt was put in charge of the railroads in the Washington area, one of his first concerns was to safeguard them as far as possible from destruction by Confederate raiding parties. Accordingly, he used the Construction Corps to construct defense positions around the machine shops and yard of the Orange and Alexandria Railroad, with blockhouses at those points most vulnerable to enemy raiders.[16]

During this period Haupt's attitude towards the enemy found expression in testimony before the Committee on the Conduct of the War.[17] When quizzed on McDowell's instructions relative to "rebel property" Haupt pointed out that McDowell ordered his officers to take not only the property of rebels but any property which was necessary for supplying the army. However, in all cases this should only have been done by proper authority. Individuals should never have been permitted to straggle over the country and plunder on their own, robbing farm houses and insulting citizens. According to Haupt, McDowell extended protection to the defenseless and to "quiet citizens" who remained at home and carried on their legitimate business of cultivating the land. Where citizens had not taken up arms against the Federal Government and asked for protection McDowell generally allowed a sentinel to be placed in their houses. When asked if McDowell ever seized enemy property, Haupt admitted that a large amount of corn was taken along the line of the Aquia Creek-Fredericksburg road, as well as a foundry and machine shop in Fredericksburg. The machine shop was converted into a repair shop for the railroad and engines and cars were repaired in it.

Apparently Haupt agreed wholeheartedly with Mc-Dowell's practice of taking any property which had military value, but also agreed that troops should not be permitted to indulge in wanton destruction. Seizure of all grain was foolish, maintained Haupt, because if the inhabitants were starved completely it would be necessary for the Federal Government to feed them. Accordingly, when grain was seized, McDowell directed that enough be left for the citizens' immediate needs as well as for seed. Unfortunately, soldiers from other units, coming into the area later, robbed the people of everything that remained.

Haupt initially was extremely naive about the attitude of the South towards the Yankee "aggressor." On one occasion he told Stanton of his disappointment over the hostility of the Southern people. Haupt, rather unrealistically, had supposed that a strong Union sentiment prevailed in the South which only required the presence of Federal armies to develop. But on arrival at the front he soon realized that little loyalty for the Union existed in eastern Virginia, and what had existed was soon extinguished by the robberies, insults, and general misconduct of the Federal troops. Haupt told the Secretary that if this anti-Union feeling prevailed throughout the rest of the South, victory for the North would be almost impossible short of extermination of the entire population.

By the time of the Gettysburg campaign, Haupt was much more realistic about how to deal with the hostile inhabitants in the areas of active operations. In a letter to General Rufus Ingalls, Quartermaster of the Army of the Potomac, Haupt complained of daily enemy attempts to wreck Federal trains. As Haupt put it—"those who appear to be farmers during the day are the parties who injure us at night." The railroader asked Ingalls to communicate with Meade and have an order promulgated giving notice to the inhabitants as follows:

> Notice is hereby given that if any attempt shall be made to destroy the track, bridges, or telegraph on any of the lines of railroad used by the Army of the Potomac, the residents in the vicinity, for a distance of 10 miles, will be held responsible in person and property and all the able-bodied citizens arrested. If the offenders can be discovered thir punishment will be death.[18]

Three days later Meade issued a proclamation[19] providing that any citizen who damaged U.S. railroads would be arrested and either confined or put beyond the lines. This order was directed especially against citizens who were sabotaging the Orange and Alexandria Railroad. People within ten miles of the railroad were notified by the order that they were held responsible "in their persons and property" for any injury done to the road, trains, depots, or stations by citizens, guerrillas, or persons in disguise; in case of any such injury the citizens would be impressed as laborers to repair all damages. Meade further ordered that if these measures failed to stop the depredations, he would direct that the entire population of the district or country along the railroad would be put across the lines and their property taken for Government uses. Haupt was so incensed at the destruction to his rail lines that he wanted all able-bodied citizens arrested and, if the offenders could be discovered their punishment should be death.[20] Shortly thereafter, Haupt was given permission to organize and drill his railroad personnel as infantry to enable them to defend the rail lines when attacked.

Haupt gave considerable thought to the physical protection of his locomotive engineers when their trains were attacked. On October 9th he wrote McCallum[21] on the advisability of placing bullet-proof cabs on the engines. Haupt had observed that men in locomotive cabs were special targets for the enemy. The cabs where the engineer and fireman were usually seated were often riddled with bullets and the men could only escape by lying flat on the floor. It was necessary to give these men a sense of security by protecting their cabs with iron. Also, it was necessary to protect other smaller but vulnerable areas of the locomotives. As a result of Haupt's recommendations protected locomotives and bullet-proof cabs were soon provided. At this time the Federals seriously considered making all their engines iron-clad as a protection against sudden guerrilla attacks. Six engines were made bullet-proof by a covering of three-eighths inch iron plating, which functioned perfectly so far as protection against small arms fire was concerned. They were not in any way invulnerable to artillery projectiles. However, the confined air, heat, and especially the impossibility of escape for the engineer and his assistants if the engine were forced off the track, led to the abandonment of the entire project.[22]

Haupt's activities during the Maryland campaign were concentrated in Virginia where he was directly responsible for preparing the rail lines to be used by the Federals in their next advance on Richmond.

It was during his service under McClellan that Haupt developed several of his inventions and technical improvements for military use. Apparently, Haupt had his own ideas on technical aspects of the Federal war effort from the very beginning. Much of the railroader's interest was centered around naval armament and harbor defenses. As early as April 26, 1862, Haupt sent an open letter to John P. Hale, Chairman of the Committee on Naval affairs, on the subject of coast and harbor defenses and armor for war vessels.[23] In this open letter, Haupt maintained that at the beginning of the war he had suggested revolving land and floating batteries as an efficient combination for defense. Moreover, these views had been presented in June 1861, to General John Wool who approved them. At that time, Haupt also submitted sketches for the following:

1. An armor clad revolving fort consisting of two parts: The lower part was to consist of solid masonry protected from shot and shell, containing the engine for rotation, fuel, supplies, magazines, etc. The upper part was to consist of a flat revolving dome with solid wrought iron embrasures. The dome was to be supplied with twenty or more guns of the heaviest caliber, rotating at such velocity as to give any desired number of discharges in any given direction per minute, free from angles or sectors without fire. Each gun was to be capable of firing in any direction, while the fort would be perfectly secure against assault. The only communication was by a gallery which could be dug so that its entrance could be at any desired distance and completely camouflaged. The principle of the Ericsson revolving turret was admitted by Haupt to be similar to his concept of the revolving fort, the chief difference being in the revolution of a part instead of the revolution of the whole structure.

2. A second sketch represented a plan for increasing the efficiency of the ordinary circular and polygonal forts by giving them flanking defense and removing the dead angles not covered by fire. This was accomplished by an

arrangement identical in principle with that which was later used in the turret of the Monitor. It consisted of building projections at each angle supermounted by revolving armor-clad domes or turrets of 20-30 foot diameters. Each of these small domes was to be pierced with one large and several small openings and armed with a single gun of great size, sweeping 180 degrees in an horizontal arc. A railway track was to connect each dome or turret with the interior of the fort where a turntable would be located, equipped with various tracks on which a reserve of guns would be placed.

Haupt also outlined suggestions for improved gun trunions and floating batteries, and forwarded the entire list of suggestions in pamphlet form for publication by the press.

Haupt's absorption in the strategical and tactical considerations involved in the war led him into both private and public criticism of the Navy Department and its chief, Gideon Welles. Some of his suggestions were practical and timely. For example, on one occasion Haupt reported extensive smuggling carried on by small boats of the enemy near the mouth of the Potomac. These boats secreted in the creeks or drawn up in the bushes were used at night to carry mail and necessities to Richmond. In his letter to Welles, Haupt pointed out that this smuggling could be broken up, or seriously interfered with, by searching for and seizing all the boats and by the establishment of an efficient river patrol. While Welles sent a copy of Haupt's letter to the commander of the Potomac Flotilla, there is no evidence that action was taken or that Haupt's letter was answered.[24]

Shortly after Antietam Haupt wrote Lincoln[25] on the subject of naval construction and rams. Letters from well-qualified professional acquaintances were cited to support Haupt's concern for the weakness of the North's harbor defenses and also the need for naval rams.

Moreover, Haupt made clear that he believed Welles should be thrown out of the Navy Department. Various successors were named, including Hiram Wolbridge of New York and Commodore Stockton.[26] No reply to this letter and its enclosures appears in the Haupt papers and Haupt must have felt that his suggestions were not especially welcome.

Appreciated or not, Haupt made his opinions known, even using the press to spell out in detail his views for improving the quality of ships of the Federal Navy! In an open letter[27] to the *Boston Evening Transcript* on November 17, 1862, Haupt pointed out that many experienced naval constructors and engineers apparently believed the Federal Navy was lagging behind in the essential requisites of modern war vessels of such powers as England and France. If this were true, Haupt went on, then the Northern metropolitan or vital commercial centers were defenseless against the armor-clad English and French-made vessels currently under construction for the Confederacy. Under these conditions, maintained Haupt, the fact should be brought prominently to the attention of those who have the power and duty to remedy the situation. Anticipating adverse comments as to his motives, Haupt warned that, in a situation which so directly affected the security of the United States, no loyal citizen should be deterred from efforts at reform, either by a fear of appearing conspicuous or by the consideration that perhaps it was none of his business anyway. One should be free to criticize the management of persons in official positions. Haupt bluntly stated that it was the duty of every citizen to expose peculation, fraud, and extravagance wherever he found it. He noted that a suggestion had been proposed for an interview between Lincoln and recognized experts in mechanical service and naval construction for the purpose of informing the President of the danger inherent in foreign superiority in building warships. However, the suggestion had been shelved for another approach—that of a written questionnaire. And it was to Haupt, himself, that the answers to this circularized questionnaire were to be sent.

The questionnaire, obviously prepared by Haupt, was prefaced by the note that answers to all questions were not expected. However, some fifty questions were listed, including the recipient's name, address, occupation, knowledge, and experience in naval construction. The questions themselves were certainly specific enough. They included, for example, the following:

"Have naval constructors been appointed by the Government who possessed no practical knowledge of the art [of naval construction]?"

"What is the power, tonnage, armament, speed, and general efficiency of attack and defense of the largest English and French iron-clads?"

"Have we any present means of protecting New York, Philadelphia, or Boston against an attack by such armor-clad vessels as are now being built in Europe?"

Haupt also asked for a comparison of U. S. vessels with those being produced in Europe, and especially for those comparisons which appeared most significant.

Three days after the publication of the *Boston Evening Transcript* article, and probably because of the furor raised by the Navy Department, Haupt wrote Welles in part as follows:[28]

I have no wish to criticize your administration but I do wish to see our Country saved. If the plans of your engineer and naval constructors are the best possible, (well, that's fine). If not, and improvements can be made, it will be no evidence of disrespect to you if they are suggested. . . . I cannot perceive that I have said or done or intended anything that should give you offence or to which you can properly take exception.

Yours with much respect,
H. Haupt

On the 22nd Welles wrote Haupt, pointing out that the Secretary did not resent the railroader's suggestions. Haupt replied on the 25th telling Welles how relieved he was that there was no hard feeling about the entire affair. However, Stanton was much displeased at Haupt's using the newspapers to present his views on the inefficiency of the Navy Department. Stanton was also annoyed at some newspaper publications of material prepared by Haupt on military railroads.[29]

Fortunately some details of Haupt's concept of harbor defenses are extant in a letter[30] he wrote another capable engineer, Brigadier General George W. Cullum, chief engineer on Halleck's staff. In his letter, Haupt described his defenses in a harbor as consisting of a series of floating vessels, hollow and capable of being loaded with sand or stones, which could be easily sunk so that enemy ships would run into them on attempting to enter the harbor. These vessels would be armor-plated and could be hooked together in pairs. Another element in Haupt's plan was that of a floating battery which could steam to the side of a crippled vessel, and by its rotating guns pour in steel bolts or shells and finish off the ship in a short time. Haupt told Cullum he had great faith in these rotating batteries. A pair of the batteries, maintained Haupt, would be worth more if used in conjunction with a line of obstructions than all the forts that could be built.

But on the subject of harbor defenses Haupt could find no one in authority who would adopt his ideas. Accordingly, on August 7, 1863, Haupt wrote Lincoln a lengthy letter[31] on the entire subject of the Navy's responsibilities in protecting the United States. After pointing out that he was not in the habit of troubling the President since "You have self-appointed advisors enough," Haupt emphasized his sincere wish to serve the Country and assist in crushing the rebellion. Haupt had corresponded with many of the leading scientific-technical experts on coastal and harbor defenses, armor, navy, and ordnance but had found that those in policy-making positions in these fields were, according to Haupt, "so firmly set in their own ideas" that all attempts to move them were useless. Accordingly, after several futile interviews with them and the Assistant Secretary of the Navy, Gustavus V. Fox, Haupt protested by letter to Fox against the 15-inch guns, and predicted that the Navy Department would very soon abandon these cannon, especially in the monitors where Haupt believed them to be particularly unsuitable.

So far as the monitors themselves were concerned, Haupt believed that by "fortunate accidents" they had performed fairly well, but would have given an even better account of themselves if they had had better armament. But they were unseaworthy and slow, fouled badly and were ill-adapted for defense of harbors or chasing enemy vessels or blockade runners.

The Federal Navy needed speed, and to get this, maintained Haupt, it was necessary to open ship designing to competitive constructors and the genius of

American inventors. Haupt believed that the plans and designs of bureau officers should not be allowed to "use their own brains in devising the best means of getting results."

Haupt, concerned about the possibility of a foreign war, emphasized the necessity of placing the harbors in a defensible condition against the improved ships and guns of England and France. Haupt believed this could be best achieved by lines of watertight crib work sunk across the channels, so arranged as not to interfere with the channels. These obstructions would be backed up by two or more revolving batteries of the type earlier proposed by Haupt, who insisted that "no vessel could attempt to run the gauntlet and escape destruction."

Nor was the railroader content to limit his remarks to the Navy. He was also outraged at the extravagance and waste only too apparent in the military operations. The rascality of government contractors was so rampant that Haupt confessed he was getting used to it, and only hoped that victory for the Union would result in these "smaller matters" being overlooked. After listing several of his contributions to the Federal war effort, Haupt expressed his gratification that department commanders were gradually accepting his plans. He closed his letter with a reaffirmation of his wish to serve the Country "without any compensation present or prospective other than the consciousness of helping a good cause."

It was during these last few months that Haupt developed some of the devices which were suggested to him during his service with the military railroads. During the Maryland campaign, especially, he had more time to perfect these devices, one of the first of which was his "blanket boat." This boat, made of ordinary rubber blankets in common issue at the time, was 64 inches long, 28 inches wide, and 16 inches deep. Each boat held one man, sitting on the bottom. The frame of the boat was made from such easily obtainable material as fence rails. The frames themselves could be constructed by means of a small pocket auger which was easily portable.[32] Gradually Haupt improved on this boat until it became foolproof enough for him to submit it to the army commander, Hooker.[33] The sample boat as viewed by "Fighting Joe" could be used in combination of 25, so lashed and tied together that they could support 9,000 pounds and would sink only 7 inches. These boats were designed for use in river crossing operations. As Haupt visualized their use in battle, the first wave of the boats would cross a river and the men could speedily throw up defensive works before the enemy could react. According to Haupt, his boats could move a substantial number of men across a river in short order.

During this period, also, Haupt developed his "bridge torpedo," which he described November 1, 1862, in a lengthy report on the general subject of bridge and locomotive destruction.[34]

NOTES, CHAPTER 8

1. Haupt, p. 136.
2. *Ibid.,* pp. 138–139.
3. *Haupt Order Book,* Library of Congress.
4. Haupt to Halleck, *Official Records,* Series I, Vol. 12, Part 3, p. 813.
5. *Haupt Order Book,* Library of Congress. It is interesting to note that the same letter was used with the June 27th order added in pencil.
6. Halleck to Stanton, October 28, 1862. *Stanton Papers.* Vol. IX, Library of Congress.
7. *Haupt Order Book,* Haupt to P. H. Watson, Asst. Sec. of War, November 6 and 8, 1862, Library of Congress.
8. Special Order No. 337, War Department, Adjutant General's Office, November 10, 1862.

9. Haupt's Report, September 9, 1863, to Secretary of War.
10. Haupt, pp. 156–157.
11. Haupt to Lincoln, December 22, 1862, Library of Congress.
12. *Report,* Committee on the Conduct of the War, Part I (1863), pp. 682–687.
13. *Official Records,* Series I, Vol. 27, Part 3, p. 1088.
14. *Ibid.,* p. 755.
15. Bigelow, John, *Principles of Strategy,* p. 115.
16. For details, see Chapter 10.
17. *Report,* Committee on the Conduct of the War, Part III (1863) pp. 429–430.
18. *Official Records,* Series I, Vol. 27, Part 3, p. 774.
19. Proclamation, Headquarters, Army of the Potomac, July 30, 1863.
20. Haupt, pp. 248–251.
21. *Ibid.,* p. 144.
22. *Scientific American,* October 24, 1863.
23. Letter from Haupt to Hale, *Boston Commercial Bulletin,* April 26, 1862, Library of Congress.
24. *Official Records of the Union and Confederate Navies,* Series I, Vol. 5, p. 226.
25. Haupt to Lincoln, September 23, 1862. Library of Congress.
26. Presumably Robert F. Stockton, who had made a study of British naval construction.
27. *Boston Evening Transcript,* November 17, 1862.
28. Haupt to Welles, November 20, 1862, *Order Book,* Library of Congress.
29. *Ibid.*
30. *Ibid.* Haupt to Cullum, June 29, 1863.
31. Haupt to Lincoln, August 7, 1863, Library of Congress.
32. Haupt, p. 286.
33. Haupt to Hooker, February 7, 1863, Library of Congress.
34. Haupt, pp. 148–150. See also Chapter 13.

9

FREDERICKSBURG

McDowell had been cooperative and McClellan passive, but the new commander, Burnside, lacked the imagination and intellect of either of Haupt's earlier commanding officers and therefore was especially difficult to serve. Haupt found that Burnside lacked the system and order which characterized McDowell. Moreover, Burnside's grasp of elementary railroad and bridge construction was limited, almost to the point of ludicrous naivete. On one occasion the new commander of the Army of the Potomac wanted a wharf built below Aquia Creek and asked his railroader how much time would be required to do the job. On being told "about three weeks" the General exclaimed: "Three weeks! I want it in three days. I will detail twenty thousand men for the service." Haupt explained that only so many men could work on the wharf's construction; more men would only be in the way. Moreover, time was needed to collect tools and materials. Burnside's idea apparently was that if 50,000 days' work were required to complete a structure, then all he had to do was to detail 50,000 men and complete the job in one day.

So far as rail transportation was concerned, the new commander early promised Haupt to issue no orders except through Haupt himself, but at times he forgot this promise and gave orders directly to subordinates. Naturally this practice led to confusion.[1] Burnside promised to back up Haupt but never really accepted Haupt's status as a railroad semi-civilian and his right to issue orders to military personnel.

On November 9th, Haupt penned a long letter to Burnside explaining the problems involved in supplying an army over a single track line. In his letter, Haupt stressed two major points. First, he emphasized that at *every* depot there should be present a force to unload a train as soon as it arrived. And secondly, Haupt pointed out the importance of establishing a depot of reserve supplies at Manassas to draw upon in case of any break in the rail line between Manassas and Alexandria. As the army advanced, wrote Haupt, depots at intervals of 30-40 miles should be established to guard against the very real possibility of breaks in the rail line due to enemy attack or sabotage by civilians.[2]

From this and other correspondence, it is plain that Haupt was becoming increasingly critical of Burnside's leadership. Haupt's loyalty to McDowell and Pope had been a personal loyalty, but his loyalty to Burnside was sustained mainly by patriotism rather than the respect accorded by a subordinate to his commanding officer.

Reconstruction and repair of the railroads were pushed. In his examination of possible rail lines to use for supporting Burnside, Haupt was unenthusiastic over the logistical value of the Orange and Alexandria.

Haupt considered the Fredericksburg line "far preferable" to the Orange and Alexandria because the sixty

miles of water communication between Washington and
Aquia Creek could not be disturbed by enemy action, and
from Fredericksburg to Richmond there would be one
hundred miles less railroad to construct and protect than
by the Orange and Alexandria route. Moreover, occupation of the Fredericksburg line would compel the enemy
to move towards Richmond and increase the distance
between them and the Federal capital.[3]

Because of these considerations, Haupt was convinced
that the necessity would inevitably arise for the reconstruction of the Fredericksburg railroad. He inquired
several times of Halleck if it would not be necessary to
prepare for this reconstruction, but the reply was usually
to the effect that an advance by this line had not yet
been decided; if it should be, then Haupt would be notified in time. However the railroader was very aware
of the difficulty and delay in getting lumber and other
construction materials. Fearing that the close of navigation would cut off supplies from the Susquehanna, Haupt
telegraphed his assistant, William W. Wright, in Harrisburg, Pennsylvania, on October 26th, directing him to
ascertain the amount of lumber at the river mills. A
day or two later, Wright sent two agents to visit personally all the mills and yards from Lockhaven to Havre
de Grace and rendered a report. On receipt of this report, Haupt went again to Halleck and told him that
navigation would soon close; that it would be best to
order lumber right away; if not needed for the Fredericksburg line, it could be used for other purposes. Halleck approved and Haupt then requested McCallum to
order immediately one million feet to add to some two
hundred thousand feet that Haupt had on hand already.
This advance order was to prove most opportune; the

lumber began to arrive on the very day when Haupt's men were prepared to begin work at the Aquia Creek base. Not only were Haupt's own working crews fully supplied with construction material all the time but men and materials were also furnished to other departments which had not anticipated the sudden demands on them.

Haupt's assignment was a difficult one; he was charged with the speedy reconstruction and opening of rail communications out of Aquia Creek Landing and Fredericksburg. This involved the additional task of rebuilding the buildings and wharf at Aquia Creek Landing. To put the facilities at the Landing into operation, Haupt decided to construct a floating wharf. Accordingly, on the 11th he wrote Meigs[4] asking him to have shipped to Aquia Creek the following material for constructing the floating wharf:

25 Schuylkill barges of uniform height and shape
 1 Pile Driver, with men to operate its supply of coal, etc. (One pile driver was in use at Long Bridge and could not be spared.)
 4 Scows
 4 Batteaux
14 Anchors
60 Piles, about 35 feet long.

Haupt made it clear that these materials had to be on hand as soon as the military took possession of the Aquia Creek area.

Haupt informed Burnside that the floating wharf could be used very well for wagons until a new track could be graded and laid and a permanent wharf constructed. The railroader informed his chief that he was all set to begin work as soon as he received orders to do so. Security against an enemy attack on the construction work would be provided by a detachment of cavalry to cover the landing of materials at Belle Plain and Aquia Creek.[5]

The day after he had written Meigs for the floating wharf material Haupt accompanied Halleck and Meigs on a visit to Burnside at Warrenton.[6] At the conference held that day, Burnside discussed his plans for the forth-coming campaign against Lee. Apparently he wished to use the Orange and Alexandria Railroad as his axis of advance, but Haupt argued against this line. Haupt was well aware of the poor facilities of the Orange and Alexandria line, and the difficulty of supplying an army four times the size of that commanded by Pope a few months previously. On the Orange and Alexandria line there were only a few switches and sidings. Moreover, neither wood nor water could be obtained at several points of the line. Soldiers were wasting water, using the wood for camp fires, and even destroying switches. Guards were needed to protect these essentials for rail-road use, but unit commanders would not cooperate to the point where they would provide guards with orders to shoot trespassers.

At this conference the availability of pontoon bridges came up for discussion. Later, when Haupt was asked if the conference members had determined exactly when the pontoons should arrive for Burnside, Haupt pointed out that he had missed some of the conference and had no distinct recollection regarding the pontoons' arrival. However, he did say that he had the impression that if the President agreed to Burnside's plan "certain things were to be done by somebody in Washington." Haupt could only infer that some arrangements had been made but could not say that there was an agreement to send the pontoon trains to the Rappahannock at a time and place agreed upon.[7]

When Burnside testified before the Committee on the Conduct of the War[8] a week after the battle, he went into some detail on the pontoon fiasco. On the morning of November 14th he began to feel uneasy about the arrival of the pontoons since he had not yet heard that they had been started on their way to his army. Accordingly, he directed his chief engineer to telegraph again about the pontoons. The engineer got off a telegram to General Daniel Woodbury or Major Ira Spaulding. However, amazingly enough, it subsequently developed that this telegram was the first indication these officers had received that Burnside wanted the pontoon train sent down to Fredericksburg, although the authorities in Washington had known of Burnside's plan, which had been sent to them November 9th. Moreover, the plan had been discussed by Halleck and Meigs at Burnside's headquarters at the Warrenton conference on the night of the 12th of November. After discussing Burnside's plan, these officers had sat down and sent telegrams to Washington which, as Burnside supposed, fully covered the case and would insure the starting of the pontoons immediately. Burnside told the Committee that he naturally assumed that the dispatch of the pontoons would be attended to at once. As he pointed out, he could have sent officers of his own to Washington to attend to the pontoons had he thought it necessary; perhaps he had erred in not doing so. Certainly Halleck thought so, later telling Burnside that he should not have trusted such details to the people in Washington.

At all events, in response to Burnside's telegram calling for the pontoon train, General Woodbury telegraphed back that the pontoons would start on Sunday morning (November 16th) possibly, but certainly on Monday morning. If the pontoons had been started on either of those dates, affirmed Burnside, they would have arrived on time to meet the General's schedule. But the pontoons did not even start until the 19th. On that day it commenced raining, which greatly delayed them. The roads became so bad that when the pontoons got to Dumfries the men were forced to float the pontoons off the wagons, send to Washington for a steamer and carry them down to Aquia Creek by water, sending the wagons around by land. The pontoons did not arrive in the area of the Army of the Potomac until about November 22nd and were only at the Lacy House, Sumner's headquarters opposite Fredericksburg, on November 27th! The engineer officer in charge later testified that two bridges could have been thrown across the Rappahannock that night (November 27th) without interference from the enemy, if the engineers had been allowed to do so.[9] If the orders had been received in time the pontoons could have been forwarded in time for Burnside to have crossed the Rappahannock.

Burnside testified that the non-arrival of the pontoons at the time he expected them had prevented his crossing at the time he expected to cross. This failure of meeting his schedule interfered with the success of his entire plan of operations.

Moreover, Burnside expected that the bridges would be built in two or three hours after they were unloaded, which was about daylight. But, on the contrary, the bridges on the right were not built until 3 P.M. in the afternoon, and therefore Burnside had only the means of getting one division over the bridges on the right. Franklin's bridges were built about noon, and were held by Federal troops on the opposite bank. This gave the enemy time to accumulate their forces.[10]

It is very probable that Haupt, in private conversation at least, made comparison of the Army professional engineers under Woodbury and the personnel under Haupt who had developed bridge building and track laying to a science. Haupt found that military personnel did not work as well as civilians on his construction projects, but he may have confused personnel of the regular and volunteer engineer units involved in the pontoon episode at Fredericksburg.

Meanwhile, Haupt had his own assignment to carry out. At the Warrenton conference (November 12th) a change of base was not decided upon. Plans for the campaign were discussed and agreed upon, but these plans needed Lincoln's approval for implementation. Haupt pointed out the impracticality of any attempt to reach Richmond by the line of the Orange and Alexandria Railroad. A whole army would have been required to maintain the communications intact. Haupt maintained that a whole brigade at a single bridge would be unable to save it if a superior force at that point decided to attack. In this connection Haupt enumerated one of his principles of military railroading: "A line of railroad cannot be properly protected by troops placed only upon the line itself; in addition to this, suitable positions in advance must be occupied."

The railroader believed that if the Federals were to depend exclusively on this line for supplies, the army would be destroyed. However, the line would be an excellent axis of approach for a force with a good proportion of cavalry and light artillery, which could move rapidly to destroy bridges and break the enemy's communications with central and western Virginia. After accomplishing this, without attempting to keep open the communications with its rear, the force could link up with some other base of supplies instead of returning by the same route.[11]

As a result of Haupt's strong recommendation, the President approved a change of base from the Orange and Alexandria line to the water route termination at Aquia Creek Landing and Belle Plain. However, construction of wharves and bridges was necessary.

On November 14th (Friday), after Haupt had been informed by Halleck that the President had approved the change of base, the railroader immediately called upon General Daniel Woodbury, commander of the engineer brigade, and upon the quartermasters for necessary transportation. The next day, Saturday, November 15th, several transports with troops were sent to Aquia Creek and Belle Plain. On Sunday morning (November 16th) Haupt went with Woodbury, Ingalls, and two assistant quartermasters to examine the localities and decide upon the plan of construction. This group landed before any of the troops were ashore, agreed on the construction plans and returned to Washington that night.

Next day, Monday, Haupt started a force under the charge of William W. Wright as engineer and superintendent. They arrived during the night, landed on Tuesday (November 18th) erected tents, and commenced work that afternoon. In four days about eight hundred feet of wharf (in length) had been reconstructed and a locomotive landed. The Potomac Run bridge was rebuilt in six days. In eight days from the commencement of work at the wharf an engine passed over the whole road from Aquia Creek to Falmouth; the Federals had reconstructed in that time two railroad bridges—one a very long one—and half a mile of railroad besides a large portion of the wharf.

In a few days Haupt arrived at Aquia Creek to see how things were going. Supplies were on the way and facilities were prepared to unload them. Several engineer companies were already ashore. An impressive list of items was labeled for shipment to the Landing, including locomotives, cars, and a complete machine shop.[12]

This supply of the Army from the Washington-Alexandria main supply base was carried out by a method which Haupt had urged for many months. Railroad cars, loaded with supplies, were loaded on barges in Alexandria, floated down to Aquia Creek where the rail trip was once again picked up. The entire trip, with no break of bulk, was accomplished in about the same period of time as was required by the army to march overland. These Schuylkill barges, so-called, were actually two separate barges bolted together parallel to each other. On them were laid railroad tracks sufficient to handle eight cars. As a result, the usual 16-car train could be transferred *as a unit* by water to Aquia Creek in two barges.[13]

This dramatic engineering feat was new in warfare. Hundreds of loaded railroad cars were sent by this method which, of course, was efficient in saving time and personnel in handling the supplies. Only six hours were required for the trip from Alexandria to Aquia Creek, with one hour at each end for getting the railroad cars

on and off the barges. According to Haupt the saving
over land transportation was about $3,000 a day.[14]

Here is a new revolutionary example of a well-planned,
scientifically executed build-up of a major logistical base
of operations, comparable to the "floating docks" used
at the Normandy beachhead some eighty years later.
But Burnside's change of base was accomplished with
much less fanfare than was that of the Army of the
Potomac's movement from White House to Harrison's
Landing a few months previously.

Work on the wharf progressed rapidly. The destroyed
railroad line began to be repaired, thus obviating the
arduous and slow hauling by wagons over execrable
"roads." The telegraph line to Burnside's headquarters
was being established. Everything was being put in readiness except for one essential—the pontoon train. Pontoons had not arrived and the river could not be crossed
by infantry and artillery unless they were constructed.
There was no permanent bridge still standing in the
Fredericksburg area which could be used.

Until the wharf was rebuilt the army was being supplied by wagons from Belle Plain. Once the railroad was
running again all complaints about shortage of supplies
ceased. During the few days the army was at Warrenton,
Haupt and his assistants not only were able to supply all
essentials to the army, but also had 200 loaded cars to
bring back, the capacity of which was sufficient to supply
an army of 150,000 men for ten days.

The railroad was completed from Aquia Creek to
Falmouth on November 27th. Meanwhile, preparations
had been made by Haupt to rebuild the bridge across
the Rappahannock the week before the Federals took

possession of Fredericksburg. Haupt had the timber cut, framed, and piled alongside the railroad ready to be loaded, not only for the bridge across the Rappahannock but also for two or three other bridges, in case of a Federal advance towards Richmond. Haupt did not have the slightest doubt that he could supply the army by means of this railroad as they advanced on Richmond if cars would be promptly loaded and unloaded. If this were done, Haupt maintained, he could supply an army of 150,000 men with a single track road, 100 miles long, if properly equipped. But if those conditions were not fulfilled an army of 30,000-40,000 men over a road only twenty miles long could not be supplied.

Although the enlisted men still created problems in smooth operating of the rail line, there was an encouraging spirit of cooperation from the officers of the line units. Whereas earlier the problem of rail supply of some 30,000 men in the Falmouth-Fredericksburg area had been due directly to interference by line officers, now the railroad personnel were let strictly alone. This non-interference was the direct result of the fact that Haupt's control of rail operations was backed by Halleck personally.

Haupt's reconstruction of this line was a remarkable feat of engineering. Five days after the track had been begun, he had completed a 1,000 foot section of wharf to accommodate large vessels. An additional wharf was constructed at Uba Dam which could hold 24 cars and could handle ships drawing 10½ feet of water at low tide. The capacity of the yards was increased by constructing sidings to connect with the main line.[15]

Until the Belle Plain and Aquia Creek bases, with their rail lines, were functioning effectively it was still necessary to supply Burnside's army over the mud roads to Aquia Creek. Although the road distance was short, the surface conditions were very bad due to heavy rainstorms. Although Haupt's railroad with the new bridge over Potomac Creek was in operation, and the roads had been corduroyed, supplying an army of about 120,000 men was a tremendous logistical effort. The tactical situation called for a rapid advance before Lee could determine exactly the axis of the Federal attack. Burnside was about to make a river crossing in the face of a veteran enemy, extremely well led. Time was all important.

Burnside, of course, was well aware of the need for speed. Disappointed and frustrated at the non-arrival of the pontoon train from Washington, he turned to Haupt's reconstruction of the railroad to Fredericksburg. Haupt, knowing his commander, was very careful to brief him thoroughly, step by step, on the progress of the construction work. He went into more detail with Burnside as to his construction methods than was his custom with other generals. In a letter to Burnside on the 22nd, Haupt pointed out that it would take several days to finish repair of the line to Fredericksburg. Cars and locomotives had to be transported from Alexandria and unloaded singly. This, of course, was time consuming.[16]

By the 27th the rail line had been completed and trains were arriving at the main depot at Falmouth. The entire army was pleased. A soldier of the 35th New York Infantry wrote[17] home about his comrades' delight that trains were finally running again from Aquia Creek to Falmouth. The soldier described the scene in picturesque fashion:

As the white steam began to roll up in snowy fleeces from behind the trees and . . . the big, black monster with his shining
harness appeared, a wild hurrah broke from the thousands of
troops. . . . Cheer after cheer went up on joyous welcome as
that pioneer train passed the successive camps on camps that
. . . [stretched] along either side of the track. . .

This soldier pointed out in his letter that the soldier in
the army appreciated the railroad because it brought
him "plenty of rations, regular mails . . . as well as
[being] a great contributor to shortening the war."

Meanwhile, Burnside was making plans for extended
aggressive operations against Lee. These operations included destruction of enemy-held bridges on the rail line
to Richmond.

About the 4th of December[18] the General conferred
with Haupt about using a substantial number of Haupt's
"bridge torpedoes." Agreement was reached and Haupt
immediately ordered 100 torpedoes by telegraph. The
following afternoon Haupt was informed that the torpedoes were made and ready. However, Haupt told
Burnside that he wanted to paste on each torpedo a
diagram of a bridge truss and instructions as to how to
use and where to apply them. To get the diagrams and
instructions lithographed in Washington would mean a
delay of a day or two, but the boxes of torpedoes would
soon be forwarded. Each box contained fourteen torpedoes, loaded, with fuse inserted, several copies of instructions, some extra fuses, friction fuse lighters, auger
and handle, complete for use.

Meanwhile, Haupt was encountering much opposition
in assembling and maintaining an adequate construction
force. As late as the day of the battle (December 13th)
Haupt informed Burnside[19] that he had been trying to

round up a detail of soldiers to load bridge timber but had to give up; instead, he would try to get 300-400 civilians (presumably contrabands) to function as a construction force for building bridges beyond Fredericksburg.

Haupt was compelled to use a small untrained construction crew of bridge carpenters and some untrained and unenthusiastic soldiers during the battle and throughout the last weeks of 1862. Haupt's old Construction Corps, organized under McDowell, had been disbanded after Pope's campaign and not reconstituted. Owing to differences of opinion as to whether civilians or soldiers should be used as construction crews, no effective reorganization had been made in time for the campaign.

Burnside himself refused to reestablish the Construction Corps. Even Halleck, who generally had backed Haupt in his suggestions to the High Command, was not in favor of Haupt's projected plan of organizing a construction-transportation corps of 500 civilians. Halleck considered that regularly enlisted engineer troops should be used for this type of service. Haupt claimed that he could use an engineer regiment if assigned to him on a permanent basis. If this were done, Haupt would organize and drill them, and train them in bridge construction. A prerequisite would be Haupt's right to select the men for the regiment and get rid of the drones. But Haupt still preferred civilians over enlisted men for construction purposes on bridges and rail lines.[20]

The day before the battle, at Haupt's insistence, Burnside ordered 200 soldiers to report to Haupt for duty the next morning. Early the next day while Burnside's artillery was shelling enemy positions in Fredericksburg and the heights beyond the city, these 200 soldiers and a

force of 30 bridge carpenters under E. C. Smeed and
G. W. Nagle began work on the railroad bridge across
the Rappahannock. However, as enemy fire became
hotter, the soldiers scattered over the hills and behind
trees, leaving only the bridge carpenters. These men continued to work for several hours under enemy fire until
the pulley-block of the hoisting apparatus was broken.
The timber on which the carpenters were working was
struck several times by shell fire and the ropes cut.[21] As
the carpenters were too few in number to get the job
done, and the bridge could be finished after the battle
in time for its scheduled use, Haupt permitted the carpenters to take cover until the next day before continuing
their work on the bridge. Work was begun the next day
and a span on each side was well advanced toward completion. However, the following night Fredericksburg
was evacuated and further work on reconstructing the
bridge had to be abandoned.

After the desertion of the soldiers from the bridge
site, Haupt went to Burnside's headquarters, reported
the situation, and asked for more men to replace the
deserters. On being informed that no men could be spared
he returned to the bridge and found it deserted. Since
nothing more could be accomplished there, Haupt returned to Burnside's headquarters and remained with the
General all day, watching the progress of the battle and
listening to reports as they came in.[22]

December 14th, the following day, Haupt went to
Washington where he reported to the High Command
and to Lincoln his personal observations of the battle
and the defeated commander. After hearing Haupt's
comments the President took him over to Halleck's office on "I" Street between 15th and 16th Streets. As a

result of the ensuing conference, Lincoln asked Halleck to telegraph orders to Burnside to withdraw his army to the north side of the river. Halleck, after pacing the floor for some time, stopped, and facing the President said decidedly, "I will do no such thing. If we were personally present and knew the exact situation, we might assume such responsibility. If such orders are issued, you must issue them yourself. I hold that a General in command of an army in the field is the best judge of existing conditions." Lincoln did not reply but was much disturbed. Haupt then remarked that he did not consider the situation as critical as Lincoln imagined it to be. The Army of the Potomac had dug itself in after its repulse and effected a safe withdrawal during the previous night. There were adequate bridges for the army to retreat on. A retreat would be adequately covered by the excellent Federal artillery which, lined up hub to hub on the northern heights, was ready to add to its record, already very substantial from Gaines' Mill to Antietam. The President was then encouraged by Haupt's description of the Army's condition.

Haupt was very favorably impressed with Halleck's position on this occasion. Although "Old Brains" was often charged with interference, Haupt disagreed with this fairly universal verdict. As Haupt pointed out, Halleck would indicate to the commander of an army the objects to be accomplished, but would leave the commander complete latitude in details necessary to implement achievement of those objects.

After the interview with the President and his Chief of Staff, Haupt prepared to return to Burnside's headquarters. Another forward movement of the army was expected and, if successful, would result in a very rapid advance towards Richmond. This advance would require a quick reconstruction of the rail line and bridges if these had been destroyed by the enemy in his retreat. Haupt had a profile of the axis of advance and knew the dimensions of all bridges involved. He had a clear idea of the work required of him in the projected movement.[23]

Haupt remained in Washington a few days trying to get civilians to work on the wharves and bridges in the Aquia Creek-Falmouth area, but with little success.

Meanwhile, another forward movement of the Army of the Potomac under Burnside was abandoned until the following month. On December 22nd, Haupt expressed his concern to Lincoln[24] about the "want of success" which had so far attended the President's war effort. Summing up briefly the situation in which the Army of the Potomac now found itself, Haupt insisted that "the experiment of the 13th . . . cannot be repeated, should it be attempted, disaster will ensue." The axis of advance for the Army was blocked. "We cannot advance; to stand still is ruin. To withdraw the Army and send it to the Peninsula would proclaim to the world that the evacuation of August was a mistake. We must go back substantially to the military position of May last when the Army of the Potomac was on the Peninsula and the Army of the Rappahannock at Fredericksburg, but General Halleck cannot, consistent with his former action, order this; and you cannot order this in opposition to him without assuming great responsibilities before the nation and losing perhaps proper cooperation from your present advisors. General McClellan's friends are numerous and powerful, but you cannot place him in position without offending opposing factions."

There is no record of Lincoln's reaction to this bluntness from his railroad expert. The President must have seriously pondered this letter. He had abundant evidence of Haupt's loyalty and ability. We must conclude that Lincoln was impressed.

The construction work at Aquia Creek and Belle Plain continued and it was obvious that if these facilities and the rail lines were to function effectively, new construction and transportation units would have to be established. Accordingly, on January 1st, McCallum and Haupt issued a joint order[25] for the organization of construction and transportation of the military railroads.

Construction and operation of military railroads in Virginia, by this order, were separated and each placed in charge of an officer as engineer or superintendent. A list of appointments of various individuals was included —naming individuals under this new order who would function as Chief Engineer, engineers, and superintendents.

Engineers and superintendents were authorized by this order to hire and fire, and were to be held strictly accountable for results. In general, all appointments were to be filled by personnel with previous military railroad experience.

Existing rules and regulations for operations of military railroads were to be revised as follows:

Engineers and superintendents could present any suggestions regarding organization or for improving the efficiency of the service that they thought expedient. The order was signed by McCallum as Military Director and Superintendent U. S. Military Railroads; and Haupt, as Chief of Construction and Transportation.

These recommendations of the two railroaders were later to be incorporated into the Federal Government's overall policy for its military railroads but for the time being apathy or outright opposition of the military still prevailed.

Meanwhile, Burnside attempted to atone for the blood-bath at Fredericksburg by an advance against Lee, commencing on January 20th. The movement was intended to be an envelopment of the enemy by way of Bank's ford. The army moved out on a crisp bright winter day with the troops in high spirits. A flaming general order indicating victory through a surprise of the enemy was read to every regiment just before the march began. But no sooner were the troops well on the road than the cold temperatures began to rise. Throughout the first two days of the advance—appropriately dubbed the "Mud March"—a pouring, pelting rain made a quagmire of the roads. The feet of men and animals, the wheels of gun caissons, and wagons cut up the mud until it became a liquid foam. Twelve horses could not move a gun; wheels of vehicles disappeared entirely; pontoons on their wagons were stuck fast in the roads, the wheels out of sight, and the boats in a fluid mud sufficient to float them if they had been free. Enemy pickets shouted over to the engineers their willingness to send a detail to help float the pontoons if "You Yanks can't do it yourselves." By the 23rd the storm abated and the army returned to winter quarters, muddy, wet, ugly, sour, and insubordinate. So general was the demoralization and so widespread the desertion in many of the best regiments that Lincoln removed Burnside on the 26th and replaced him with Fighting Joe Hooker.

Although Burnside's prestige suffered permanent damage for Fredericksburg and the "Mud March," his railroader, Haupt, continued to impress his fellow officers and civilian railroad personnel.

An interesting sidelight to Haupt's prestige during this period was the following letter dated December 12th, from J. O. D. Lilly to McCallum:

> Myers Baldwin and Co. have the first engine very far advanced and will have completed by 25th inst. I have taken the liberty without any instructions on the subject, to call the first one. . . . Genl. H. Haupt. . . . Suggest the name of the Deceased Son of the President for their second engine.[26]

This naming of locomotives for prominent figures became a popular custom. On the military railroads operating out of Alexandria by October 1863, there were 60 locomotives, many bearing such military titles as Mars, Hercules, and the names of leading Federal generals. *The Scientific American* quoted[27] some of the comments on the engines:

> What are you going to do with General Hooker?
> Put on a new blower.
>
> How is General Burnside?
> A screw loose.
>
> Where is General Couch?
> Played out.
>
> How is the J. H. Devereux?
> Always ready.

Amusingly enough, the soldiers noted that the General Burnside, like its namesake, was constantly getting stuck. As late as March 1864, soldiers riding on a train pulled by this locomotive pointed out that the engine was completely in character; it "couldn't make the grade" and was constantly having to back up and try again.

Notes, Chapter 9

1. Haupt, pp. 306, 309.
2. Haupt, *Order Book,* November 9, 1862.
3. It is significant to note that Grant also used the Fredericksburg line in the initial stages of his 1864 campaign against Richmond.
4. Haupt to Meigs, November 11, 1862, *Order Book,* Library of Congress.
5. *Official Records,* Series I, Vol. 28, pp. 549–551, 571–572, 587.
6. *Report,* Committee on the Conduct of the War, Part I (1863), pp. 681–686.
7. *Ibid.,* p. 682.
8. *Ibid.,* pp. 651–655.
9. Stackpole, Edward J., *Drama Along the Rappahannock,* pp. 68–69.
10. *Report,* Committee on the Conduct of the War, Part I (1863), pp. 651–655. Burnside's testimony of December 19, 1862.
11. *Ibid.,* p. 682.
12. *Official Records,* Series I, Vol. 21, p. 764.
13. Haupt, pp. 165–166.
14. *Ibid.,* p. 179.
15. *Official Records,* Series III, Vol. 3, pp. 119–120.
16. *Ibid.,* Series I, Vol. 21, pp. 789–790.
17. Smithe, Geo. C., *Glimpses,* p. 29. Smithe wrote the letter on December 1st while his regiment was encamped at Brook's Station on the rail line.
18. *Official Records,* Series I, Vol. 21, p. 827.
19. *Ibid.,* pp. 850, 855.
20. *Ibid.,* p. 855.
21. *Ibid.,* Vol. 27, Part I, pp. 23–24.
22. Haupt, pp. 176–177.
23. *Ibid.,* pp. 177–178.
24. Haupt to Lincoln, December 22, 1862, Haupt Letters, Library of Congress.
25. U. S. War Department, USMRR Office of Construction and Transportation, Washington, D. C., January 1, 1863, Library of Congress.
26. Haupt Papers, Library of Congress.
27. *The Scientific American,* October 24, 1863.

10

CHANCELLORSVILLE

When Lincoln appointed Hooker to the command of the Army of the Potomac, he sent the letter, now famous, in which the President, promised him all assistance possible, and urged him to "go forward and give us victories."[1] The President appointed Hooker knowing full well that the general was a trouble maker and was openly stating that the Army and the Government needed a dictator. "Be a successful general," said Lincoln, "and I'll risk the dictatorship."

In a genuine spirit of cooperation and exhibiting a correct appreciation of the problems confronting the newly appointed commander, Haupt briefed Hooker on the current status of the military railroads insofar as these railroads would support Hooker's plans for the spring campaign. This briefing took the form of a letter written by Haupt January 27th, the day after Hooker received his appointment. First of all, the railroader tactfully congratulated Hooker on his elevation to the Army of the Potomac command and expressed the hope that Hooker's assignment would bring the success to the Federal cause which the justice of that cause merited. Haupt assured the new commander of complete cooperation by the military railroads because "the success or failure of a movement is often a question of prompt supply.[2]

Haupt emphasized that, despite the "innumerable" difficulties inherent in the operation of the military railroads, because of the cordial support of Halleck, McDowell, McClellan, Pope and Burnside, he had always been able to keep the Army of the Potomac supplied. This could only be achieved, stated Haupt, by a regular schedule of trains and prompt loading and unloading of cars. The organization as set up on January 1st, was working very satisfactorily. Assignments of such men as Devereux, Wright, and Adna Anderson were excellent ones. So far as McCallum was concerned, Haupt pointed out that he attended to the routine and red-tape business! Haupt, himself, was generally present when active operations were in progress. Haupt added that it might be necessary for him to be absent for some weeks during the current session of the Massachusetts Legislature, but arrangements had been made to keep everything going during his absence. Hooker was asked to consult Wright on any problems of railroad transportation and Anderson on railroad construction.[3]

Actually, the situation was well under control. Haupt and his subordinates had worked hard. The condition of the military railroads when Hooker assumed command was described in some detail by Stanton in his annual report of December 1, 1862. Stanton pointed out that with the advance of Federal armies into the enemy's country, it had become necessary to take possession of and repair the railways abandoned by their owners. Among the roads thus occupied in the East were parts

of the Orange and Alexandria, the Norfolk and Petersburg, Seaboard and Roanoke, the line from Beaufort to
Newbern, as well as several water routes. In the West
the Federals had seized parts of the Tennessee and Ohio,
Memphis and Ohio, Memphis and Charleston, Central
Alabama, Nashville and Chattanooga, Mississippi Central, and some others. Most of these lines had been, to
some extent at least, repaired, equipped, and run by the
Quartermaster Department of the Army.

Stanton also pointed out that losses in locomotives and
rolling stock during the course of active military operations had been substantial. East of the Blue Ridge alone,
some 11 locomotives and 400 railroad cars had been
destroyed or lost. Although some engines and cars had
been captured from the enemy, these probably did not
make up for the Federal losses.

The Secretary then went on to specifically mention
McCallum and Haupt in the East and Captain James B.
McPherson, John B. Anderson, and Colonel Thomas
Swords in the West as having been especially outstand-
ing in the continued operation of rail lines for the
Federals.[4]

Before Hooker replaced Burnside, Haupt and Mc-
Callum had gotten together and prepared a much needed
delineation of authority. On New Year's Day this was
put into words in a radical move by the Federals in a
War Department order[5] in which the military railroads
were definitely separated into two components, the construction force and the operating force. Each was henceforth to be under its own officer as engineer or superintendent. Both McCallum and Haupt signed the order,
and the order of their signing is both curious and significant. The *first* signature is that of McCallum, *junior* in

rank to Haupt. McCallum signed as Colonel and Military Director and Superintendent U. S. Military Railroads. Haupt, a brigadier general, signed his rank and position as Chief of Construction and Repair. From this, it can logically be inferred that it was considered advisable to clearly define the duties and responsibilities of McCallum's and Haupt's respective positions in the military railroad service. Somewhat subtly also was the deliberate placing of McCallum first in the order of signing; this could well have been some of Stanton's work, since the Secretary's approval was necessary for the issuance of War Department orders.

This McCallum-Haupt order was a well-conceived clearly defined directive for the military railroads for the coming campaigns. Experience gained during the previous year had brought to the fore some excellent railroad men in the service of the military railroads. These men were now given recognition and responsibility commensurate with their abilities and past services. McCallum and Haupt took this opportunity to put in key positions the men on whom they knew they could depend and who were to render such excellent service at Chancellorsville, Gettysburg, and in the 1864-1865 campaigns.

Adna Anderson, whom Haupt considered "very superior" and thoroughly familiar with all details of transportation and accounts, was announced as chief engineer of military railroads in Virginia. From bitter experience, it was found necessary to appoint a superintendent for the military railroads which terminated at Alexandria with their connecting roads. For this important position John H. Devereux was selected. Haupt maintained that a more efficient superintendent could not have been found. An experienced railroader, James J. Moore, was assigned to Devereux as "engineer of repairs." William W. Wright, who had served under Haupt both as a student and assistant engineer on the Pennsylvania Railroad, was named as superintendent and engineer of repairs of the military railroad which terminated at Aquia Creek. As superintendent and engineer of repairs of the Norfolk and Petersburg and the Seaboard and Roanoke Railroads, E. L. Wentz, a man little known to Haupt, was selected.

To insure a vigorous prosecution of military operations, these new appointees were given strong power. They were to be held strictly accountable for operations in their spheres of responsibilities, including authorization to engage the services of all persons for whose acts they were held responsible as well as the right to dismiss subordinates when the interests of the service would thereby be promoted. Appointments in the military railroad service were to be filled by those with service in military railroads, and, all other things being equal, by those with seniority in the service.

So far as the jurisdiction of individual superintendents and engineers was concerned, those officials were to make decisions themselves, but if conflict of jurisdiction between them arose, they were to appeal to the military director. Moreover, the military director was to fix the rate of compensation for all employees. Superintendents and engineers were required to report monthly the names, duties, and compensation of all subordinate officers and artificers, as well as the number and pay of all laborers employed.

The order closed with a statement that the existing rules, regulations, and orders concerning military railroads would be revised and reprinted. In the meantime, superintendents and engineers were permitted to present constructive suggestions to improve the efficiency of the service.

The long interval from Hooker's assumption of command in late January until Chancellorsville was a period of preparation for the coming campaign against the Army of Northern Virginia. Hooker's confident spirit was impressed on his men; he improved morale by personal visits to the lower units, commanding and rewarding by furloughs men who had not been home for months. Desertion was checked and the men's spirits rose by the personality of a vigorous, combat-tested general whose very presence was like a shot in the arm. Pride in fighting units was enhanced by a system of corps badges, inaugurated under Hooker at this time, which only a fighting soldier can appreciate. This was the same type of organizational pride which later generations felt in their divisional "patches."

While the Army was in winter quarters Haupt visited Massachusetts, presumably to keep in touch with the Hoosac Tunnel project. His visit was interrupted in February when he was called upon by the Committee on the Conduct of the War to testify on the Second Bull Run campaign.

Haupt's testimony, occupying some sixteen pages of the Committee's *Report*,[6] was mainly a resumé of his service with the military railroads leading up to and including the Second Bull Run campaign. At the conclusion of his testimony on Pope's campaign, Haupt emphasized that if McClellan's troops, after debarkation from the transports which evacuated them from the Peninsula, had been marched immediately to Manassas instead of waiting several days for rail transportation, they could have rendered Pope "efficient support." Their presence would have given the Federals a decisive victory, maintained Haupt, although he professed ignorance as to who was responsible for the delay in forwarding the troops.

The Committee then asked Haupt for a comparison of the efficiency of military railroads in Virginia and those in the West. Apparently the Committee was especially interested in Haupt's professional opinion, based on his fine record through Fredericksburg—a record which had become respected throughout the army.

In his reply, Haupt spoke very decidedly against running the military railroads by contract. Whatever saving could be effected in money would be more than offset by the loss in efficiency. When the committee asked Haupt to compare the expenses of military railroads in Virginia with those in the West he reiterated his inability to answer this since no centralized railroad bureau existed; no reports on railroads were made to any bureau in Washington. There was no place in Washington, or anywhere else for that matter, where one could find essential data on conditions of roads and bridges, officers in charge of rolling stock, prices and wages, and details on personnel. Haupt quoted Halleck in saying that Stanton was "too much engaged" to give the establishment of such a bureau his attention.

The Committee expressed an interest in Haupt's military status, specifically whether he had accepted a military commission. Haupt assured the Committee that he had not been sworn in for a commission, emphasized his financial sacrifices in leaving the tunnel project, and stated that acceptance of a commission would restrict his freedom to act and speak in the public interest when incompetency or dishonesty in official positions would appear. Haupt closed his testimony with a statement that he had good reason to know that Halleck, Hooker, and the War Department itself were satisfied with the arrangement which had been worked out. The railroader told the Committee that he considered himself as merely a "temporary attache" to the War Department—a sort of appendage—who would serve until no longer needed and then would retire from the scene.

After completing his testimony, Haupt went back to Massachusetts; in late March he received a message from Stanton to come to Washington as soon as possible. On arrival in the capital, March 24th, he reported to the Secretary who asked him for his opinion of conditions of railroads used for Government transportation in the West and Southwest. Haupt told Stanton that although nominally in charge of the United States military railroads he knew nothing about conditions of the Western and Southwestern lines.

Stanton, pointing out that the lines were being run for the benefit of speculators, contractors, and sutlers, ordered Haupt to go immediately and straighten things out. Haupt indicated his readiness to carry out the Secretary's directive, but pointed out that he must first report to Hooker and also must insure that railroads for the Army of the Potomac were in readiness for Hooker's forward movement, which might be under way before Haupt returned from the Western tour.

Haupt returned to his office, drew up a set of orders defining his responsibilities and authority, and presented the orders to Stanton for approval. The Secretary, deeming them "pretty strong," told Haupt he wanted a few days to think them over. Haupt assured him that the trip would be a waste of time without such authority as was called for in the orders.

On leaving Stanton, Haupt went on to Falmouth and told Hooker of Stanton's plan. Hooker was opposed to Haupt's leaving, claiming, rightly, that once the army began its advance, the personal presence of the railroader was indispensable, because it would move rapidly and that Haupt would be expected to reconstruct the bridges and railroads and keep the army in supplies. Haupt's absence could possibly wreck his campaign, Hooker noted.[7]

Fighting Joe meant exactly what he said, for on Haupt's return to Washington the railroader was informed by Stanton that Hooker had telegraphed the War Department that Haupt should stay with his army and some other Western plan be adopted. Accordingly, Stanton ordered that Haupt "cause an inspection . . . be made of the railroad transportation service" in the West, report on his findings to the War Department, including his recommendations. Haupt, by this order, was to submit names of individuals to Stanton to carry out this inspection.[8]

On receipt of Stanton's order, Haupt appointed F. H. Forbes of Massachusetts, a loyal friend and long-time newspaper reporter, who apparently was ideally suited to ferret out the irregularities in the Western railroads. Haupt's detailed instructions for this "Special Agent" were approved by Stanton. Both Stanton and Quartermaster General Meigs issued orders to all officers to cooperate with Forbes in the execution of his mission.

After arrival in the West, Forbes sent back reports which certainly bore out Stanton's belief of widespread corruption in the Federal transportation services in the West. Steamboats were kept moored at their landings until their captains paid substantial sums for their release. Apparently Government property was sold and the proceeds appropriated by sutlers, while hardtack was permitted to be ruined by the weather so as to be condemned in order that new supplies could be ordered—all for the benefit of contractors. As Haupt said, some large game was hit in Forbes's reports; and Haupt himself received letters from parties who asked him to suppress Forbes's reports. In reply, Haupt informed the writers of these letters that the reports were being forwarded to Stanton, and if they wished to add explanations or denials Haupt would be only too happy to forward them along with the reports. After the inspection tour had been going on for some weeks, Stanton himself went out to the Western Theater and on his return he removed Forbes and sent him back to Massachusetts. Haupt never learned if, or in what manner, the abuses uncovered by Forbes were corrected.[9]

Although Haupt had been ordered by Stanton to report such suggestions and recommendations as would promote efficiency and economy, he never received authority to correct abuses or remedy defects. Nor were Haupt's recommendations acted upon while he remained in the service. In his final report[10] he emphasized that the abuses uncovered in the West could only be corrected by a uniform code of rules, regulations, and signals for the operation of *all* military railroads of the United States. In other words, Haupt reiterated his appeal for a central railroad bureau at Washington.

The chaotic condition of U. S.-controlled railroads in the West was glaringly evident in the fall. On September 9, 1863, Federal troops occupied Chattanooga and at once ran into difficulty in obtaining supplies. Rail lines were pitifully inadequate for the sudden demands made on them. The Louisville and Nashville Railroad, for example, could only send 16 carloads a day at a time when 65 carloads were needed. Moreover, this line, charging 25 per cent higher prices than other rail lines, gave private business priority over the needs of the Government. A complete change in the line's management was imperative.[11] Matters were brought to a head by the Federal defeat at Chickamauga and Meigs personally went out on an inspection tour of his own. That an improvement was effected was dramatically demonstrated shortly thereafter by a brilliant display of logistical planning and execution—the transfer by rail of two army corps from Virginia to Rosecrans's forces in the West.

Throughout the spring and summer Haupt and his railroad colleagues were directly concerned with the draft laws which threatened to take away some of their best men. By the draft of August 4, 1862, calling for 300,000 men, a list of automatically exempted men had been drawn up, including, *inter alia,* all engineers of locomotives on railroads.[12] This list was later added to as railroad owners requested exemption of certain key personnel. In this they met with only indifferent success. The operation of the draft continued to be a bone of contention between the Government and the railroads and was never satisfactorily resolved.

The Government had even drafted such key personnel as railroad superintendents, freight agents and paymasters.[13] Stanton, in response to a query as to whether firemen and conductors "who are essential to the running of trains" would be exempt, merely reaffirmed that only locomotive engineers were exempt from the draft.[14] Stanton was reasonably inclined towards a proposal that all railroad workers who had been employed at least three months prior to the draft (August 1862) be exempt. These employees, however, (between the ages of eighteen and forty-five) would be enrolled in companies and would have to drill once a week and be subject to field service in case of emergencies.[15] However, by General Order No. 99, Adjutant General's Office, August 9, 1862, the only exemption was for "all engineers of locomotives on railroads."[16]

In a letter to Stanton[17] after Gettysburg, Haupt discussed the problem of employees of the United States Military Railroads who were being drafted into military service. As Haupt pointed out, all men were not equally important to maintenance and operations of railroads— but some unquestionably were indispensable. Haupt recommended to the War Secretary that men be kept in the military railroads so long as they performed satisfactorily, but if dismissed or if they decided to leave the USMRR for personal or other reasons, their names should be sent to the draft boards. Apparently no action was taken on Haupt's recommendations.

With the approach of the spring thaws Haupt began to take necessary steps for the support of the coming offensive. On March 28th he wrote Adna Anderson ordering him to take measures to have everything ready to support Hooker in the forthcoming campaign. Anderson was enjoined to spare no labor or necessary expense in carrying out this order. Haupt told Anderson to have a well-organized force of skilled men on hand, completely equipped, to perform the necessary tasks. Reliable foremen and mechanics would be required to be available at all times. However, when no construction work was necessary, Anderson's men were to assist in transportation, help the quartermasters, commissaries, or military engineers, and in general make themselves useful. The skilled personnel at Anderson's disposal could be especially valuable in constructing blockhouses for the protection of bridges. And when nothing else remained to be done, Anderson's men could use oxen to haul wood and ties and the men could get practice in the construction of board and trestle bridges.

During the lull before active operations commenced, Haupt was very busy getting the military railroads in shape. The Army of the Potomac was encamped on the north side of the Rappahannock opposite Fredericksburg and supplies were forwarded by river and rail via the base at Aquia Creek. Trains ran on schedule and Haupt turned his attention to improving the reactivated Construction Corps and to improvement of various devices and inventions designed for military use, especially in relation to bridges, rail lines, and river crossings.

Haupt kept his Construction Corps very busy during the preparations for the coming offensive. He perfected its organization, procured material, and got it in readiness for rapid advance movements wherever it should be ordered. The Corps as now constituted consisted of about 200 bridge carpenters and 300 "contrabands." Haupt finally was given permission to have the Corps and some of the employees in the Transportation Department receive daily drill under the direction of a Lieutenant Colonel, John Clark. Permission for this military instruction was later extended by Halleck to include organizing, arming and drilling of all employees of military railroads, a force of about 1,000 men. Haupt won his point on this, pointing out that these men were often exposed to enemy fire and that they should be able to defend themselves. The men entered into the program with enthusiasm and were soon in shape to put up a good defense if attacked by hostile raiding parties.[19]

In addition to getting his men ready, Haupt collected the equipment and supplies needed to reconstruct rail lines and bridges with a rapidity exceeding anything which the Construction Corps had previously accomplished. About 1,600 lineal feet of bridging were prepared, including 1,000 feet of bridging prepared in 60-foot spans. The trusses for these spans were to be carried on railroad cars to the termini of the rail line and then hauled by oxen to the bridge sites where they would be hoisted into place as a unit by means of a special hoisting apparatus. About seventy carloads of material were in readiness for Hooker's "On to Richmond" offensive. Haupt tested his Corps and their equipment by replacing the trestle bridge over Potomac Creek with a substantial truss-bridge, using the new materials and techniques. The new bridge was erected and the old one removed without delaying railroad traffic although Headquarters had not thought this possible when Haupt first suggested the plan.

Standardization and interchangeable parts characterized Haupt's innovation in bridge construction, and made it possible to build this excellent bridge very rapidly. The new bridge was designed as a general type structure adaptable to any span or location. It could be built in advance and kept on hand for an emergency. No skilled labor force was necessary to set it up and the auger and saw were the only tools required to put it together. All parts were alike and interchangeable, any timber could be reversed end for end and would fit equally well. This type of bridge could be raised in one-half or one-third the time of any other bridge of the period. The trusses of Haupt's Potomac Creek bridge, 400 feet long in three spans, were raised in about a day and a half. This was the first bridge of its kind ever constructed.[20] Henceforth Federal military bridges were to be erected with a speed which amazed professional soldiers, both here and abroad.

It was also during this lull preceding the Chancellorsville campaign that Haupt perfected and tested several of his unique contributions to military railroading. In general terms, these innovations involved new methods of facilitating railroad transportation, reconstructing roads and bridges, destroying and repairing communication facilities, and moving troops rapidly across streams in the immediate presence of the enemy.[21]

On April 7th, McCallum, as Military Director and Superintendent of Military Railroads, reported to Stanton[22] on the condition of the railroads for the coming campaign. In this report, McCallum brought Stanton up to date on the condition of railroads in the East. Supplies for the armies in the Eastern theater were being received at the Baltimore and Ohio station in Washington, while in the same cars the quartermaster's and commissary supplies were taken to the Sixth Street Wharf. Forage and munitions were forwarded to Alexandria, Vienna, Fairfax, Union Mills, and then on to Fredericksburg via Aquia Creek, without breaking bulk; loaded cars were shipped on barges either at Washington or Alexandria, towed to Aquia where they were transferred to the railroad and run out to Falmouth. After unloading, these cars were returned empty to Alexandria. Thus, a train of sixteen cars handled in this way saved wharf room, transports, crews and laborers. The trip, as originally conceived by Haupt, took only twelve hours from Washington to the major base at Falmouth.

McCallum took this opportunity to point out the problems created by lack of shelter for rolling stock, change of termini, and necessity for repairs of locomotives and railroad cars. To complicate the picture even further, the engine house at Alexandria had become useless, because the roof had collapsed. It had been necessary to rebuild the turntable. By a special order, the shop at Alexandria had been used to repair boilers and machinery of Government transports and to manufacture ironwork for military suspension bridges. Federal locomotives and rolling stock were kept in repair and running order but only through the exertion of constant vigilance and hard work. Some of the locomotives had to be practically rebuilt because they had fallen into the hands of the enemy or had been thrown down embankments by raiding parties.

McCallum went on in his report to outline what specific steps had been taken to get the railroad lines themselves in readiness for the spring campaign. With supply and repair elements well organized, especially at Alexandria, the Federals had concentrated their attention on the rail facilities around Washington and Alexandria and the route from Aquia Creek to Falmouth. The Washington, Alexandria, and Georgetown Railroad, and the Orange and Alexandria as well as the Loudoun and Hampshire Railroads, were involved in the forwarding of troops and supplies. Between January 1st and March 1st the average movement of loaded cars had been 178 daily.

At the front, the Richmond, Fredericksburg, and Potomac Railroad took over as the main line for the Army of the Potomac. The Federals had taken this line over on November 17th during the preparations for

Burnside's advance. At Aquia Creek a new wharf, 1,000 feet long and 16 feet wide, had replaced the destroyed one. Despite the construction of new sidings for the railroad and a large addition to the new wharf, it was soon evident that the base would not be sufficient to supply Hooker's army unless additional unloading facilities were constructed. Accordingly, a branch railroad, one and one-half miles long, was built to Yuba Dam, where a wharf was constructed with a capacity of 24 railroad cars. Vessels drawing 10½ feet could come up to this wharf at low tide. The addition of this wharf and rail spur line increased the rail capacity for the Richmond, Fredericksburg, and Potomac Railroad by nearly fifty per cent.

Under Haupt's direction, the buildings on the main wharf and most of the buildings on shore were created by the Construction Corps. This had been made possible by Haupt's accumulation of building materials beforehand.

The results of this extensive construction of wharf and rail facilities at the major Federal supply base— Aquia Creek—was that the supply of Hooker's army was assured. A month before Chancellorsville an average of 140 cars passed daily over the Richmond, Fredericksburg and Potomac Railroad. During the period, November 25, 1862-March 1, 1863, there were transported over this road, exclusive of construction materials and special trains, a total of 8,812 cars. Estimating ten tons per car, there were transported 88,120 tons, or an average of 800 tons per day.

The class of supplies transported is an excellent illustration of priorities as developed under Haupt and McCallum. The following table from McCallum's report shows the number of cars utilized in carrying essential supplies and personnel during the period of November 25, 1862-March 1, 1863:

Type of Load	Number of Cars
Quartermaster supplies	915
Food rations	2,346
Forage	4,663
Railroad supplies	112
Ordnance and ammunition	132
Mail and passengers	644

Protection of trains from enemy attack continued to be a problem. On April 23, 1863, Haupt informed Hooker of instructions which were being promulgated to the superintendents of military railroads in Virginia. Haupt directed the superintendents to forward trains with supplies to any point to which they were ordered. But in cases where military protection for such trains was absent or insufficient, and where such trains were in danger of capture by the enemy, any orders would have to come from the general in command of the department and not from any subordinate officer.[23]

As Lee's invasion of the North gradually unfolded itself, Haupt became increasingly worried about the exposed condition of the vital rail facilities at Alexandria. In mid-June he expressed this concern to Halleck and proposed a line of palisades extending from the Potomac River at the foot of Duke Street to Hunting Creek. Batteries of artillery and gunboats would supplement the infantry units which would be stationed behind the palisades. Haupt realized that a raid by two or three hundred cavalry could attack these installations at night and destroy the buildings, shops, rolling stock, engines, and other equipment and get away unscathed. The forts surrounding Washington were so distant that before notice could be given and a force collected the damage could be done and the enemy far away before any pursuing force could be of any value.[24]

Halleck gave Haupt permission to go ahead, and soon the Construction Corps had built a stockade and a system of block houses which were reminiscent of the stockades built for defense against Indians. Haupt's men apparently enjoyed building the stockade, which was solid enough to stop a cavalry raid but which would have been of no use against artillery. Later in the war such stockades would have been reinforced with 25 feet of dirt banked up in front. These defenses of Haupt's were never tested in battle, but they remained in Alexandria for some time as a memento of the great crisis which culminated at Gettysburg in July.

As late as June 27th, Haupt telegraphed J. H. Devereux, Superintendent in charge of the Alexandria depot, to push the stockade as rapidly as possible. Haupt ordered Devereux to use any lumber he could find after using up the cross-ties. No men were to be permitted to work on any other project until the stockade was finished. As a special precaution, Haupt ordered Devereux to run all the spare locomotives to Maryland Avenue or some other convenient place in Washington.[25]

Despite the urgency of the military situation and the obvious need for protecting the rail facilities at Alexandria, the military engineers charged with the defenses of Washington complained to Stanton that Haupt had constructed an interior line of defenses which interfered with their overall defense system! Haupt added an endorsement to the long list of red tape notations that he was unable to see how the construction of a fence around the depot grounds of Alexandria could interfere with the defenses of Washington. Stanton took no action.[26]

Hooker's preparations for his battle with Lee began to take definite shape. As early as about April 1st, Haupt had been ordered to report to army headquarters immediately by Hooker. Haupt left Washington at once, arrived at Aquia Creek at daylight, breakfasted with Wright and then went by locomotive to Falmouth, reporting to Fighting Joe as the General was about to have breakfast. The commander turned over to Haupt a written plan of operations of the Army of the Potomac, enjoining him not to discuss the plans with anyone, stating that even his own staff would not know them until they were to be put into operation. Hooker told Haupt that when the army moved, it would move very rapidly and that he was depending on Haupt for supplies. Success or failure could very well hang on how well Haupt performed and accordingly, the commander was giving Haupt advance notice of his plans for fighting the Army of Northern Virginia.

Haupt assured Hooker that everything would be ready and returned to Potomac Creek where he replaced the old bridge, very susceptible to destruction by a sudden freshet, with a new military truss-bridge of Haupt's own design. The new bridge was completed in three or four days and the line was ready for the forthcoming operations.

Haupt's primary assignment in the upcoming battle was to construct a railroad bridge over the Rappahannock as soon as Sedgwick had carried Marye's Heights by storm.

On May 1st, Hooker's Chief of Staff, Dan Butterfield, at 7 P.M. informed his chief that Sedgwick was advancing, with eight days' rations in each man's haversack and knapsack. After pointing out that a spy[27] reported that 59,000 rations had been issued to Lee's army, Butterfield told Hooker that "Haupt was ready to spring with the bridge."[28]

Butterfield's dispatch is interesting in that it demonstrates the marked increase in accuracy of reporting by Federal secret agents since the days of Pinkerton, who had so grossly exaggerated the strength of Lee's army during the 1862 campaign. The spy who reported Lee's men receiving 59,000 rations was amazingly close to the actual figure of 57,352 Confederates engaged in the battle of Chancellorsville.[29] Credit for the excellent intelligence work performed under Hooker must go to Pinkerton's successor, Colonel George H. Sharpe, 120th New York Infantry, whom Hooker had appointed to head a new intelligence organization, the Bureau of Military Information, on March 30th. Before Sharpe's appointment Hooker could not have been more ignorant of what was going on across the Rappahannock if his opponents had been in China.[30] But Sharpe, and an excellent staff of carefully selected men, mostly from the ranks, kept not only Hooker but the subsequent commanders of the Army of the Potomac well informed of their enemy.

Sedgwick carried Marye's Heights in a brilliant assault which, strangely enough, has never received the acclaim such an operation merits. During the assault Haupt stood by ready to build his bridge as soon as the order was given.

On the morning after the battle, while waiting for

orders to commence building the railroad bridge at Falmouth across the Rappahannock, Haupt walked over the site of Sedgwick's charge at Marye's Heights. Haupt's photographer, Captain A. J. Russell, got several good photographs at this time, including one of Haupt and W. W. Wright looking at the wreck of an artillery limber chest which had received a direct hit during the shelling which preceded Sedgwick's assault.[31]

Haupt tells us[32] that he and Wright came under enemy rifle fire as they went out in front of the lines to examine a pile of lumber to see if it could be utilized in building the railroad bridge. However, as neither man was in uniform, the Confederates did not shoot them, apparently mistaking them for citizens of Fredericksburg.

The next day (May 5th) Lincoln was notified of Hooker's intention of retiring across the river. Haupt was not called upon to build his bridge, and all the extensive preparations for the army's forward advance, so carefully prepared by Haupt, were rendered useless. Meanwhile, Haupt had been assigned the steamer *John Brooks* to evacuate his railroad force. But he declined the use of the steamer and remained at Aquia Creek awaiting further orders.

Meanwhile the Chief Quartermaster of the Army of the Potomac, Rufus Ingalls, was in close contact with the quartermaster at Aquia. Because of the danger involved in a continued enemy advance, Ingalls ordered that supplies on vessels at Aquia Creek be kept on board and not unloaded until further orders. Ingalls telegraphed Haupt at Falmouth not to construct the bridge but to be sure that the rolling stock was protected against any enemy raid. To this, Haupt assured Ingalls that his wishes had been anticipated, pointing out that all rolling stock not needed at Falmouth had been returned to Alexandria. Haupt asked Ingalls if it would not be advisable to keep supplies at Falmouth at a minimum. To this Ingalls informed Haupt that no more supplies should be moved up until further notice. He then told Haupt that he hoped Haupt would ask for protection at Aquia in case of necessity, though "we trust to fight out in excellent style yet."[33]

The actual conditions of affairs were not evident for several days. As late as the 7th of May, Ingalls telegraphed Haupt that Stoneman, the cavalry commander, was approaching Rappahannock Station after having performed "most splendid" service. Ingalls urged Haupt to get his trains moving at once and have supplies for Stoneman on his arrival. Ingalls informed Haupt that Hooker was asking that extraordinary exertions be made to have the supplies available and told Haupt that Hooker "knows he can rely on you." The Quartermaster ended his telegram[34] with the statement that Stoneman had cut the enemy communications in every direction.

Ingalls followed this up with a dispatch to the quartermaster at Alexandria the same day, ordering him to run trains out to Rappahannock Station at once, loaded with one to two days' supplies for men and horses. To expedite and coordinate this, the quartermaster was to contact Haupt. Workmen and guards were to go out with advance cars. Supplies were to be taken to the Rappahannock where they would be rafted over, since the river was not fordable. In this message also, Ingalls showed his unawareness of failure of Stoneman's operations, which he had characterized as "most successful."[35]

Actually Stoneman, who had been given command of

the newly constituted cavalry corps, had failed miserably throughout the entire campaign. Ignoring the main supply depot of the enemy (Guirney's Station on the Fredericksburg and Richmond Railroad) Stoneman went after comparatively unimportant targets. The supplies at Guirney's Station were only lightly guarded and their capture or destruction would have forced Lee to fall back despite his victory at Chancellorsville. Stoneman failed to use his entire command as a fighting unit but sent small detachments out to destroy bridges and railroad installations. These small groups, usually of brigade or regimental strength, were defeated in detail by the alert enemy. Thus, Stoneman's primary mission of destroying the enemy's communications and supply depots was not accomplished. The Cavalry Corps, numbering 10,000 men, lost only 17 killed and 75 wounded in the entire operations. Hooker replaced Stoneman with Pleasonton and shortly after Gettysburg Stoneman was appointed to head the newly created Cavalry Bureau in Washington, July 18, 1863.

With Hooker's retreat the troops were pulled back but continued to be supplied from Aquia Creek. The base there was retained until mid-June when orders were received to abandon it. Accordingly, on June 13th, Ingalls informed Haupt of the proposed withdrawal from Aquia Creek of wounded and supplies to Alexandria. Characteristically, Ingalls assured Haupt of his complete cooperation, stating that Ingalls's best quartermasters would be stationed at various key spots on the Orange and Alexandria Railroad.[36]

Never was Haupt's tremendous energy more in evidence than in the evacuation of Aquia Creek. In three days from the receipt of the evacuation order, all the

military supplies left by Hooker's army, all railroad
property, and about 10,000-12,000 sick and wounded
men from the hospitals had been moved to the landing
and safely loaded on vessels. This evacuation involved
more than 500 carloads of men and material. This was
no mean logistical accomplishment, even by today's
standards. As Haupt himself tells us[37] an equally successful removal of supplies could have been effected on the
occasion of the former evacuation under Burnside if
Haupt had been given the opportunity, but there seemed
to be no desire at that time to save property. Moreover,
the efficiency of the railroad Construction Corps was
such that it no longer was necessary to submit to the
destruction of a major supply base, with the attendant
loss of much rolling stock and material.

After the abandonment of Aquia Creek, Hooker
marched west toward the line of the Orange and Alexandria, which again became the main supply route. However, it functioned as such for only a short time. During
its use this rail line was under constant attack by roving
guerrilla parties who burned bridges, obstructed track,
and fired upon the trains. It became necessary to run
all trains with 30-50 men as guards. On one occasion a
bridge was found burning in the middle and at both ends;
as the train drew closer to the burning bridge five guerrillas were seen making their escape on horseback.

After the successful evacuation of Aquia Creek Haupt
concentrated his energies on replenishing the supplies of
the army by utilizing the Orange and Alexandria line.
The flow of supplies was in the direction of the main
axis of the army's northern movement towards Frederick, Maryland.

By the 26th of June, Haupt was involved in setting

up a supply depot at Frederick, Maryland. Ingalls hoped that this depot could be operative within a day or two.[38]

In the Frederick area the Baltimore and Ohio line took over as the main supply route. But here again, Haupt ran into his perennial headache—the detention or appropriation of trains by the military with no regard to the railroad superintendent of the line. Having relieved a stoppage caused by interference of the military, Haupt then took military possession of the Western Maryland Railroad, which extended from Baltimore to Westminster, Maryland, and used this line during the ensuing Gettysburg campaign.

While Lee was moving North on his invasion of Maryland, Haupt went to Hooker to see what support the General would need. Fighting Joe was in a bad humor, telling Haupt that he would not move at all to forestall Lee until he got some orders and then would only obey such orders literally since all his suggestions were given a bad hearing by the powers-that-were in Washington. Haupt, alarmed at Hooker's belligerent and defeatist attitude, hastened on to Washington where he briefed Halleck on the situation. Halleck informed Haupt of Hooker's distortion of the facts of the case and stressed Lincoln's insistence that a swap of Washington for Richmond would be a very poor exchange.[39]

Friction between Hooker and his superiors increased, especially because of the Administration's refusal to permit the evacuation of Harpers Ferry, and on June 27th, Hooker, at his request, was replaced by Meade as commander of the Army of the Potomac. The same day, Haupt by a Special Order, Adjutant General's Office dated June 27th, was authorized and directed to do whatever he might deem expedient to facilitate the transportation of troops and supplies to aid the armies in the field in Virginia, Maryland, and Pennsylvania. Halleck signed the order.[40]

Haupt, deeply involved in supporting the operations of the Army of the Potomac, was now to work closely with his West Point classmate, George Gordon Meade, as the latter desperately tried to interpose his army between the advancing enemy and the rich prizes of Harrisburg, Philadelphia, and New York.

NOTES, CHAPTER 10

1. *Official Records,* Series I, Vol. 25, Part 2, p. 4.
2. Haupt, p. 185.
3. *Ibid.*
4. Annual Report, Secretary of War, December 1, 1862, pp. 67–69.
5. *Official Records,* Series III, Vol. 3, pp. 1–2.
6. *Report,* Part I (1863) pp. 370–386.
7. Haupt, p. 188.
8. *Ibid.,* p. 189.
9. *Ibid.,* pp. 189–190.
10. *Ibid.,* pp. 277–278.
11. *Stanton Papers,* Vols. XIV and XIX Dana to Stanton.
12. *Official Records,* Series III, Vol. 2, p. 334. Issued as a War Department General Order No. 99, August 9, 1862.
13. *American Railroad Journal,* November 1, 1862.
14. *Official Records,* Series III, Vol. 2, p. 322.
15. *Ibid.,* p. 323.
16. *Ibid.,* p. 334.
17. Haupt to Stanton, August 15, 1863. Stanton papers.
18. *Official Records,* Series I, Vol. 25, Part 2, p. 161.
19. Haupt. p. 279, for further details see Haupt's contributions as discussed in Chapter 13.
20. *Ibid.,* pp. 272–275.
21. For example, on March 14th, Haupt demonstrated his inventions, including the "torpedoes" and "immense floats" for transporting loaded railroad cars, to General M. R. Patrick, Provost Marshal, Army of the Potomac. Sparks, p. 222.
22. *Official Records,* Series III, Vol. 3, pp. 118–120.
23. *Ibid.,* Series I, Vol. 25, Part 2, p. 245.
24. Haupt, p. 190.
25. *Official Records,* Series I, Vol. 27, Part 3, p. 359.

26. Haupt, 190–193, 278–279.
27. A member of Sharpe's Bureau of Military Information.
28. *Official Records,* Series I, Vol. 25, Part 2, p. 329. The bridge was a railroad bridge, *Ibid.,* p. 378.
29. Livermore, p. 99.
30. *Photographic History,* Vol. 8, p. 264.
31. *Ibid.,* Vol. 2, p. 125.
32. Haupt, p. 195.
33. *Official Records,* Series I, Vol. 25, Part 2, p. 400.
34. Ingalls to Haupt, May 7, 1863. Library of Congress.
35. *Official Records,* Series I, Vol. 25, Part 2, p. 439.
36. *Official Records,* Series I, Vol. 27, Part 3, p. 94.
37. Haupt, p. 196.
38. *Official Records,* Series I, Vol. 27, Part 3, p. 339.
39. Haupt, p. 205.
40. *Official Records,* Series I, Vol. 27, Part 1, p. 24.

11

OLD CLASSMATES MEET AT GETTYSBURG

As Lee's army moved northward, the two Pennsylvanians, Meade and Haupt, very conscious of the fact they were fighting on their own soil, put every effort into their respective assignments. They were backed by Stanton who granted his subordinates extraordinary powers and discretion to get the job done. Orders went out to impress tugs, steamers, or anything else necessary. Meigs was told to get his supplies in any way possible, but to get them; while Haupt was given comparable freedom of action with regard to the military railroads.

Although Haupt was unaware of what the future held for him, this was to be his last campaign. The war was only in its "high-water mark," half over; but Haupt was soon to leave the service and was not privileged to serve under the last commander, Grant, in 1864 and 1865. However, for this crucial campaign, Haupt was peculiarly fitted. He had the confidence of the new commander, a classmate from West Point days; he had available a well-trained construction crew; and he was operating in a territory he knew thoroughly. Haupt had lived and taught in Gettysburg. His home had been on Seminary Ridge and during the battle one of Longstreet's batteries was to be set up in his front yard.[1] Haupt entered into the spirit of urgency with that remarkable energy which was one of his most valuable characteristics.

Although the new commander, Meade, and Haupt had graduated in the same class from the Military Academy, they had never become close friends. Dignified and courteous, Meade was reserved and definitely lacked personal magnetism. Actually Haupt had been only a casual acquaintance of Meade's during their cadet days and had only met him briefly on the occasion of Meade's marriage before the war.

Meade had not at all expected the appointment to the command of the Army of the Potomac, and his promotion found him unaware of the location of Lee's forces and even his own! Meade originally did not intend to fight at Gettysburg. His intention, as he told Haupt[2] shortly after the battle, had been to fall back towards Baltimore and take up a defensive position. But circumstances were to force Meade to change his plans.

As Lee pushed north, the situation grew more serious hourly, and Haupt, eager to get in the midst of things, called on Stanton, but the Secretary kept him waiting two or three days until "very impatiently" he went to Halleck who agreed the railroader should be in the field, not in Washington. Halleck advised Haupt to go to Stanton and say that unless the Secretary had more important duties for him, Halleck wanted Haupt to leave at once. Stanton let Haupt go.

Meanwhile, by a special order dated June 27th, Halleck authorized Haupt to do whatever he deemed expedient to facilitate the transportation of troops and supplies to assist the armies in the field in Virginia, Maryland and Pennsylvania.[3]

The situation was worsening rapidly. Meade had moved northward to intercept Lee's army, which had cut the Baltimore and Ohio Railroad. Haupt believed that his immediate mission was to go to Harrisburg, ascertain the military situation in Pennsylvania, especially the numbers and position of the Federal forces that had been gathered in that area to oppose Lee, and then to make his way, either on horseback or foot, and give Meade all the information he had been able to gather.[4]

With his mission thus in mind, Haupt went to Baltimore on the 29th, intending to join Meade at Frederick. But rail and telegraph communications were down; the enemy still held key positions on the rail line, and Haupt went on to Harrisburg. Here he spent several hours with Governor Andrew Curtin and Haupt's protege, Thomas A. Scott, who briefed him on the situation. Scott had been very active and had seen to it that the Pennsylvania Railroad was getting as good protection as the short time would permit. However, Scott had misinterpreted completely the intentions of the enemy. Some of Lee's forces had occupied the opposite side of the Susquehanna River in large force, and at an early hour had begun to retreat so rapidly that provisions had been left uncooked while their artillery had passed through Mechanicsburg at a fast trot. Scott interpreted all this as evidence that the enemy had been duped by the Federal claim of having 60,000 men available to defend Harrisburg when actually there were only 15,000 raw recruits. As Scott saw it, the enemy was unwilling to attempt the crossing of the river in the face of such strength and Lee had therefore decided to retreat. During this briefing, Haupt pointed out that Lee was aware of Meade's dispersion of forces and intended to take advantage of that dispersion. The major Eastern cities—Washington, Baltimore, Philadelphia, and New York—would be in real danger if Meade's army were beaten, Haupt pointed out. Once again the railroader had put his finger exactly on the crux of the problem. Haupt realized that Lee had concentrated his forces very rapidly and was moving toward Gettysburg to crush each element of the Army of the Potomac before this army could fully concentrate or its new leader could get it well in hand.[5]

With the enemy's intentions clearly in mind, Haupt now proceeded to get telegrams off to Halleck and General Robert C. Schenck (the department commander whose troops were guarding rail lines and patrolling the north bank of the Potomac) to alert them to the developing situation. Haupt suggested that a locomotive be run from Baltimore to Westminster, and also that a mounted courier be dispatched to Meade. The dispatch got through and certainly helped to confirm other intelligence reports which were pouring into Meade's headquarters. Haupt's intelligence came from the rear of the enemy and fitted in well with the information which Meade was getting from his front intelligence-gathering elements.

On Wednesday Haupt returned to Baltimore and went on to the Relay House. He then examined the condition of the Western Maryland Railroad, a line of critical value to the Federals in this emergency. Haupt found the Western Maryland to be completely unprepared, both in equipment and facilities, for the duties which immediately confronted it. This road had no experienced managerial personnel, water stations, sidings, or turn-tables. Available supplies of wood were sufficient for only two or three trains per day, but the Army of the Potomac would need thirty trains per day in both directions.

Haupt ordered locomotives and rolling stock, complete with train hands, sent out from Alexandria. To supply the shortage of fuel, split wood was sent along with the trains. Water was dipped from a dam by buckets; an old turntable was set in operation again, while the lack of sidings was overcome by prompt unloading of the cars on the main track. Haupt, as was his custom, gave personal credit in his final report both to the quartermaster in charge as well as to Adna Anderson, chief engineer of construction, U.S. Military Railroads, for their "extraordinary service" in getting this line in operation so quickly.

Haupt's leadership in preparing the Western Maryland for service typifies the tremendous and efficient effort he could bring to bear on a major logistical problem in remarkably short time. Moreover, the situation was complicated by the continuing harassment caused by the prolific source of military railroad troubles, the detention or appropriation of trains by military authority exercised independently of the superintendent of the line. Haupt took immediate steps to solve the problem by taking military possession of the Western Maryland extending from the Relay House, outside of Baltimore on the Northern Central Railroad, to Westminster, Maryland.[6] Moreover, Haupt's insistence on a schedule system for railroads under his control really paid off during those hectic days. The schedule was of prime importance in making the Western Maryland so valuable an element in logistical support of the Army of the Potomac during this campaign.

With the Western Maryland functioning smoothly, Haupt placed its management in the hands of Adna Anderson and turned his attention to reopening communication with Harrisburg, by means of the Northern Central Railroad. On this road there were nineteen bridges down; some of the larger of which were completely destroyed. These bridges had to be rebuilt and time was all-important. For this emergency Haupt divided his Construction Corps into two divisions, and each of these were in turn subdivided into lesser working groups. One of the main divisions went to Harrisburg and began working south on the line, while the other main division began working north. Haupt took personal charge of a subdivision of this second major group and concentrated on the reopening of communications with Littlestown and Gettysburg.

Much of Haupt's success in repairing the rail lines and bridges during these days was due to the excellence of the Construction Corps, which he had organized and trained. With the exception of its higher officers and foremen, the Corps as constituted for the Gettysburg campaign consisted almost entirely of "contrabands." Thousands of these ex-slaves had flocked into the Washington-Alexandria area. From their number were selected several hundred able-bodied men familiar with the use of the axe. These Negroes worked with enthusiasm, and each gang tried to excel the others in the progress made on each job within a specific time limit. The Corps functioned smoothly and rapidly in its pri-

mary function of restoring communications. Permanency
of construction, naturally, was not the prime requisite.
The men worked with such speed that neither months
nor even weeks were considered, as with permanent
structures, but rather hours and minutes. The Corps
rebuilt all nineteen bridges on the Northern Central in
a few days; all the bridges on the branch lines leading
to Gettysburg were rebuilt during or shortly after the
battle, and communications were established with Washington by noon of the day after Lee's retreat!

With these unsung heroes of the Construction Corps,
Haupt worked his way towards Littlestown, repairing
the railroad and bridges as he came to them. But in the
course of this reconstruction of rail facilities, Haupt was
keeping his superiors informed of military events as they
developed. As during the Second Bull Run campaign,
Haupt sent and received a large number of telegrams
which, in the light of events as we now know them, portrayed a kaleidoscopic but accurate blow-by-blow account of the fast-moving action as it developed in late
June and early July.

The first[7] in the series of these dispatches was sent
by Haupt from Harrisburg at 6 A.M. July 1st, the first
day of the battle. Haupt, knowing of an enemy drive
towards Harrisburg, informed Halleck that Lee had received information of the removal of Hooker and his
replacement by Meade. Apparently Lee, knowing that
the Federal communications had been cut by Jeb Stuart,
had decided to profit from the confusion arising from
poor communication facilities and change of commanders. It was obvious that Meade was going to have difficulty in getting his forces together, and if Lee could
quickly concentrate his scattered forces he could fall on

Meade, crush him; and Washington, Baltimore and Philadelphia would all be at the mercy of the invader.

In this valuable dispatch, Haupt estimated Lee's strength as 92,000 men and 236 guns, and also pointed out the current location of the individual corps of Lee's army. This is an excellent military report and surprisingly accurate. According to a competent authority, the numerical strength of Lee's army at Gettysburg was 75,054 effectives.[8] It must be emphasized that this figure excludes sick, deserters, and stragglers, as well as losses in the preliminary skirmishes preceding July 1st. Therefore, it is reasonable to assume that Lee entered Maryland with an army fairly close in size to the estimate sent by Haupt. Lee had 287 guns[9] a figure not at too much variance from Haupt's estimate. Haupt was uncertain about the number of artillery pieces in Hill's corps. His figures, broken down by corps, were as follows:

Infantry		Artillery Pieces
Ewell	23,000	48
Longstreet	30,000	122
Hill	24,000	40 (?)
Early	15,000	26
	92,000	236

Ewell's forces had been counted in Carlisle on Friday, June 26, as they passed through the town.[10] Although anxious to return to Baltimore, Haupt remained in Harrisburg long enough to get a telegram off to Halleck as a result of information received at 12:45 P.M. This latest intelligence, Haupt told Halleck, definitely indicated that Lee was concentrating his forces in the Gettysburg area rather than at Chambersburg as Haupt had earlier predicted. The enemy was moving very rapidly and Meade should by all means be informed and alerted to a sudden attack from Lee's whole army. Unfortunately, there was a 12-hour delay in forwarding Haupt's message to Meade by a courier from Frederick. While Haupt's dispatch would not necessarily have influenced Meade in his hurried tactical dispositions, the dispatch does show very clearly that Haupt was correct in his analysis of the tactical situation.

At 6 P.M. of the same day, July 1st, Haupt sent a longer intelligence summary and also informed Stanton about the state of affairs in the Harrisburg area. This accomplished, Haupt returned to Baltimore, taking by necessity a long route through Philadelphia because Lee's men had destroyed many bridges and culverts on the rail line.

By the time Haupt arrived in Baltimore the battle at Gettysburg was well under way. Haupt could now take stock of what he had accomplished and what there yet remained to do to aid Meade's army. The Western Maryland Railroad was operating despite an original lack of telegraph lines to handle train units, sidings, and adequate scheduling. Haupt had corrected these deficiencies and had established a train convoy system with adequate guards to protect the line and its many small bridges from sabotage by Confederate sympathizers. The Western Maryland line was in running order.

Haupt saw that his rail communications from Baltimore to Westminster and thence to Gettysburg were slow and uncertain, and were interfering seriously with the supply trains. Accordingly, he at once inaugurated a Pony Express system at intervals of three hours, with relays every seven miles, running day and night. Since the distance from Baltimore to Westminster is only twenty-eight miles, and the road is a good turnpike, this alternate method of communication was a sensible one. With no telegraph line, and with a longer rail distance (usually requiring five hours) the horse express method worked well. The time required by horse was only three hours. This express route was extended to Meade's headquarters on the 2nd of July.[11]

The continued functioning of Meade's army, now engaged in bitter combat with the invaders, involved the forwarding of troops and supplies, and the evacuation of wounded. On the 2nd of July, Haupt was able to telegraph McCallum that the Western Maryland Railroad to Westminster, the Baltimore and Ohio to Frederick, and the Northern Central to Hanover Junction were running smoothly.[12] This had been accomplished despite the destruction of nineteen bridges on the road to Hanover Junction alone, while three bridges had been destroyed between the latter place and Gettysburg.[13] The battle of Gettysburg is a classic in military supply preparations and evacuation of wounded and prisoners. The credit is unquestionably Haupt's. As early as the afternoon of July 2nd, Haupt could report to Stanton that fifteen trains a day would be put into Westminster, and that 150 cars, in returning, could carry from 2,000 to 4,000 evacuated wounded. Meanwhile, repair crews were working on the Northern Central, and Haupt assured Stanton that as soon as the military situation permitted, he would have the line into Gettysburg in operation.

Meanwhile, trouble arose over the attempted seizure

of civilian railroads by the military. General Darius Couch, commander of the Department of the Susquehanna, impatient at some trouble with railroads in his area of responsibility, appointed Colonel W. W. Wright, U.S. Military Railroads, to the position of "Superintendent of Railroad Transportation" in the Department of the Susquehanna with implied orders to take military possession of any or all railroads. Haupt promptly refused his subordinate this power pointing out that "it is best to operate roads by and through the regular officers and agents." As Haupt pointed out, the Pennsylvania, Northern Central, and Lebanon Valley Railroads were managed by experienced personnel. To assert or exercise authority over such lines, unless absolutely necessary, would have been unnecessary and unwise. In fact, Stanton himself expressed unqualified appreciation to the Superintendent of the Northern Central (J. N. DuBarry) for his energetic cooperation.

By the evening of the 3rd, fighting had been going on for three days. Lee was badly defeated, having suffered very heavy losses in men and material. Federal casualties were staggering also, and Stanton directed Haupt to spare no efforts in evacuating the wounded by rail. Or, if the rail lines were clogged, the railroader was to get the wounded back by any means available. But to get to Gettysburg itself was no easy task. Shortly before noon, Haupt reported to Halleck[14] that a locomotive had gone to Hanover Junction the previous afternoon, and then, using the Gettysburg railroad, had managed to get to within seven miles of Gettysburg; but a burned bridge had prevented its getting any closer to the scene of the fighting. Men on the locomotives reported "excessively heavy firing and much smoke" in the Gettysburg area. This very probably was the charge of Pickett. The locomotive returned at midnight after this unsuccessful attempt to get all the way to the battlefield. Due to the large number of railroad bridges down, Haupt dispatched half his bridge construction personnel, with a train, to Harrisburg by way of Baltimore and Philadelphia. This group worked south, while the other half of the "bridge corps" worked north towards them. However, the Northern Central line to Gettysburg was still in bad shape. The line itself was of the "very poorest description" with curves of 300 foot radius, around which ordinary locomotives could not run. Haupt assured Halleck that he would do the best he could, but that not much logistical support could be expected from the Northern Central. Therefore, Haupt suggested that some supplies be sent to Meade's army by wagon. Haupt closed his dispatch with the statement that he was leaving for Westminster.

Due to delays, however, Haupt spent most of the 4th (the day after the battle) at Hanover Junction, forwarding supplies and making arrangements for wholesale evacuation of the wounded. During the day he went to Littlestown to superintend repairing of a bridge and evacuating the wounded from that point. Meanwhile, his men had completely rebuilt the bridge at Hanover Junction. At 4 P.M. he sent a dispatch to Halleck informing him that he had made arrangement to bring General Daniel Sickles by special train to Washington. The controversial commander of the 3rd Corps had lost a leg by a cannon projectile on July 2nd. This injury had been received after Sickles had placed his corps in such an unfavorable tactical position as to cause it to lose about one-third of its strength in some four hours.[15]

After amputation, Sickles, with a strong escort, had been carried on a stretcher to Littlestown, some twelve miles southeast of Gettysburg. Here Haupt found him. Sickles's stretcher was placed across the backs of two seats on the train and, with 1500 other wounded, proceeded to Washington, arriving on Sunday, July 5th.[16]

Meanwhile Haupt had informed Stanton[17] that the construction crews had passed over the Northern Central to Hanover Junction, and on over the Hanover and Gettysburg branches to Oxford, only seven miles from Gettysburg. However, due to the presence of the enemy, the reconstruction and operation of the Gettysburg branch of the rail line from Oxford to Gettysburg would not be feasible at the present time. Haupt told Stanton that as soon as Federals had full and undisturbed control of the area around Gettysburg, he could quickly open up the rest of the branch line to Gettysburg itself.

While still at Oxford, Haupt finally was able to open up direct telegraphic communication with Washington. A telegram[18] to Halleck arrived at its destination in only 15 minutes. In this telegram Haupt, now organizing his headquarters to support Meade, was able to give Halleck a first-hand account of the military situation. Haupt could pass on his interpretation of the condition of the Army of the Potomac, as well as an analysis of Meade's plans for following up Lee's defeat of the previous three days. But Haupt was not pleased at all with what he had to report. Apparently Meade was content to refresh his men and collect supplies while Lee was effecting his escape. Haupt pointed out to Halleck that a good force on the line of the Potomac could prevent Lee's crossing the river and the Confederates could be destroyed. Turning to the supply situation, Haupt informed

Halleck that by 11 P.M. that night, some 2,000 tons of supplies should have been forwarded since the previous day to Meade's army.

Haupt followed up this telegram to Halleck with a second, sent at 4:20 P.M., in which he reaffirmed his intention of doing everything possible to get the wounded away from the battlefield area and suggested the establishment of a hospital at York, which Haupt hoped would be linked up with good rail connections in two days. Meanwhile, temporary arrangements for the wounded could be made. Haupt then assured Halleck that he would be kept informed of all important developments.[19]

About an hour later, Meigs informed Haupt that the Adams Express Company had offered to organize and send forward a "hospital corps," complete with men, supplies, and spring wagons, to remove the wounded from Gettysburg. The Company was asking Haupt for transportation to Westminster for this ambulance train. Stanton, having accepted this offer, called on Haupt for assistance in providing the necessary rail transportation, so long as the forwarding of supplies necessary for pursuing the enemy was not slowed down. Pointing out that Meade's army had some 1,100 ambulances, the Secretary curtly told Haupt through Meigs to let nothing interfere with the supply of rations to the men and grain for the horses.

Stanton's special order providing for this unique ambulance service by the Adams Express Company is of special interest. The Secretary's order provided for the organization of a hospital corps which was to furnish supplies and transportation of officers and men wounded in the Gettysburg battle. Stanton ordered that Adams Express Company's "agents and servants" be permitted

by all personnel in the Federal service to pass within
the military lines of the United States, with their wagons, ambulances, and horses, to and from the battlefield
and its vicinity with food and hospital supplies. This
was all well and good, but contrasted sharply with Stanton's reactions to similar proposals made by Surgeon
General William A. Hammond the previous summer.
What an opportunity was presented here for enemy
espionage! And Stanton had opposed Hammond who
had endeavored to organize this very type of service
within the military!

Despite these incongruities in the actions of the Secretary of War, Haupt bent every effort to arrange a
prompt, smooth-flowing evacuation of wounded from the
Gettysburg battle area. And he succeeded. In an official
report of July 25th, Medical Inspector Edward P. Vollum attested to Haupt's efficiency. Amidst the destruction of bridges and telegraph lines, reported Vollum,
Haupt managed to get things so well organized that the
medical personnel were able to perform efficiently, with
no further delays until some two weeks after the battle
was over.[20] By that time, Haupt had left the area and
was no longer involved in caring for the Gettysburg
wounded.

At 11 P.M. Saturday, July 4th, while Haupt was still
at Oxford, seven miles from Gettysburg, he informed
Halleck that the railroad and telegraph lines had been
opened to Gettysburg. Supplies were moving into the
battle area and wounded moving out. Earlier, 5:30 P.M.,
Meigs urged Ingalls to stand on no ceremony in getting
horses to follow up the victory. Remounts were needed
to replace cavalry and artillery horses lost during the
three-day battle.[21] Quartermasters all over the North

(even as far west as Indiana) were ordered to forward horses immediately to Meade's army. Haupt sent telegrams to railroad officials to expend every effort to get the animals through.[22]

Meanwhile, troop commanders closer to the Gettysburg area were being ordered to concentrate all their forces against Lee with the intention of inflicting on him a *coup de grace*. Before noon on the 4th, Halleck had ordered Federal troops at Cumberland to move at once and be prepared for a rapid flanking attack against Lee. "No time is to be lost" urged Halleck.

Haupt realized that Lee was anxious to get his army back into Virginia and therefore hoped the Federals would not attack while this retreat was in progress. It was not necessary to attack Lee's entrenched position. Lee was down to 35,000 effectives but still could exact a heavy toll from the attacking Federals. Meade should have held a strong defensive position with part of his army, while the remainder, a strong force, crossed over the Potomac—the two elements still remaining in mutually supporting distance—and then moving on to seize the south bank of the river and denying to Lee any opportunity to bridge the river for his escape.

Throughout the 4th, all Washington had been impatiently waiting for news from the Army of the Potomac. Fragmentary reports drifted in from time to time. Toward evening, Haupt's report of Lee's retreat arrived and gave the expectant crowds an exhilarated feeling of final victory. This was soon followed by Meade's congratulatory order to his troops, in which the General thanked his army for the "glorious result" of the recent operations. Meade said that an enemy superior in numbers, after an unsuccessful attempt to destroy the Army of the Potomac was now utterly baffled and defeated and "forced to withdraw from the country."[23] Meade closed his order with an urging for his army to exert even greater efforts to drive the invader from "our soil." All loyal people were disappointed but no citizen more than Lincoln who could not refrain from his famous outburst:

> Drive the invaders from our soil! My God! This is a dreadful reminiscence of McClellan. Will our generals never get that idea out of their heads? The whole country is our soil![24]

The next morning, Sunday July 5th, the day after Lee began his retreat southward, Haupt went by buggy into Gettysburg. On arrival in the town square he found General Marsena Patrick (Provost Marshal of the Army of the Potomac) who directed him to Meade's headquarters. On arrival, Haupt found Meade and General Alfred Pleasonton and told them that by noon there would be both rail and telegraph communication with Washington. Both generals were surprised and pleased; they thought that the destruction of bridges had been so complete that two or three weeks would be necessary to make them servicable again.

Meade and Pleasonton proceeded at once to rapidly brief Haupt about the battle situation. After the briefing Haupt asked Meade as to the next movements of the army since it would be necessary to furnish the transportation and supplies for such movements. Haupt pointed out that he assumed the army would march at once to the Potomac and cut off Lee's retreat.

Haupt listened incredulously as Meade replied that the army could not start immediately. The men required rest! Haupt, bitterly disappointed, retorted that the men were well supplied with rations, they had been stationary behind stone walls during the battle and therefore could not be footsore; the enemy troops had been on their feet much more than Meade's men; and it was but little more than a single day's march to the Potomac. If prompt advantage were not taken of Lee's present predicament, he would escape.

Meade replied with the observation that Lee had no pontoon train and the river was swollen by rains and not fordable. Haupt persisted, "Do not place confidence in that. I have men in my Construction Corps who could construct bridges in forty-eight hours sufficient to pass that army, if they have not other material than such as they could gather from old buildings or from the woods, and it is not safe to assume that the enemy cannot do what we can."

More conversation followed. Haupt spoke bluntly to his old classmate but he could not inspire the spirit of aggressiveness which the situation obviously demanded. Meade insisted that his men needed rest.

Much discouraged, Haupt listened as Meade went on to say something about moving his headquarters, but there was nothing to indicate any intention of pushing forward with the bulk of his army to crush Lee.

Haupt clearly saw that here was presented a golden opportunity to destroy Lee's army. Knowing the terrain and surrounding country thoroughly, Haupt urged immediate pursuit. Repeatedly Haupt urged his classmate to pursue Lee and crush him because this was the critical moment of the war. And Haupt was right! Lee's men, as he pointed out, were worn out and hungry. The Confederates had about exhausted their ammunition and supplies. Any supply trains moving up from the South could

be cut off easily. The enemy was in dire straits, like a
"rat in a trap." Haupt insisted that Meade could whip
and capture his adversary.

But all his pleadings were to no avail. Meade, sobered
by his own heavy casualties and a profound appreciation
for the fighting capabilities of Lee's army, refused to
launch an immediate offensive against the enemy.

Swift action was necessary. That night Haupt took a
locomotive and rushed back to Washington to report to
Halleck in person early the next morning (Monday,
July 6th). He explained the situation to Halleck, and
then called upon Stanton and the President separately.
After his interview with Halleck, Haupt returned to his
Washington office and wrote the General "for the
record" the entire situation of Meade's army vis-a-vis
the enemy. Haupt clearly pointed out in his letter of
July 6th[25] the probable line of retreat of Lee's army and
what could be done to intercept him before he could
escape across the Potomac. As Haupt accurately indicated:

> In this condition of affairs, the railroad would be indispensable,
> and as the country must not be nearly clear of the enemy, a
> very small force could occupy the Gaps of the Blue Ridge,
> make descents into the valley to cut off any trains of supplies
> sent to relieve Lee and put the Manassas Gap and Orange and
> Alexandria Railroads in condition for use, if sudden demand
> should be made upon them. Even if Lee's army should be
> captured or dispersed north of the Potomac, I suppose the rail-
> road will be required for a movement south to strike rapidly
> and follow up our advantages until every strong place has
> fallen and the rebellion be completely crushed.

Unfortunately Meade, like McClellan, was not of the
aggressive type who would follow up an advantage and

crush the opponent. Haupt realized that Lee's retreat was stopped by an impassable river. The Confederates were in a trap; they either had to stall for time until the river became passable, fight another battle (and that with few supplies and rounds of ammunitions), or surrender. But Haupt did not command the Army of the Potomac! Haupt realized that once the enemy succeeded in crossing the river, any attempt to catch him would be futile. "It would be like a tortoise attempting to catch a greyhound." Lee would be moving towards his base and growing stronger by the minute, while Meade would be leaving his base, extending his line of communications, and weakened daily by guerrilla and cavalry raids.[26]

As a result of his three-hour conversation with Meade on July 5th, Haupt was convinced that Meade was culpable in permitting his antagonist to escape. Lee had ten days—July 4th to the 14th—to effect his escape, and this was twice the time Haupt would have needed to have built bridges over the Potomac. Haupt respected Meade personally and had no desire to detract from the General's victory at Gettysburg, but in later years he was very emphatic about Meade's blunder. While Haupt was not sure in his mind that McClellan could have prevented Lee's escape after Antietam, he was sure that Meade could have prevented the Confederate retreat after Gettysburg. According to Haupt, Meade lost his great opportunity by dilatory tactics in the ten days following Pickett's repulse.

Although the main body of the Army of the Potomac was "resting" on Meade's orders, Haupt continued to assist other forces in their frantic efforts to intercept the fleeing enemy. While still in Washington, Haupt received an urgent request from one of his subordinates to hurry back to Baltimore all U. S. Military Railroad and Baltimore and Ohio cars because they were needed to move supplies to Frederick.[27] On the same day, July 7th, Ingalls, at headquarters of the Army of the Potomac, complained of detention of trains serving Meade's army. Haupt soon learned the cause: General W. H. French at Monocacy, Maryland, had held up ten entire trains with troops, thus causing the blockade of Federal rail movements at Frederick.[28] French was incompetent and arbitrary in the extreme. His excuse for his interference with the troop trains was the lack of railroad officials at spots they were needed. It is significant that French never held an important command after Gettysburg except at Mine Run where he again displayed his incompetence. Soon Haupt succeeded in ironing things out with French. Here again, it was the old problem of failure to unload trains as they arrived. It developed that French had detained some twenty trains at Frederick, while another fifteen were on the road going west. French had not permitted the first trains to be unloaded, hence the bottleneck. At 8:20 that evening (July 8th) Stanton received a telegram from Haupt saying that the blockade at Frederick had been removed and everything was moving smoothly. This done, Haupt told Stanton he was on his way to Harrisburg to open the Cumberland Valley Railroad, which had now become essential for the continuance of military operations.[29]

Meanwhile, Meade continued to procrastinate. On July 8th, he telegraphed Halleck that his army was short of rations and barefooted, a statement in direct conflict with Meigs's report that the army had sufficient supplies for three days. In fact, on July 5th, when Meade's "pur-

suit" began, the army had more supplies than the men
wanted to carry with them.[30]

Haupt continued to push the opening of rail communications on the 30-mile stretch of track between Hanover
Junction and Gettysburg as well as the reconstruction of
the Hagerstown line. He used civilian railroad workers
to augment the work of his own crews. He had to
straighten out the great confusion on the Gettysburg
line, which had become blocked. Cars were not being
unloaded; supplies had been ordered to Gettysburg only
to stand on the tracks for long periods of time, completely preventing all movement. Wounded were lying
for hours on trains, unable to be evacuated, all because
the simple rule of prompt unloading and returning cars
was being violated.[31]

To expedite repairs Haupt ordered up additional
track repair crews from Alexandria to Gettysburg, to be
sent by wagon to Chambersburg for repair of the
Hagerstown road. By Saturday, July 11th, Haupt was
able to inform Ingalls that his track crews, using impressed teams, had started on toward Chambersburg but
damage to the Hagerstown line would delay reconstruction. The next day, July 12th, Ingalls told Haupt that
the Army of the Potomac was receiving supplies in sufficient quantity and the enemy had taken up a defensive
position in front of Williamsport, Maryland.[32] Soon
thereafter Lee crossed the Potomac and the campaign
was over. On the 14th, Meigs telegraphed Haupt to
withdraw the Construction Corps from the Northern
Central and return to Alexandria.[33] Lee had gotten away.
The reconstruction of the Hagerstown road was abandoned, and Haupt sent his men, oxen, and equipment

back to Virginia to secure the Orange and Alexandria and the Manassas Gap railroads.

The campaign was over and the Federal leaders took stock of their accomplishments and failures. Haupt's achievements had been no less brilliant than the previous summer at Second Bull Run. The almost incredible transformation of single track railroads in Maryland and Pennsylvania for direct supply of Meade's army showed Haupt at his best. Using local assets, especially in materiel, Haupt improvised and reconstructed damaged lines with great rapidity. His system of train convoys where telegraph lines were nonexistent, and especially his rule of prompt unloading and return of empty cars went far to overcome the lethargy or incompetence of such men as General French and his subordinates. Moreover, Haupt and his men had developed the rebuilding of bridges and straightening of bent rails to a science. During the period July 9th-August 1st, 15,580 wounded men were evacuated by rail lines under military control.[34] Haupt was largely responsible for this. According to Jonathan Letterman, Meade's Medical Director, Haupt had also succeeded in getting medical supplies to the Army of the Potomac, once Haupt assumed control of the rail line.[35] Medical Inspector John M. Cuyler reemphasized Letterman's report when he reported[36] that the railroads had been in no condition for evacuating wounded until Haupt arrived on the scene. After Haupt arrived and assumed military control there were no further delays in moving the wounded out of the battle zone for about two weeks. On the 18th, a bridge on the rail line to Harrisburg collapsed under the weight of a cattle train and for the next five days trains had to go to

Baltimore and York rather than to New York. Of course, this detour of trains was after the tide of battle had receded and was in no way a lapse on the part of Haupt who had displayed great energy and drive throughout that entire campaign.

Prompt evacuation of the wounded had been made possible by Haupt's convoy system, whereby the rail line supplied 1,500 tons of supplies per day to the front and returned with 2,000 to 4,000 wounded men daily. This system required about 150 cars daily; each convoy had five 10-car trains. Twice a day, at 10 A.M. and 5 P.M., a long train of baggage cars, each car supplied with straw and open at both ends, left Gettysburg for Baltimore, or to Elizabethport (from which they went by boat to David's Island, New York).[37]

During the rest of July Haupt was back in Virginia, disappointed over Lee's escape but intent on keeping the vital line of the Orange and Alexandria Railroad in operating condition. On the 14th, Meigs pointed out the necessity of occupying the gaps of the Blue Ridge with troops to keep this vital rail line operating. On the same day Haupt informed Ingalls that the Winchester line was useless for transportation. The rails were of strap iron type, the supports were rotten, and as a result even the lightest locomotives were constantly running off the track. Haupt went on to tell Ingalls that he was moving all his crews to Alexandria because Lee had escaped and there was no point now in trying to catch up with him. Implied was the truism that Lee had to be intercepted to be caught. Ingalls, informing Haupt that army headquarters would be at Berlin, Maryland, the next night (i.e. the 15th) emphasized Meade's orders that the Orange and

Alexandria and Manassas Railroads be kept at operational efficiency.

Throughout the rest of the month Haupt concentrated his efforts on Meade's directive regarding the rail line. But the track was in such run-down condition from grass and weeds that it was necessary to cut off all the cars. Even locomotives could not move until Haupt's men had placed sand and pebbles on the road. To add to Haupt's difficulties, enemy guerrillas became extremely active. On the 22nd the train from Alexandria to Manassas was fired into at Accotink, some eight miles from Alexandria. In the space of one hour about 50 shots were fired at the train but with no damage. Haupt at Fairfax Station informed Halleck[38] that he would take a train guard and deploy them as skirmishers when he reached the scene of the attack. Ingalls, who was with Haupt at the time, was thus afforded an opportunity of seeing the wisdom of Haupt's insistence on military training for guards and railroad personnel.

A small body of skirmishers pressing an elusive enemy was not the solution and Haupt knew it. On the morning after the Accotink attack, Haupt alerted General Rufus King at Centerville about the nature of these attacks. Guerrillas, mounted on horses, had removed rails and had placed obstructions on the track. Although Haupt's track men had repaired the damage, the threat from these men of "Mosby's gang" was a serious one. Haupt told General King[39] that cavalry pickets and mounted patrols were needed to protect his rail lines. As Haupt pointed out—every civilian of draft age, not in the army, had to be regarded with suspicion and closely watched, because many of these men had been exempted from the

Confederate draft on condition they join Mosby's band. Obviously train guards were of little protection against these men.

General King replied the same day, assuring Haupt that he would employ his cavalry in scouting along the line of the Orange and Alexandria as far as Bull Run. These cavalrymen would be instructed to watch carefully all suspect people and to look especially for the guerrillas of Mosby's gang. Haupt also contacted Federal cavalry commanders on guarding railroad bridges, rail lines, and key fords.

But the attacks continued. On the 26th, Devereux reported to Haupt[40] that a train, 1½ miles east of Burke's Station, had come on a section of line where a rail had been removed. The engineer reversed his engine, the brakes were put "hard down," and the engine jumped the break and two cars also passed over safely. But if the rail had been removed from the opposite side, the whole train would have run off the track and gone over a 12-foot embankment. This train had been ambushed by twelve Confederates, some in gray uniform and others in blue coats and pants. All were armed. They came out from bushes along the track and engaged the train's guard, composed of men from the 4th Delaware Infantry. This guard saved the train by a determined resistance and the enemy escaped to the woods. But Devereux, disgusted that a handful of the enemy could impede the army's progress, asked that 200 men be immediately stationed from Accotink to Burke's Station. A week later Devereux again called for adequate protection for trains, pointing out that in addition to the normal traffic of trains loaded with supplies and troops, paymasters with large sums of money were also using the line. Moreover, such critical points as wood storage depots were in danger, while some sixty Negro workers were understandably nervous because of inadequate protection and were difficult to keep on their job. Apparently the enemy guerrilla force was some 150 strong. These men lurked in the woods, waiting for a favorable moment to attack.

Haupt, in a report to Ingalls[41] at army headquarters on July 27th, described the enemy derailment attempt and pointed out that similar attempts to derail trains were occurring daily. Unless this sabotage could be stopped, Haupt informed Ingalls, the Army's communications were going to be in constant jeopardy. Despite orders from the army commander,[43] this enemy sabotage continued.

NOTES, CHAPTER 11

1. Haupt, p. 311.
2. *Ibid.*, pp. 310–311.
3. *Official Records,* Series I, Vol. 27, Part 1, p. 24.
4. Haupt, pp. 208–211.
5. *Official Records,* Series I, Vol. 27, Part 1, p. 22–24.
6. Haupt's final report to Stanton, September 9, 1863.
7. *Official Records,* Series I, Vol. 27, Part 3, pp. 476, 477.
8. Livermore, p. 103.
9. Stackpole, Edward J., *They Met at Gettysburg,* p. 116.
10. *Official Records,* Series I, Vol. 27, Part 3, pp. 476–477.
11. *Ibid.,* p. 494.
12. Haupt to McCallum, July 2, 1863, Haupt letters, Library of Congress.
13. Haupt, p. 216.
14. *Official Records,* Series I, Vol. 27, Part 3, p. 511.
15. *Ibid.,* Vol 27, Part 1, p. 178.
16. Tremain, Henry E., *Two Days of War,* p. 99.
17. *Official Records,* Series I, Vol. 27, Part 3, pp. 521–522.
18. *Ibid.,* p. 523.
19. *Ibid.,* p. 522.
20. *Ibid.,* Vol. 27, Part 1, p. 26.

21. *Ibid.,* pp. 524–568.
22. *Ibid.,* Vol. 45, pp. 523–524.
23. General Orders No. 68, Army of the Potomac, July 4, 1863.
24. Rice, Allen T. (Ed.) *Reminiscences of Abraham Lincoln by Distinguished Men of His Time,* New York 1888, p. 402.
25. Haupt, pp. 227–228.
26. *Ibid.,* pp. 229–230.
27. *Official Records,* Series I, Vol. 27, Part 3, p. 575.
28. *Ibid.,* p. 392.
29. *Ibid.,* pp. 609–610.
30. Haupt, pp. 238, 239.
31. Haupt to Meigs, *Official Records,* Series I, Vol. 27, Part 3, p. 619.
32. *Official Records,* Series I, Vol. 27, Part 3, p. 669.
33. Haupt, p. 243.
34. McCallum's Report, pp. 7–8.
35. *Official Records,* Series I, Vol. 27, Part 1, p. 196.
36. *Ibid.,* p. 26.
37. Anonymous, *The United States Sanitary Commission,* pp. 128–130, 145.
38. *Official Records,* Vol. 27, Part 3, pp. 750–751.
39. *Ibid.,* pp. 155–756.
40. *Ibid.,* pp. 770–771.
41. *Ibid.,* p. 774.
42. Headquarters, Army of the Potomac, July 30, 1863, Meade's Proclamation.

12

HAUPT LEAVES THE SERVICE

Haupt's final weeks with the military railroads were occupied mainly with combating guerrilla activities directed against the Orange and Alexandria Railroad. Active campaigning by the Army of the Potomac had practically ceased—not to be resumed until Grant assumed command the next spring. In Haupt's area of responsibility bridges were destroyed and rebuilt (that over Bull Run for the seventh time!). Trains were still harassed by the ubiquitous guerrillas, and contraband articles were smuggled into the camps by sutlers and others. Haupt applied for and received authority to arm and drill personnel of the military railroads so that they could protect themselves, to some extent at least, against guerrilla attacks.[1] With this protection the railroads would function better during the coming campaign.

During this comparative lull, Haupt forwarded reports on his experiments both in repair and destruction of railroad facilities. While engaged in the preparation of recommendations for improving the organization of the military railroads, Haupt's service with the railroads came to an abrupt end, due to a series of incidents instigated by Governor Andrew and abetted by Secretary Stanton.

From time to time throughout his military service, Haupt had gone up to Massachusetts to look after his Hoosac Tunnel interests. These visits annoyed Governor Andrew greatly. Andrew had apparently endeavored to thwart Haupt and the tunnel project but without success so far; the Governor had been worsted in every bout, and even the committees which had been packed against Haupt, eventually turned and reported in the railroader's favor.

In late August Andrew visited Washington and was in daily conference with Stanton. Some of Haupt's friends, who worked at Stanton's office, as well as one of the assistant secretaries, told Haupt that he was a frequent topic of conversation between the Governor and War Secretary. Haupt was further informed that the decision expressed in these conferences was that it had been arranged that Stanton would compel Haupt to accept his commission unconditionally and then would assign him to some post which would exclude any possibility of going to Massachusetts "to trouble the Legislature with . . . [his] claims for compensation for expenditures made in construction of the Hoosac Tunnel."

Andrew, despite the unanimous endorsement of Haupt by investigating committees and in opposition to the advice of his Executive Council, had insisted that the work be taken out of Haupt's hands and placed under the control of commissioners, and that Haupt not be paid one dollar for the expenditures he had made on the tunnel.[2]

According to Flower, Stanton's biographer, the War

Secretary was compelled to yield to Andrew because Stanton could do nothing without the active and hearty support of the loyal governors of the North, of whom Andrew was a leader. It was Haupt or Massachusetts, and Stanton promptly chose Massachusetts. Governor Andrew was a recognized leader of the abolitionists and Lincoln's administration needed the support of Massachusetts in prosecuting the war.

Although absolute proof is lacking, there is evidence that McCallum may well have been party to Andrew's decision to handcuff Haupt. More correctly perhaps, it is quite possible that McCallum was not averse to having a competitor removed from his prominent position. As early as April 22, 1862, immediately after Haupt reported for duty with the army, Andrew replied, in an extremely ambiguously worded letter,[3] to a communication sent on the 18th by McCallum to the Governor. While it is impossible to trace the references made by Governor Andrew in his letter to McCallum, their correspondence shows conclusively that the two did exchange ideas, and, moreover, Andrew's letter of April 22nd is especially interesting when he hints as follows: "I beg to add, Colonel, the assurance that if in any way, and at any time, I can be of possible service, I am to the extent of my power always at command." While all this may not be in any way pertinent to Stanton's intention of cooperating with Andrew on restricting Haupt to field service away from Massachusetts, it is still not possible to ignore McCallum's jealousy of Haupt's successes and official approbation. One of the tangible evidences of official recognition of Haupt's services was his promotion to brigadier general in September 1862. But McCallum, whose commission as colonel antedated Haupt's by some two months, was only brevetted a brigadier general and that not until the war was nearly over.[4]

During the lull in active operations Haupt carried on an active correspondence with various civil and military personalities. On August 7th, he penned two letters[5] to Lincoln. One was a short letter informing the President that Halleck had promised a West Point appointment to Haupt's son, Lewis M. Haupt. As Haupt pointed out to Lincoln, he was aware that the President had made this possible, was appreciative of the favor, and believed that the son would make his mark, Haupt closed his letter with the query as to whether the appointment would be issued in time for Lewis to enter West Point in September. It was. Lewis Haupt graduated and was commissioned a second lieutenant of engineers, July 17, 1867, but resigned from the army September 20, 1869.[6] Like his father, he received his education at the Nation's top military academy but served a minimum of time before entering civilian engineering practice.

The second letter written that day reveals Haupt's fatal propensity for unwisely speaking his mind about organizations and people and meddling in affairs which were none of his business. This second letter did not reflect credit on Haupt and may very well have been a major reason for Lincoln's reluctant acquiescence in Haupt's removal the following month. While Haupt was doubtless sincere in his criticisms, he was out of order in writing so sweeping a denunciation of men and measures as appeared in this rash letter to the President.

Haupt began his letter by reviewing his reasons for serving the Country and his belief that this service had been an unselfish and valuable one to the Federal war effort. Haupt then proceeded to attack one of his favorite targets—the Navy Department. He had done this before, but now he went into very considerable detail. Haupt stated that he had consulted with "many of the leading scientific and mechanical men of the Country" on coast and harbor defenses, armor, ordnances, and naval matters in general, but those in charge of the Navy Department were "so firmly set in their own ideas" that all attempts to move them were unavailing. After several interviews and some correspondence with the Assistant Secretary of the Navy, Haupt now put on record his protest against the 15-inch guns, especially for use on the monitors. Haupt pointed out to Lincoln that his prediction as to the unsuitability of these guns had been fulfilled and the Navy was now using smaller caliber guns which could be fired with approximately equal velocity to the 15-inch guns, but did not burst.

Haupt conceded that the monitors had had some success but believed they would have done even better with different armament. He correctly pointed out that they were unseaworthy, slow, fouled badly, and unmaneuverable. Haupt insisted that the Navy needed speed, fuel economy, and effective armor in its ships. If the Navy Department would permit competitive bidding and not be so inflexible in prescribing plans and designs, the Country would save money and would soon lead the world in its naval craft. Haupt maintained that the Country's harbors were "perfectly defenseless" against the "improved ships and ordnances" of England and France in the event of a war with those countries. Here he was sadly in error. The Federal navy by August 1863 was superior to France and England, who had refused to change their fleets from wooden sailing ships and obsolete armaments, except for a few armored ships.

Haupt was on surer ground when he went on to criticize the "extravagance, waste, and disregard of the public interest" so prominent in military operations and in the conduct of government contractors. He closed with a brief resumé of his successes in developing new methods of transportation and construction, including his inventions and improvisations as outlined in the photographs and accompanying descriptive literature he had previously sent the President.

Although well-intentioned, Haupt did himself no good in criticizing his superiors, and he definitely was out of order in his attack on the Navy Department. Certainly one of the bright spots in Lincoln's administration was the efficient leadership of the blockade and war at sea under Secretary Welles. Haupt's animadversions with respect to the Navy Department must have made Lincoln much more ready to accept Stanton's abrupt dismissal of Haupt whose excellent service in the field was marred by his proneness to meddle in areas where he definitely did not belong.

Meanwhile, Haupt's personal relations with Stanton had been steadily deteriorating since shortly after Gettysburg. On July 17th, Haupt sent a lengthy letter to Halleck,[7] stating that Stanton was holding up approval of his pay account, pending consultation with Halleck. Although Haupt had gone in person to Stanton, the railroader's explanations had not been considered acceptable by the Secretary. The matter was serious enough to Haupt's peace of mind for him to write this letter to Halleck, describing in detail his entire service and emphasizing the problem of nominal acceptance of his commission without being formally mustered into military service. Haupt pointed out that he had never had a staff, servants, or horses which were allowed a brigadier gen-

eral by army regulations, nor had he ever charged or
received more money than was actually required to replace cash paid out in the public service. In fact, maintained Haupt, even this amounted to less than one-third
the pay and allowances due a brigadier general. He
reiterated his need for freedom of action to be free to
act since "the outrageous conduct of the present State
administration in Massachusetts has for the time robbed
me of everything." Haupt assured Halleck that he was
aware that the position he was occupying was exceptional,
but unavoidable, and not inconsistent with performance
of his duty.

However, Stanton had made up his mind. On September 1st, he had the following letter[8] sent to Haupt:

Washington, September 1, 1863
General: I do not observe on file any acceptance of your appointment as Brigadier-General. Inasmuch as the Secretary of
War has ordered that all appointments the acceptance of which
shall not have been on file by September 5, 1863, be taken as
vacated, it becomes necessary to file your acceptance at once.

Very respectfully,
Your obedient servant
James A. Hardie
Assistant Adjutant General

Stanton's order arrived at Haupt's office on the 2nd
while the railroader was out of Washington. One of
Haupt's subordinates (George L. Fall) promptly answered the letter, acknowledging receipt of the order for
Haupt to accept his appointment as brigadier general
by the 5th or vacate the commission. But Fall had to
inform Stanton that Haupt would probably not return to
Washington before the 5th and, at the present time, he
did not know Haupt's precise whereabouts.[9]

However, Haupt got back to Washington on the 5th and promptly dispatched a lengthy letter[10] to Stanton reiterating his reasons for refusal to accept military rank. And here Haupt made a point which possesses validity and which the Secretary could well have accepted had he been so inclined. Haupt asked why it was necessary for him to be fettered by a commission. As he pointed out:

> The members of the Cabinet are civilians; the Asst. Secretary of War, and of the Navy are civilians; the chiefs of some of the Naval Bureaux are civilians. Why cannot the officer who directs the operations of the Military Railroads be a civilian also, if you will clothe him with the powers necessary to secure efficiency and prevent military interference with his duties?

Of course, Haupt was right on this point. Stanton had not been hesitant to grant unusual powers to other civilians when so inclined. But as Haupt no doubt suspected, Stanton had no intention of acting *ex cathedra* in his case. Moreover, because Stanton had questioned Haupt's pay accounts, the railroader made no further attempts to explain those accounts, but would pay the expenses he incurred out of his own account.

Haupt then called Stanton's attention to the bad condition of railroads in the West and compared it with the smooth-running railroad system in the East "where results have been attained, with which I am much gratified and where I can keep things straight with very little personal attention." Haupt went on to suggest to Stanton that he would serve in any capacity and in any theater of war. However, Haupt pointed out, he would have to know at once what the Secretary should decide, since necessary family arrangements for the Haupts would be directly affected by Stanton's decision.

And Stanton's action *was* immediate. A few days later he sent for Haupt, much irritated that the railroader would not accept the commission unconditionally.[11] He pointed out to Haupt that the commission had been granted for meritorious services, that it was a high honor, and that refusal to accept it was an act of disrespect to the President and the Government, and that he could not be paid lawfully unless the commission were accepted. Haupt countered by stating that pay was no consideration; he was losing many times the amount of pay by neglecting his private affairs. Moreover, Haupt said, the Secretary could pay him from contingent funds if he were so inclined. This was true. Haupt then reminded Stanton of their first meeting when the Secretary had stated that Haupt's services would be required for only a few weeks, but that he had been willing to remain as long as his services were needed. Haupt conceded that when those services were no longer needed, the Secretary had the power to relieve him. Stanton exploded. "I will relieve you at once, Sir!" Although Stanton's order was not promulgated for several days, his dismissal of Haupt became public knowledge in Washington almost at once.

The dismissal occasioned considerable surprise in official circles. Congressional members of the Committee on the Conduct of the War went to Stanton to remonstrate but with no success. Lincoln, although apparently regretting the action, refused to interfere. Haupt had a letter[12] from an undisclosed source, dated September 27, 1863, informing him that if he would use his pen and tell what he knew, there was an element in Congress, both in the House and Senate, which would bring sufficient pressure as to compel Stanton to resign. But Haupt was not disposed to do this, nor apparently was he at all sure it would succeed.

On the 9th Haupt rendered his final report[13] to the Secretary of War. This was Haupt's last official act in connection with the United States Military Railroads and is an extensive discussion of his service from April 1862 to the end of his service. Haupt made a special point of emphasizing the need for a uniform code of rules, regulations, and signals for the operation of all military railroads, a central bureau in Washington, and a system of regular periodical reports, giving the location, condition, amount of rolling stock, miles in operation, and other pertinent details for the military railroads. Haupt also listed the various inventions and innovations which he and his subordinates had introduced into the military railroad service. Haupt submitted with his report a complete set of photographs illustrating these contributions to military railroading construction and transportation.

On September 11th, Haupt, in separate letters[14] to Stanton and Lincoln, put in written form his reaction to the Secretary's unceremonious removal of him from active service. In his letter to Stanton, Haupt pointed out that he needed no more than 10 to 20 per cent of his time to attend to private affairs (e.g. the Hoosac Tunnel controversy). He bluntly but clearly outlined the conditions on which he could continue to serve. These involved the establishment of a central bureau of military railroads, removal of the problem of interference by commanding generals with railroad operations, and the granting of the chief of the railroad bureau sufficient freedom of movement, to inspect personally the operation of the railroads as well as permission to attend to "such other public or private business as might require his attention." Appended to this letter to Stanton was a proposed order which would implement Haupt's concept of a "Bureau of United States Military Railroads" and the appointment of Haupt as its chief.

A copy of this letter to Stanton was enclosed in Haupt's letter to Lincoln, which, in the main, was a reiteration of Haupt's inability to accept a commission unconditionally and an appreciation of the consideration which Lincoln had shown the railroader. Haupt assured the President of his willingness to serve again if he could be of use to the Country.

The official order relieving Haupt appeared on the 14th. It read as follows:

> Washington, Sept. 14, 1863
>
> Sir: You are hereby relieved from further duty in the War Department.
>
> You will turn over your office, books, papers, and all other property under your control belonging to the United States, to Colonel D. C. McCallum, Superintendent of Military Railroads.
>
> Very respectfully,
> your obedient servant
> *Edwin M. Stanton*
> Secretary of War

The order was very terse and official. There was no word of appreciation for Haupt's contributions nor mention of his services in the recent Gettysburg campaign. Stanton was in no mood to express the nation's gratitude!

Haupt responded in kind. On the 14th he sent Stanton a curt acknowledgment of the removal order. He wrote that he had just received Stanton's written order and was certainly "much *relieved*" by the Secretary's actions. Haupt went on to remind Stanton that he had not solicited the appointment but rather that Stanton had telegraphed *him* to come to serve; in fact, he would be willing to come again if he could be useful to the country. He closed the brief letter with the statement that a report of the operations of the military railroads was being prepared and would be sent on to Stanton.[15]

Full official publicity was given Haupt's removal. In the service journal, *Army and Navy Gazette*, for September 15th, the order was printed in full, with the caption "Relieved from Duty" in bold black letters.[16] The prominence given Haupt's removal is interesting. A careful perusal of War Department general orders and notices of similar action against other officers fails to reveal instances of other officers receiving such abrupt treatment, unless they had been convicted of serious military crimes or misdemeanors. Thus, Haupt, still a comparatively young man at forty-six, left the service. His achievements and experience had been very substantial and he left Washington to go on to demonstrate his abilities in a very brilliant career of nearly half a century. In his later years, Haupt, softened by a long career which was eminently a successful one, looked back on Stanton as a man of "marked ability" but impulsive and headstrong. Haupt always realized that Stanton deliberately sided with Governor Andrew and refused support to Haupt himself.[17]

After Haupt returned to Massachusetts he was kept continually aware of Governor Andrew's animosity. In a letter to one of the Governor's most outspoken critics, General Benjamin F. Butler, dated October 1st,[18] Haupt said that the Governor's treatment had been "infamous" and he expected another free-for-all fight during the winter. Haupt told Butler that affairs in Massachusetts had precluded his accepting a commission unconditionally but Stanton would agree to no conditions. Haupt pointed out that he offered to manage the railroads as a civilian without pay, but Stanton, "probably at the insistence of Andrew who was with him at the time" tried to force Haupt to accept a commission. This Haupt refused to do; strong language was used, and Haupt was relieved from command. In conclusion Haupt reiterated his concern over the poor condition of the Western military railroads. "Confusion regns supreme, and Stanton is responsible," Haupt told Butler. Despite Halleck's urgings, the Secretary had refused to grant authority to remedy defects and correct abuses. Moreover, Haupt asserted, "Inefficiency characterizes both the War and Navy Departments."

As Haupt prophesied, trouble with the Troy and Greenfield Railroad continued into the winter. On January 20, 1864, the Boston *Post* printed a "memorial" of Haupt to the Massachusetts General Court, charged that during his absence on military service, John W. Brooks, Chairman of the Board of Commissioners of the Troy and Greenfield, made certain statements about the financial status of Haupt's firm which conveyed the impression "entirely at variance with the facts." These statements, according to Haupt, were made without any official request. Haupt, insisting he sought no financial compensation arising from Brooks's action, did state his request for an investigation before an honest and impartial board.[19]

Haupt, meanwhile, still angry at his removal, had written Lincoln on January 16, 1864, a letter[20] of explanation of the facts of his removal. This letter was occasioned by Haupt's conversation with a lady who said

that Lincoln expressed the opinion that Haupt was "relieved at his own solicitation." Haupt denied this, pointing out that he was relieved by "an impulse of irritation"
on the part of the Secretary of War caused by Haupt's
refusal to accept unconditionally a commission which
would thereby place himself entirely in Stanton's power.

The letter, a very long one, added little to what Haupt
had already stated about his position vis-a-vis Stanton.
Haupt did state that his military service entailed a loss
of possibly more than $200,000 by giving his Massa-
chusetts enemies the opportunity to pass a bill taking the
Hoosac Tunnel project out of his hands. Moreover,
Haupt told the President, he was not sure that the desire
of Governor Andrew to prevent Haupt's return to Massachusetts may not have had something to do with Stanton's attempt to compel him to accept the commission—
"the failure of which so much irritated . . . [Stanton]."

Haupt then went on to comment on the poor organization of the railroads in Kentucky and Tennessee—where
supplies had to be transported by wagon more than 100
miles—all because Stanton had refused to sign an order
which would have guaranteed a proper organization of
the entire military railroad system. After a summary of
some of his bridge and track destroying inventions,
Haupt, rather foolishly, expressed his lack of confidence
in the leaders of both the War and Navy Departments.
While one cannot approve his sweeping denunciation of
Welles, partly because Haupt was never in a position to
be actually conversant with the workings of the Navy
Department, his strictures on the Secretary of War came
from personal observation and certainly merit posterity's objective consideration. Haupt told Lincoln that
"Stanton is so irritable, so prone to act hastily and with-

out investigation, that even the personal liberty of a citizen is not safe who incurs the displeasure of some secret informer." As Haupt pointed out, any individual could do his duty faithfully in Washington, but if he ran afoul of any of Stanton's "operators," he was almost sure to land in the Old Capitol Prison. Haupt did not ascribe the responsibility for this situation to any lack of integrity on Stanton's part, but rather to the Secretary's propensity for lending an ear to informers. Haupt maintained that these individuals were not worthy of Stanton's confidence, and actually committed great injustices.

NOTES, CHAPTER 12

1. Haupt, p. 254.
2. *Ibid.,* p. 261.
3. Andrew to McCallum, April 22, 1862. Haupt papers, Library of Congress.
4. September 24, 1864. He was later (March 13, 1865) brevetted a major general.
5. Haupt to Lincoln, August 7, 1863. Haupt letters. Library of Congress.
6. Hamersly, Thomas H. S., *Complete Regular Army Register . . . 1779–1879,* p. 499.
7. Haupt to Halleck, July 17, 1863. National Archives.
8. Haupt, p. 261.
9. George L. Fall to Stanton, September 2, 1863, Haupt papers, National Archives.
10. Haupt to Stanton, September 5, 1863, National Archives.
11. Haupt, p. 263–264.
12. *Ibid.,* p. 267.
13. *Ibid.,* pp. 268–280.
14. Haupt to Stanton, September 11, 1863, Haupt to Lincoln, September 11, 1863., Library of Congress.
15. Haupt to Stanton, September 14, 1863, National Archives.
16. *Army and Navy Official Gazette,* Vol. I, No. 11, September 15, 1863, p. 169.
17. Haupt, p. 301.
18. Butler, Benjamin F., *Private and Official Correspondence of General Benjamin F. Butler,* Vol. 3, pp. 117–118.
19. Haupt papers, Library of Congress, Boston *Post,* January 20, 1864.
20. Haupt to Lincoln, January 16, 1864, Library of Congress.

13

HAUPT'S CONTRIBUTIONS TO
MILITARY RAILROADING

Haupt's first venture in writing on his professional
field, his classic, *The General Theory of Bridge Construction,* was published in 1851 and ran through several
editions. It consisted of 268 pages and 16 plates showing
the bridges in use on such railroads as the Pennsylvania
and Baltimore and Susquehanna lines.

Except for Haupt's and Cullum's manuals for bridge
construction the only other American work on military
bridges to appear during the war was a pamphlet published by the Quartermaster's Department in 1862. This
brief study, entitled *Instructions for Transport and Erection of Military Wire Suspension-Bridge Equipage* was
issued in limited quantities to the various armies in the
field.[1] Only a few copies were printed and the pamphlet
saw very little use.

In 1864, Haupt came out with his *Military Bridges,*
a truly professional study of 310 pages and 69 plates.
The subtitle was "Suggestions of new expedients and
constructions for crossing streams and chasms, including

also, designs for trestle and truss bridges for military
railroads." This work embodied Haupt's field service
experience. It discussed in detail the type of bridges,
floating railroad bridges, blanket boats, floating docks,
warehouses, transports and other innovations. Included
also were suggestions for protecting military railroads
and bridges, as well as the use of military telegraph as
an auxiliary to the movement of troops and supplies by
rail. Haupt also discussed the use of buried shells as
mines, blockhouses, and the use of his "bridge torpedo"
as well as the most efficient means of disabling locomotives. With characteristic generosity, Haupt devoted an
entire chapter to a discussion of Cullum's india-rubber
pontoon bridge. The appendix of this work emphasized
the advantages of blanket boats (by "blanket" Haupt
meant the India-rubber blanket). With units of India-
rubber blankets, said Haupt, it is entirely feasible to
construct boats, rafts, ferries and bridges.

Shortly before his death, Haupt published his *Reminiscences,* a limited edition of 900 copies, with notes and a
personal sketch by Frank A. Flower. It appeared in
1901. The ironic element here is that Flower also, some
four years later, wrote an extensive biography of Haupt's
old nemesis, Edwin M. Stanton! The end result was that
neither Haupt's Reminiscences nor Flower's biography
of Stanton really discuss frankly the Haupt-Stanton feud.
In his preface to Haupt's work, Flower expressed his
conviction that Haupt was a man of "unselfish patriotism" and "fruitful deeds." Most of Haupt's autobi-
ography had been written as early as 1889 but Flower
had hesitated about publishing it until convinced that
posterity should have the opportunity to examine certain
aspects of Haupt's Civil War service "which had entirely

escaped the attention of historians." Flower acknowledged that in his preparation of Stanton's biography he had discovered the historical value of Haupt's service and also Haupt's "almost abnormal modesty" which had resulted in so much self-submergence as to entirely deprive him of many important honors to which he was incontestably entitled.

Recent appraisals of Haupt's war service have tended to give him a more prominent position in the Civil War. The importance of railroads in the War has been stressed by several competent scholars in recent years. Certainly the military railroads of the North were, in the main, an efficient service of the War Department, comparable to the military telegraph, signal corps, and balloon service in interest, novelty, and substantive contributions.

Much credit is due McCallum for the amazingly rapid and smooth transfer by rail of the 11th and 12th Army Corps some 1,200 miles from Virginia to Chattanooga in 1863, after Rosecrans's defeat at Chickamauga. The two corps, with all impediments including ambulances, wagons, horses and food supplies, were moved over this route, not in the 40-60 days originally deemed necessary but in about half that time.

Haupt's influence extended to all theaters. In the West, where crucial campaigns were to be waged in 1864 and 1865, many of Haupt's subordinates played key roles for Grant and Sherman. Such men as Adna Anderson, E. C. Smeed, and W. W. Wright had served in the East under Haupt, from whom they received their basic training in military railroading. Haupt deserves credit for inculcating his principles of railroad management in these men. They, in turn, deserve credit for applying the lessons they learned in their new areas of activities. Haupt's organizational genius had "rubbed off" on these subordinates who were successful in applying his methods and principles in the vast expanses of the Western theater of war.

It was not until after Haupt's adverse report on conditions in the West that the railroads there began to function smoothly. In February 1864, McCallum's authority was extended to include the Western railroads. And it was in Sherman's operations from Nashville and Chattanooga in 1864 that Haupt's precepts were most dramatically and convincingly borne out. Without question, the amazingly efficient supply of Sherman's men in their advance on Atlanta from the base at Chattanooga was a classic in efficient military railroading. In this campaign it was necessary to supply an army of 100,000 men and 60,000 animals from a base 360 miles away, over a single track railroad, located deep in enemy country, constantly susceptible to surprise guerrilla and saboteur attacks.[2]

In his *Memoirs* Sherman frankly admits his indebtedness to the railroads, "To have delivered [the necessary supplies] . . . by ordinary wagons would have required 36,800 wagons, of 6 miles length, each, allowing each wagon to have hauled two tons 20 miles a day, a simple impossibility in such roads as existed in that region of the country."[3]

In his final report, McCallum told Stanton that the United States Military Railroads operated 2,105 miles of road, using 419 locomotives to haul 6,330 cars, at a net expenditure of some thirty million dollars.[4]

Since the Federals were generally operating in enemy territory, one of their main problems was rapid construction of rail lines destroyed by the enemy in retreat.

In the early months of the war, the Confederates destroyed rail lines by piling ties and fence rails in a heap, putting rails on top of the heap, and setting the pile afire. After a considerable period of heating, the rails would bend of their own weight. To replace these rails was a slow and costly process. Accordingly, Haupt experimented with this method of destroying rails and found that if they had been bent into a radius of less than one foot, they could be straightened without even having to be reheated. This was possible by means of a simple gadget developed by Haupt, consisting of 5 blocks of wood, each 10 inches square and 5 feet in length. The top block was so notched as to receive the bottom of the rail and cause it to lie with the plate of the base in a vertical position. Using 3 x 3s or 4 x 4s some 12-16 men at each end could, by pressure, straighten out the rails in two or three minutes. These rails, now almost perfectly straight, were ready to be spiked back into place. Trains could run over them with no danger at all. Other methods were developed also to straighten rails. If rails were too bent to be straightened in this manner, they were put aside and straightened later by means of improvised kilns. All of these apparati were portable, simple, and effective. They worked![5]

By 1864, bridge construction by the Federals had become a science. Equipment and men were available for incredibly rapid construction of bridges in front of the advancing armies. When a large stream was encountered, the Construction Corps went smoothly and expertly into action—the result of many hours of patient training under Haupt. The key to this efficiency in bridge construction was to be found in Haupt's specialized training of his Construction Corps and his system of prefabricated interchangeable parts for the frame bridges.

Haupt had patented a truss design for bridges before the war and adapted the design to military bridges in 1862. His men, trained to work as a team, consisted of axemen, and teamsters, framers, raisers, and surveyors. Each man had his specialty. These men only built the frames of bridges; they did not roof them over or board them in the sides, since speed of erection was all-important. Moreover, covered bridges, although well known to Northerners, were much more easily burned than simple frame structures with a minimum of wood on them. Even the bridges across the Potomac in the Washington area were cut down to bare essentials. Long Bridge had a floor bed so constructed that planking could be taken up at night to prevent a surprise Confederate cavalry raid on the Capital.

Another precaution was the constant need for troops to break step when crossing bridges. Civilian bridges often had signs warning horsemen to walk their horses across the bridge or pay a fine, but a large body of soldiers marching in step posed an even greater threat. On one occasion, a band struck up a march while leading troops across a bridge in Maryland. Fortunately, an alert officer grasped the danger in the concentrated rhythm of hundreds of feet hitting the bridge at the same instant and scattered the band by riding his horse right into their midst. The musicians leaped for safety to avoid being crushed by the horse, their tune ceased abruptly, and the bridge was saved from being shaken to pieces.

Destruction of bridges, a monopoly of Confederate raiders and saboteurs in the early months of the war, gradually became an art practiced by Federals as well. And once launched on this profitable form of military diversion, the latecomers became quite expert in it.

Haupt's bridge-destroying torpedo was the most efficient means developed during the war. In an instruction manual, dated November 1, 1862, the War Department put in printed form Haupt's precepts on use of the torpedo as well as the scientific art of bridge destruction itself.[6] (See Appendix E for Haupt's instructions on the use of the bridge-destroying torpedo.)

This bridge torpedo was the answer to the need for a rapid method of destroying bridges. Also necessary was some method to render locomotive engines useless to the enemy. Cavalry could penetrate far into the enemy's country, reach bridges, or important communication lines, whose destruction would be especially desirable in active operations. In a retreat, the destruction of a bridge might be essential to the army's safety, while there often wasn't sufficient time to burn the bridge in the usual manner, or, if set on fire, the bridge could be saved by the enemy promptly extinguishing the fire or repairing the bridge. Haupt's torpedo effectively destroyed the bridge, rapidly and completely. Moreover, in his report, Haupt pointed out the best way to destroy a locomotive. This consisted of firing a cannon ball through the boiler. The damage thus rendered could not be repaired without taking out all the flues. The usual method of disabling engines was burning the flue by letting out the water and making a fire in the fire-box. However, this operation was usually done in such a hurried fashion that the enemy soon got the engine in order again. So far as destruction of railroad cars was concerned, Haupt sarcastically pointed out that the destruction of more than 400 cars by Federal troops in the past six months showed that no instruction in this was necessary and "no room left for winning fresh laurels in this field."[7]

On May 16, 1863, Haupt sent a lengthy letter to Halleck,[8] describing in detail a portable track-wrecking apparatus. Conceding that the enemy had hitherto been more successful than the Federals in destroying track, Haupt informed Halleck of the results of a series of experiments on the most rapid and effectual way to destroy rail lines. From his own experience, Haupt was well aware of the fact that when rails were merely bent, they could be quickly straightened out and used again. He realized that the only way to really ruin them was to give them a spiral twist, like a corkscrew. When a rail received this treatment it had to be recast. In the early period of the war, the Federals used a bulky apparatus of steel hooks, with sockets for the insertion of poles to get leverage for bending the rails. The hooks forced the heads of the spikes but did not extract them; moreover, the spikes passed through the "chairs" of the apparatus and were difficult to remove. More equipment (wedges and hooks) was necessary, and even then, several minutes were needed to remove each individual spike.

A subordinate of Haupt's, E. C. Smeed, solved the problem with his invention of a simple portable gadget which enabled Haupt's men to destroy track in one-sixth the time required by the enemy to lay it. But more important, the rails so destroyed were twisted and bent in such a fashion that they were completely unfit for further use.

Smeed's invention was almost childishly simple. Basically it was claw-shaped like a "U" with the parallels slightly bent and tipped with hooks at their ends, and with a hole pierced for a wooden handle which could be inserted for leverage. In use, the hooks were put under the ends of a rail, pressure was applied by the handle, and the rail was ripped off the tie in less than thirty seconds, thus breaking the "chair." By removing a rail in this fashion it was possible to simultaneously twist the rail into a corkscrew. And Smeed's apparatus, consisting of a set of claws, weighed only six pounds and could be carried by one man.

Haupt tested the apparatus and compared its efficiency with other methods of track destruction. In the testing he accumulated two piles of dry wood, one pile consisting of thirty-two cross-ties with eight rails atop; the other pile was about half as large. He then poured a gallon of coal oil on each pile and set it afire. After three hours the rails were still not heated to any extent. By the following morning the ties had been completely burned up but the weight of the rails had not been enough to bend them to the extent necessary to render them useless. In contrast, Smeed's invention destroyed the rails in minutes completely—while the ties could be burned later if time permitted. The essential thing was to insure definite destruction of the rails—a commodity which the enemy was finding almost impossible to replace.

One of Haupt's major contributions to military railroading was his development of rapid and efficient means of constructing and destroying rail lines, bridges, and railroad facilities.

Haupt's Construction Corps, as organized at the beginning of 1863, brought the laying of track and construction of bridges to a science. Constant practice coupled with clever use of interchangeable parts enabled this force to rapidly repair the damage done by Confederate raiders and guerrillas. Even after Haupt left the service, his training of the Construction Corps paid off in big dividends for Federal military operations. The

Corps' splendid performance in 1864 in Georgia, North Carolina, and Virginia is a tribute to the basic groundwork done by Haupt.

Moreover, Haupt's daring and imaginative innovations in bridge construction were to aid Federal advances immeasurably in the 1864-1865 campaigns.

Paradoxically, Haupt's Construction Corps could well have been dubbed the "Destruction Corps," so effective had its personnel become in destroying enemy rail lines of supply. While such early methods of destroying rails by placing them on burning ties was used extensively before Haupt's arrival at the front (and later in some of the combat areas), his quick appreciation and adaptation of Smeed's novel method is indicative of the man's alertness. E. C. Smeed discovered that rails bent by the new method could be destroyed effectively when only a few laborers of the Construction Corps were available for the destruction of a rail line.

Haupt's unique organization, the Construction Corps, was largely instrumental in the success of Federal rail and bridge construction during military offensive operations in the enemy's territory, while at the same time it had become very adept at destroying rail facilities essential to the enemy's movements. The Corps, eventually consisting of some 200 bridge carpenters and 300 contrabands, was kept busy by the indefatigable Haupt in advance movements, cutting wood, piles, and cross ties, straightening rails, building block-houses, and frame bridges. When not engaged in active operations of the Army of the Potomac, the Corps, under Haupt's direction, built the stockade to protect the railroad depot at Alexandria. At the same time Haupt had equipped the men with repeating rifles.[9] Despite complaints by

War Department engineers that the defense of Washington was their responsibility, Stanton did not interfere.[10]

With respect to the railroads' chief function, prompt supply of men and material, Haupt got "much gratification" from the fact that the army never suffered for lack of sufficient equipment and rations; in fact, it is probable that rapid movement was somewhat retarded by the very superabundance of supplies and the adequacy of supplies was achieved by two factors, according to Haupt, who was always generous with prompt recognition of the contributions of others. First of all, the great efficiency of the superintendents and their subordinates contributed substantially to the successful operation of the railroads. And second, they were loyally supported by Halleck, whose stringent orders finally successfully prevented interference with train movements by the military. Prior to Haupt's arrival at the front, the interference by officers in train operations had been the primary cause of incessant and critical stoppages along key rail lines.[11]

When double-track rail lines were in use, Haupt formulated the following principles for their effective operation.[12]

> Allow trains of 20 cars to start at intervals of 15 minutes, each car carrying 50 men. With this schedule 96,000 men can be moved in 24 hours to a distance of 250 miles. The number moved and the distance travelled per day are simply questions of equipment and celerity of handling. Some colonels could get a regiment into the cars in 10 minutes; others would waste half a day, and derange the whole line.

This estimate did not include the baggage or horses, and artillery.

A unique contribution was the establishment of a courier service to expedite military news by means of relays of fast horses. This service was supplemented by telegraphers who reported back the fluctuations of combat by means of compact telegraphic instruments. The reporting of Haupt proved itself to Lincoln during the Second Bull Run campaign, and the War Department issued orders that Haupt's couriers be admitted at any time of day or night. In fact, Lincoln and Stanton were usually better aware of the overall military situation than many of the responsible commanders at the front. Haupt was a superior reporter of timely, accurate military information.

In his role as unofficial advisor to the Federal Government on railroad affairs in all military areas, Haupt rendered significant long-range service when he analyzed conditions in the West. Although his report was not published (for reasons known only to Stanton) Haupt was successful in presenting his views on railroads in the Western Theater. These views and suggestions formed a basis for improvements later implemented in time for the 1864-1865 campaigns. Haupt pointed out the inefficiency, inexperience, and probable corruptness in some quarters among the Western railroaders. He made a special point of the imperative need for military men to appreciate the role of civilians in military railroading. But unfortunately, said Haupt, "there has existed a thorough contempt for civilians, particularly on the part of officers of low grade." Haupt noted that the remedy for this situation was that supplied by Halleck to railroads in the East—where orders were issued that any officer who interfered with the movements of the trains would be dismissed from the service.[13]

This basic problem, one never completely solved while

Haupt was in service, but one which he considered of great importance, was pointed out by Thomas A. Scott, Assistant Secretary of War, to Stanton as early as March 1, 1862. Scott told the Secretary that few military men knew anything about railroads and that transportation of supplies to army depots should not be placed in the hands of the military.[14] The railroad men were primarily civilians. The locomotive engineers, firemen, dispatchers, conductors—even the superintendents and Haupt himself—were civilians. All were in the employ of the Federal Government but were not under any direct control of army personnel. The antipathy of army officers toward civilian employees of the railroads was at its worst among Quartermaster Department personnel, who had to work closely with Haupt's men. Haupt, although by training a professional soldier, decided to keep the railroads out of control of the military. In this decision he was supported by Halleck. Much of the final success of Federal military railroads was due to Haupt and Halleck in their unwavering insistence on non-interference by military men in railroad operations. By 1864, this paid off when both Grant and Sherman, recognizing the railroads' essential role in their operations, adopted and enforced Haupt's principles, worked out in the East in 1862-1863.

Cooperation with the Quartermaster Department was never easy to maintain. Had it not been for the fact that Meigs was a high-minded officer who recognized Haupt's worth the situation would have been well-nigh hopeless. As it was, much friction and a constant frustration were encountered with some of the junior quartermaster officers. Eventually all the military railroads came under the Quartermaster Department. On July 4, 1864, the

Quartermaster Department was reorganized into nine divisions. The fourth division of this reorganization was charged with operating the railroads and telegraph lines. About three weeks later Congress approved this reorganization.[15] Haupt's dream of an independent bureau of military railroads was never realized.

Although never implemented, Haupt's concept of a central railroad bureau in Washington was an eminently sound one. The Federals needed a uniform code of rules, regulations and signals for the operation of all military railroads of the Country. This central bureau would, in Haupt's opinion, have established a system of regular periodic reports, giving the names, location, condition, miles in operation, amount of rolling stock, as well as such essential data as responsible officials, salaries, and similar basic statistics.

As pointed out earlier, Haupt utilized the comparatively new field of photography to supplement his textual material on new methods of rail transportation, reconstruction and destruction of rail lines and bridges, and the rapid conveyance of troops across streams.[16]

There were several innovations developed by the railroads during the war to which Haupt made only an initial contribution. In the case of armored trains Haupt's role was confined to protecting the locomotive cabs. This is especially curious in the light of his frequent (and unfortunate!) challenging of the Navy Department on *their* work with armored turrets, forts, and ships. During the war the Federals developed armored railway cars for both offensive and defensive operations. In both cases, the armored car preceded the engine on the track. Often the sides of these cars were pierced for riflemen and for cannon. The Baldwin locomotive works built

such a car for the Philadelphia, Wilmington, and Baltimore Railroad. An armored railway battery was constructed of boiler iron rivetted on 2.5 inch oak planks
mounted on a 30-foot platform car. The sides of this
car were 2.5 feet high. It was equipped with a 6-inch
cannon.[17] From such experiments were to come the railway artillery of later wars and the railway batteries
used in coast defense installations during succeeding
decades.

So far as interest in the transportation of wounded
was concerned, Haupt was mainly preoccupied with the
prompt loading, dispatch and unloading of such trains.
However, as with the development of armored trains,
the Federals made major contributions to methods of
moving wounded men by rail. As early as 1861, an inspector[18] for the U.S. Sanitary Commission wrote as
follows:

> Twenty-seven cases of fever had been embarked at Otterville
> on Saturday morning, at 10 o'clock in a box car. The men
> were laid in their blankets on the floor. With the sick was
> laid the body of an officer, in a coffin. A single nurse, without
> stores, appliances or money, could do little else than bring wa-
> ter to the sick. . . . In the middle of the same afternoon, they
> were stopped, to have the road open for (another train). For
> this object they waited until 1 A.M. of the following day, when
> the word came by telegraph that it would not pass during
> the night. They finally arrived at 3:30 of a raw morning at
> Jefferson . . . two were already dead on the floor, the rest
> faint and cold. . . . The inspector got some tea and food from
> the nearest inn and brought it to them, for which they were
> very grateful. Finally, they reached St. Louis at 10 o'clock on
> Sunday evening, having been 36 hours on the road. Three
> men had died in transit; a fourth followed in a few hours—
> 4 of 27!

This barbarous system was little if any improvement on the primitive methods employed during the Italian war of 1859.[19]

Under McClellan on the Peninsula in 1862, wounded and sick were brought from Savage Station to White House by rail. These men made the trip merely lying on the bare floor of flat cars. The most critically wounded were put inside the covered cars—"close, windowless, boxes"—sometimes with a little straw or a blanket— more often without either. They finally arrived a "festering mass of dead and living together."[20]

Much of the credit for the concept of hospital cars belongs to Doctor Elisha Harris, who witnessed the agonies of the wounded being transported in so primitive a fashion. Under Harris's urgings and suggestions, the U. S. Sanitary Commission drew up plans and specifications for hospital cars. During 1863, ten of these cars were in operation while additional ones were added thereafter until the end of the war. Each car had twenty-four removable stretchers suspended from uprights on heavy rubber bands. The stretchers were used to carry wounded soldiers from the battlefield to the railroad car, and later directly from the car to the hospital. This reduced to a minimum any unnecessary moving of badly wounded men. Each hospital car was equipped with a medicine closet and chairs and a couch. A kitchen (6 feet by 3 feet) equipped with a water tank, wash basin, cupboards, and copper boilers completed the equipment. Extra-stiff springs were placed on the ends of the car and double springs underneath the body of the car proper. These cars were equipped with ventilation, heating, and lighting fixtures, and were made of variable gauge for use on different railroads.[21] Active also in the development of hospital trains was the Medical Director of the Department of Washington, who ordered construction of several complete hospital trains. These trains, of ten ward cars each, were run on a regular schedule during the 1864 Atlanta Campaign. Hospital trains were distinguished by brightly painted smokestacks on their locomotives—a brilliant scarlet for daylight runs, with a row of three red lanterns by night. The enemy respected these hospital trains although they were never averse to destroying any other type of railroad equipment within reach!

Nevertheless, transportation of wounded remained an ever present problem for commanders throughout the war. As late as Sheridan's victory at Cedar Creek, October 19, 1864, wounded men suffered greatly because the enemy had captured all the ambulances. The result was that the "walking wounded" were compelled to march all night and then ride for sixteen hours over a rough road in springless army wagons. As one of the sufferers told the author[22]—such a plight was not calculated to prompt any undeserved laudation of Uncle Sam's medical facilities. The men realized that the Government was doing its best, and were finally rescued by a train which took them to a large, palatial base hospital of the North. When they eventually arrived at such establishments as the Mower General Hospital in Philadelphia they "thanked God for a Government whose resources and tenderness are alike inexhaustable."

Haupt's restless imagination did not permit him to confine his attention to military railroading. Long buried among his papers are some strikingly original concepts on the subject of coast and harbor defenses as well as armor for war vessels. Details of Haupt's ideas, with accompanying sketches, appeared in correspondence from Haupt to John P. Hale, Chairman of the Committee on Naval Affairs, dated April 26, 1862.[23] This correspondence had no doubt been triggered by the recent (March 9, 1862) epochal battle between the *Monitor* and the *Merrimac*.

Haupt asserted in a letter to Hale, that at the beginning of the war he had suggested that revolving land and floating batteries were essential for defense of Northern ports. Moreover, according to Haupt, as early as June 1861 he had presented his views on these batteries to General Wool, who had approved them. At that time Haupt also submitted sketches for an armorclad revolving fort, consisting of two parts—the lower of solid masonry protected from shot and shell. This part would contain the engines for rotation, fuel, supplies, magazines, etc. The upper part, consisting of a flat, revolving dome with solid wrought-iron embrasures, would be equipped with twenty or more guns of the heaviest caliber, rotating at such velocity as to permit any desired number of discharges per minute in any given direction, free from any dead angles not covered by fire. Each gun was to be so situated and rotatable that the fort would be perfectly secure against assault. The only communication was by a subterranean gallery, the entrance and exit to be at any desired distance and completely masked and camouflaged.

There can be no question that Haupt was way ahead of his contemporaries, including perhaps Ericsson himself. The contract for Ericsson's *Monitor* was formally entered into with John Ericsson on October 4, 1861.[24] But it was not until October 29th that actual construction was begun on the model craft which Ericsson had finally succeeded in selling to the Board on Ironclad Ships in Washington.

In his letter to Hale, Haupt conceded that the principle of Ericsson's revolving turret was similar to Haupt's revolving fort, the chief difference consisting in the rotation of a part instead of the whole of the turret. Haupt also supplied a second sketch of his plan for increasing the efficiency of the ordinary circular and polygonal forts by giving them flanking defenses and removing the dead angles and blind sectors. This, according to Haupt, was accomplished by an arrangement identical in principle with that which had recently been incorporated in the turret of Ericsson's *Monitor*. Haupt's arrangement involved the extension of projections at each angle, supermounted by revolving, armor-clad domes or turrets of 20-30 feet in diameter. Each of these small domes was to be pierced with one large and several small openings, and armed with a single gun of great size, sweeping a circumferance of 180 degrees. A railway track was to connect each dome or turret with the interior of the fort, where a turntable cleared the various tracks as in a locomotive roundhouse, where reserve guns were to be located.

Haupt also outlined suggestions for improving gun trunions, floating batteries and various other military items. He concluded his prospectus with the acknowledgment that he had "communicated here only general ideas" since lack of time prevented his working out the details—but the details "present no serious difficulties."

There was some justification for Haupt's concern over defense of Northern seaports. Bitter experience with British naval attacks during the revolution and 1812 wars heightened this natural apprehension. Although

Ericsson's model for his Monitor, consisting of a re-volving turret armed with two 11-inch Dahlgren guns, had been approved in mid-September 1861, the South had already had a headstart. For two months prior to Ericsson's initial go-ahead order, the Southerners had been working on their ironclad. As Welles pointed out, men in New York—sensible in most matters—were the most easily terrified and panic-stricken at the thought of a Confederate naval attack on their city. These men were sincerely concerned lest an ironclad were to make a sudden attack on their city and destroy it before they could do anything to prevent the catastrophe.

Lincoln had great confidence in Haupt's technical knowhow, and accordingly chose him as an adviser in the mobilization of technology for the Federals.[25] This mobilization began when some individual (not identified) suggested to the President that he convene a council of engineers and naval constructors. The purpose of the meeting of these experts was to inform Lincoln of the current status of the Federal military and naval tech-nology. Before long, Haupt, who soon took charge of this council, sent out a questionnaire, October 28, 1862, concerned mainly with naval technology. Unfortunately, this questionnaire (which should have been kept in the official family) somehow got into the newspapers and in the mails. Haupt, characteristically blunt, was some-what less than the epitome of tact when he worded the preamble:

Many experienced naval constructors, engineers, and practical men appear to think that our American Navy does not keep pace with the improvements of the age in any of the essential requisites of modern vessels of war, and that our chief cities and harbors are without suitable protection against maritime attacks.

After this challenging preamble, there followed some fifty questions, many calling for long and detailed answers. The questions were so formulated as to ascertain the addressee's technical competence, the relative cost and efficiency of private persons versus government construction techniques, and the most recent military and naval technological advances. What happened to the questionnaire and the entire project is a mystery. Haupt, in his reminiscences, never mentioned the affair. Perhaps this is natural since, as a member of the military establishment, he very definitely was out of order in focusing his attack on the Navy Department. Strange indeed, however, is the fact that Dahlgren, the naval ordnance expert, not only did not figure in the affair at all, but he said nothing about it in his journal. The only hint we now have about Haupt's questionnaire is in a diary entry by Welles[26] on January 18, 1864, and an article in the *Boston Transcript* of November 17, 1862. According to Welles, his Department had received a "batch of letters" from the Provost Marshal, disclosing a fraud and intrigue by "a set of assuming men that is as amusing as reckless." According to Welles, the principals in this affair included Haupt and some government personnel, among them the eminent naval architect John W. Griffiths. Griffiths possessed an international reputation for his brilliant designing of ships. His ship designs and writings were largely instrumental in elevating the United States to a leading position as a producer of fast vessels, both clipper and steam. However, the files of the Navy Department disclose no such batch of letters to which Welles alluded. Dahlgren, who was apparently unaware of this entire affair, stayed on as Lincoln's technical adviser.

Within the army itself, Haupt's abilities were well recognized during his military service. For example, when General Nathaniel P. Banks, commanding the Department of the Gulf, wanted his railroads put in efficient running order, he turned to Haupt. Banks, needing an expert to bring order out of chaos in his railroad system, wrote Halleck that Haupt would be the best man for this purpose.[27]

Haupt's railroading precepts were followed in areas outside his own theater of operations. For example, on July 7, 1863, Major General John G. Foster, commanding the District of North Carolina, reported[28] that when his men destroyed a section of the Wilmington and Weldon Railroad, they used "the plan of . . . Haupt, whilst the remainder of the force (3rd New York Cavalry) were thrown out as pickets, and kept mounted for defense." This force successfully destroyed telegraph wire, track, and culverts.

In the course of an attempt to clarify Haupt's actual status in the Federal Army during the war, a Congressional Committee on Military Affairs issued a report[29] designed to give a "proper historical recognition" of Haupt's services, both military and civil. The Committee received substantial support from the Adjutant General of the Army whose files formed the basis for a fairly complete listing of Haupt's contributions. This list, which divided Haupt's contributions into the categories of "military and civil engineer," "author," and "inventor" is indeed an impressive one. (See Appendix for the complete list.)

NOTES, CHAPTER 13

1. Published May 13, 1862. Consisted of 24 pages and 10 folding plates. Copy in author's collection has Meigs's signature, but he has not been able to identify the author.
2. McCallum's Final Report to Stanton.
3. Sherman, W. T., *Memoirs,* Vol. II, pp. 398–399.
4. McCallum's Final Report to Stanton.
5. Haupt, pp. 255–256.
6. Haupt, pp. 148–150; *Official Records,* Series III, Vol. 2, pp. 708–710.
7. Haupt's *Order Book,* June 2, 1862.
8. Haupt to Halleck, May 16, 1863, Haupt. pp. 197–203.
9. Haupt's final report to Stanton, September 9, 1863.
10. Haupt, pp. 190–193.
11. Haupt's Final Report to Stanton, September 9, 1863.
12. Bigelow, *Principles of Strategy,* pp. 75–76.
13. Haupt's Final Report to Stanton, September 9, 1863.
14. Scott to Stanton, March 1, 1862, Stanton Papers, Vol. IV.
15. General Orders No. 30 Quartermaster General's Office, Washington, D.C., July 30, 1864.
16. Haupt's final report to Stanton, September 9, 1863.
17. *American Railroad Journal,* October 18, 1862, See also *Official Records,* Series I, Vol. 37, Part I, p. 356 and Vol. 51, Part I, p. 1069.
18. Robert Collyer in Sanitary Commission Pamphlet No. 40, p. 87, December 1861.
19. Otis, George A., *A Report on a Plan for Transporting Wounded Soldiers by Railway in Time of War* (Washington, 1875).
20. Wormeley, Katharine P., *The Other Side of War with the Army of the Potomac,* p. 129.
21. Wormeley, Katharine P., *The U. S. Sanitary Commission,* p. 288.
22. Francis H. Buffum, 14th New Hampshire Infantry to author. Buffum was shot through the body but survived the war, dying in 1927.
23. Published in pamphlet form by the *Boston Commercial Bulletin* April 26, 1862. Haupt papers, Library of Congress.
24. *Battles and Leaders,* Vol. 1, p. 619.
25. Bruce, Robert V., *Lincoln and the Tools of War,* pp. 216–217.
26. Welles, Gideon, *Diary,* Vol. 1, p. 511.
27. Banks to Halleck, May 21, 1863. *Official Records,* Vol. 26, Part 1, pp. 498–499.
28. *Ibid.,* Vol. 27, Part 2, pp. 859–860.
29. House Report No. 682, 62nd Congress, 2nd Session (Private Calendar No. 88). Haupt Papers, National Archives.

14

AFTERMATH

On February 4, 1864, McCallum was appointed general manager of all railways in the possession of the Government, or that might from time to time be taken possession of by military authority in the Departments of the Cumberland, Ohio, Tennessee and Arkansas. He replaced John B. Anderson, who was relieved from duty as general manager of said railroads and directed to turn over to McCallum all property, moneys, contracts, and papers of every kind and description belonging to the Government or in anywise appertaining to or concerning these railroads.[1]

McCallum's assignment to the West was made with the High Command's belief that the railroads in northern Virginia were either functioning smoothly or were no longer of paramount importance in the 1864 offensive. In May 1864, the Alexandria railroads ceased to be of real significance, while various other lines were not maintained because of the shift of military operations. On May 9, 1864, repairs were begun once more on the railroad at Aquia Creek, and by the 17th it had been opened to Falmouth—a distance of fourteen miles. The Potomac Creek bridge was readied for rail traffic and soon this line was busily engaged in removing wounded from the battle of Spottsylvania. On May 22nd the line was abandoned and was not used again, as a military rail line.

The shift was now made to City Point and the Petersburg front. By the end of June, the City Point and Petersburg Railroad had been occupied to Pitkin Station, only 8 miles from City Point. During the fall and winter of 1864-1865, the Construction Corps built eighteen miles of new rail line, passing to the south and southwest of Petersburg. Grant's army received its principal supplies by this new route. The Richmond and Petersburg Railroad was opened April 4, 1865, from Petersburg to the south bank of the James River, and was run by the U.S. Military Railroad until July 3rd when it was turned over to the Virginia Board of Public Works.[2]

As a belated recognition of Haupt's previous recommendations, McCallum appointed Adna Anderson General Inspector of Military Railroads. This order was issued as a circular October 27, 1864, and was long overdue.

The Construction Corps was expanded from its small complement of some 300 men in 1863 to nearly 10,000 serving i nall theaters of war. These skilled workmen were formed into divisions, gangs, and squads, in charge respectively of supervisors, foremen, and sub-foremen, furnished wit htents and field equipemnt. Storehouses were established at key points, with ample supplies of tools and materials.

Greatest expansion of the Corps occurred in the West, due mainly to the longer distance involved, plus poorer and fewer transportation facilities. The Corps was organized into six divisions in the Middle Division of the Mississippi where its maximum strength was nearly 5,000 men. The organization was as follows:[3]

DIVISION HEADQUARTERS

Division engineer	(1)
Assistant engineer	(1)
Rod man	(1)
Clerk	(1)
Messengers	(2)
Total	6

DIVISIONS

		Number of men
No. 1	Bridges and Carpentry	356
2	Track	356
3	Water Stations	15
4	Masonry	13
5	Ox Brigade	20
6	Train crew	11
		771

Divisions 1 and 2 had the elements necessary to be self-supporting.

McCallum, like Haupt, experienced great difficulty in procuring a sufficient force of competent railroad men for construction and transportation. Due mainly to the rapid expansion of the railroads during the war, the supply of trained railway men remained constantly at a premium. Many had gone voluntarily into the army in various capacities, some had been drafted, while the expansion of civilian railroads in the North had placed a high demand on the services of those who remained in their prewar positions. There was a constant demand for skilled railroad men back home. When the U. S. Military Railroads sought to induce these men to leave their secure posts, great difficulty was met in trying to pry these men loose from their safe and lucrative jobs to enter upon a new and often dangerous field of activity. The difference between the civilian and military railroads was marked. Not only were employees of the Military Railroads continually exposed to very real danger from the regular forces of the enemy, guerrillas, and scouting parties but, owing to the hasty construction and erratic operation of military railroads at the front, what were considered ordinary risks for civilian railroads were vastly increased on military lines.

As McCallum correctly pointed out, the hardships and dangers for train employees at the front were much greater than for any other class of civilians working for the Federal Government. Their service was directly comparable to that of the soldier of a line unit engaged in a raid in enemy country. It was not unusual for train personnel to be out with their trains for five to ten days without sleep, except for what they could snatch on their locomotives and cars while the latter were standing, waiting to be loaded or unloaded. Food was often scanty—if available at all—for days on end. And these conditions persisted for days for men whose every nerve was strained to the limit in an atmosphere of very real and unexpected danger. Destruction as well as construction became a science. Even line units participated.

An observer from the 65th Ohio Infantry has left us a graphic description of the destruction of a rail line. This soldier was astonished to see some 5,000 men, arranged on both sides of a rail line for the distance of a mile. The men, wearing their accouterments and keeping their muskets in reach, were using axes, sledge-hammers, levers and "claws" to wreck the rail lines. First, a few spikes were quickly drawn at intervals of two or three hundred yards. Then the men laid hold of the rails on one side, gave a mighty yell, and in an instant the track was turned over into the ditch. By vigorous blows with sledge hammers, the ties were quickly separated from the rails. Meanwhile other soldiers had started a hundred fires all along the rail line. On these fires the ties were loosely piled, including available fence rails, brush, and dry limbs. The rails were picked up—some twelve men to each—and laid across the blazing fires. In half an hour the rails were at a red heat for six to eight feet in the middle. Then came the final process, by which the destruction was completed. With grappling irons, made for the purpose, the rails were twisted around two or three times, like doughnuts. The still-glowing rails were then bent entirely around the trunks of standing trees, where they were left to cool.

Much of the lack of general knowledge of Haupt's Civil War service is due to McCallum's final report[5] of May 26, 1866, which incredibly makes no mention of Haupt at all. Not only is there no mention of Haupt, but credit for Haupt's innovations and contributions to military railroading were either assumed by McCallum himself or given to Stanton. A glaring example was Haupt's principle of prompt unloading of cars to prevent delay in operations. In his report, McCallum quotes "the order of the Secretary of War, the wisdom of which has been so abundantly vindicated by experience. . . ." Actually, it was Haupt's persistent insistence which finally resulted in the issuance of this order (November 10, 1862) and credit for its ultimate promulgation belongs not to Stanton, but to the oft-maligned Halleck. The wording of McCallum with respect to this order is illustrative of his obsequiousness to Stanton and his flagrant disregard of fair play in giving Haupt credit for bringing about passage of the order. McCallum reported that "having had a somewhat extensive railroad experience both before and during the rebellion, I consider this order of the Secretary of War to have been the very foundation of success; without it the whole railroad system . . . would have been not only a costly, but ludicrous failure." McCallum closed his report by naming his principal assistants "who assisted him at various times during the war."

Haupt took pride in the accomplishments of military railroads, both under his direction in the East, and also in the West during the latter half of the War. Certainly an important lesson of the war was the value of rail lines in moving troops and supplies in strategical and tactical planning. The Federal high command came to realize the potentialities of the new instrument of warfare. Beginning with a mere seven-mile stretch from Washington to Alexandria, the U.S. Military Railroads were operating 2,105 miles of railroad by 1865.

The war was scarcely half over when Haupt left the service. Although no longer an active participant after September 1863, Haupt followed the progress of military operations with keen professional interest. Presumably, also, he noted with interest the military use of railroads in Europe during the wars of 1864, 1866 and 1870-1871.

In these wars Prussia, and to a lesser extent the other belligerents, realized the strategic role of railroads in warfare. Both Prussia and Austria utilized their rail lines to move large units from deep inside their own countries up to the zone of active operations. The Prussians had a head start because they had begun early to examine the military potential of the railroad. In 1864, directly influenced by what their observers had reported from America, they added a railway section to the General Staff. In May 1866, on the eve of the war with Austria, the Prussian war ministry created a field railway section modeled directly on the Construction Corps of the Federal Army and designed to perform similar functions. However, the Prussians soon realized that there is no substitute for actual experience in the field. A former Federal Corps commander[6] while observing the Prussians in their war with France, noted that in improvising and repairing railroads and bridges, they had done nothing "worthy to be compared with our own work during our war." Nevertheless, this officer, whose service had been in the West, did point out that the Prussian failure in rail and bridge repair was very probably due to lack of experience, and in fact the Americans themselves were not proficient at such repair in the early months of their war.

Nor were the Prussians alone in their appreciation of the role of railroads in wars of the future. Lessons had been learned in the United States as the war had progressed. For example, the *United States Service Magazine,* early in 1864, pointed out the strategic importance of rail junctions, and the desirability of cutting rail communications. This semi-authoritative journal cited as examples the triangle of Chattanooga, Cleveland, and Dalton, as well as Memphis, Corinth, and Jackson.[7]

Several astute military writers in England saw the handwriting on the wall. A very penetrating treatment, entitled "Railways Strategically Considered," came from the pen of Captain H. W. Tyler.[8] At about the same time another British officer was pointing out that in future wars railroads would play a significant strategic role. "Armies will reach their destination not only much more speedily, but in much better. . . (condition). . . On the offensive, armies may be organized far away from the frontier, and yet become concentrated there with amazing rapidity."[9] The prophecy of this officer (a lieutenant in the Queen's Own Light Infantry) was painfully accurate to the French six years later when they faced the rapid concentration and movement by rail of the invading Prussians in 1870.

Not only were broad strategic implications of military railroading often lost on the Europeans. In such basic problems of moving cavalry and artillery units it was obvious that American experience had either not been noted or had been disregarded. For example, Prussian cavalrymen invading Denmark in 1864 remained seated on their horses while being transported by rail! In the British service, cavalrymen rested on stools or hammocks at their beasts' heads and, for short distances, the animals were kept saddled and packed. This reduced the number of horses per railroad car to three to nine, depending on the size of the car.

Most of the European countries had failed to profit from the wartime experience of the Federal forces, who had discovered early in the war that transporting horses by rail was a unique problem and that inexperience was extremely costly in horseflesh. In 1861-1862, Federal commanders had been prone to assume that once the horses were loaded in the cars, all would go smoothly. Moreover, these commanders quite often left the horses in the cars unattended for protracted periods of time. The result was a large proportion of weak or useless animals on arrival at their destination. The Federals, however, gradually came to appreciate the absolute need for care of their animals en route, which included scheduled rests, feeding, and exercise. By late 1863, when the horses of the 11th and 12th Corps were shipped by rail (along with the men and impedimenta of those corps) sensible precautions were taken to insure that the animals arrived in good condition. These precautions paid off handsomely. Although the trip was 1,200 miles (from Manassas Junction and Brandy Station, Virginia, to Bridgeport, Alabama) by using specially prepared cars the horses arrived in good shape. By 1865 rules and regulations[10] had been specifically laid down for the transport of horses by rail; moreover, these rules were being adhered to in all major commands.

Despite his initial bitterness over being removed so abruptly from military service, Haupt had no inclination to remain idle. For several years after the war he very actively practiced his profession as a consulting engineer in Pennsylvania. He was a member of the Franklin Institute, the American Philosophical Society, and the Pennsylvania Historical Society.

The Hoosac Tunnel controversy dragged out for years. Haupt fought every inch of the way—never losing a point when only facts of the case were involved. He was continually harassed and circumvented by Governor Andrew and other officials of Massachusetts. Had they not been so hostile to Haupt, the State of Massachusetts would have had its tunnel without a cent of cost to the State. As it was, the State, in the end, sold to the Fitchburg Railroad for $7,000,000 a work which had cost $20,000,000!

In 1889, Haupt stated that shortly before his death, Governor Andrew admitted that he had made a mistake in his Hoosac Tunnel policy and that he had done Haupt great injustice. Haupt was nearly ruined in this drawn-out litigation but later recovered by his successes in other engineering projects.

Honors came to him from abroad as well. In 1867, he went to Europe on the invitation of the Royal Polytechnic Society of Cornwall and explained his system of mining and tunneling by power machinery to the members of that organization. A rock drill which he used in the Hoosac Tunnel project was exhibited and received the highest honors awarded by the Society. This was the same type of drill which performed so well in the great St. Gothard tunnel—a drill which functioned with great rapidity.

Three years later in Boston he examined and reported on preservative processes applied to wood pavements. Haupt's report was unfavorable and the processes were abandoned. That same year (1870) he located the Shenandoah Valley Railroad, a line which subsequently was built.

In 1874, Haupt was appointed general manager of the Richmond and Danville Railroad system and, in this capacity, prepared the plan for organization of the Southern Railway and Steamship Association.

Four years later, 1878, Haupt achieved his greatest peacetime success—the organizing and planning of a pipeline for the transportation of crude petroleum from the Allegheny Valley wells to the tidewater districts. Working for his organization—the Pennsylvania Transportation Company—Haupt conducted innumerable topographical surveys in the areas through which the pipelines would run. He decided that the successful functioning of a line hundreds of miles in length over mountains and through valleys would require a series of pumping stations so located topographically that mechanical devices, i.e. governors, would be needed to have the pumps be synchronized and regulate each other automatically. Despite the active hostility of the Standard Oil Company, Haupt and his company eventually won out and the "Tidewater Pipeline" developed into one of the agencies which furnished inexpensive "illuminating fluid" to the people.

Haupt then turned his attention to the developing of processes for the anti-corrosive treatment of steel and iron. Although meeting with some success the firm, of which Haupt was consulting engineer, ultimately failed, and he soon thereafter was appointed general manager of the Northern Pacific Railroad. During his service with this line, 1881-1884, Haupt prepared a pamphlet protesting the constant interference of states with railroad properties and management. Several thousand of these pamphlets were printed for general distribution of railroad companies.

In 1884, Haupt was elected President of the Dakota and Great Southern Railroad and shortly before his death was President of the American Nutrient Company.

During these later years of his life he wrote extensively on a number of technical subjects including elevated railroads, city heating systems, and river navigation. In 1893 he published a book on comparative costs of construction and operation of all the urban and suburban railways known to be operating at that time.

Active until the very end, fittingly enough, his death (from a sudden heart attack) came while on a train returning to Washington, December 14, 1905.

NOTES, CHAPTER 14

1. General Orders No. 3, Headquarters Military Division of the Mississippi, Nashville, Tenn. February 4, 1864.
2. McCallum's report, May 26, 1866.
3. *Ibid.*
4. Hinman, Wilbur F., Lt. Col., 65th Ohio Infantry *Corporal Si Klegg and His Pard,* pp. 649–651 (Cleveland, Ohio, 1887)
5. Report of Brevet Brigadier General D. C. McCallum, May 26, 1866.
6. Hazen, W. B., *The School and the Army in Germany and France,* p. 133.
7. *The United States Service Magazine,* Vol. 1, March 1864, No. III, p. 271.
8. Tyler, H. W., in the *Journal* of the Royal United Service Institution, VIII (1864), pp. 321–343.
9. Steinmetz, A., "On Great Modern Invasions and the Strategic Application of Railroads," *Colburn's United Service Magazine,* CCCCXXI (October 1864), pp. 177–178.
10. Brinkerhoff, Roeliff, Captain, *The Volunteer Quartermaster,* pp. 97–98.

APPENDIX

A

SUGGESTED ORGANIZATION FOR CONSTRUCTION OF A BRIDGE SIMILAR TO THE ONE AT POTOMAC CREEK; THE BENTS OR TRESTLES BEING IN THREE STORIES.

ORGANIZATION AND DUTIES OF SQUADS

SQUAD NO.	DUTIES	NO. of MEN
1	On top of bridge, to move out sliding beams and put on ties	6

293

2 To attend to top of second trestle and bottom
   of third   5
3 To put bents together, put lower legs in sills
   and heels of second bents in place   8
4 To attend to framing and carrying timber on
   bank   7
5 To frame round timber and put sills on cribs   30
6 To run in timber at grade and haul on ropes   12
7 To put timber down bank and haul on ropes   12

On the south side all these will be duplicated except Squad 5.
And the number of squads should be continued, which will ex-
tend the number to 13.

                                                        50
14 For cutting timber in woods, 20 men with axes   20
15 For loading trucks with logs   20
16 To assist in clearing woods and loading logs
    in woods   12
17 Drivers of ox-teams   10
              Total force for work   192

If relieved at noon, and 100 men allowed for guards, sick, and for
sentrymen, the proper allowance would be 500 men; but the work
can be done with a much smaller number if efficient and well
organized.

TRANSPORTATION

If the bridge is to be built entirely of round logs, hauled, say ½
mile in woods and transported by rail 1 mile at each end of bridge,
20 yoke of oxen, 1 pair of mules, and 1 car would be required at
each end, to vary according to circumstances.
I pair of mules extra should be provided with wagon and driver.

              Total—Yoke of oxen   40
                     experienced herdsmen   2
                     pairs of Mules   3

EQUIPMENT

Axes   50
Shovels   20
Broad-axes   20

Picks	12
Handsaws	25
Crosscut saws	20

Ropes 4 (500 ft. each 1¼ inch in diameter)
8-inch pulleys
4-inch pulley
Trussed beams
24 Iron bars (from 2½ to 4 feet long)
50 kegs boat spikes 3/8 x 3/8x7

Specified nails, mauls, chains, timber wheels, files, bolts, etc.

Tools should be numbered and assigned to individuals by number with a record kept.

Bugle should be blown by direction of the officer of the day at hours for assembling squads to fall in and march promptly to place of rendezvous. Officer of the day will go around constantly to see if men are present and at work.

Each squad to be under a designated leader—who reports absentees.

Pay should be by the hour, to be reduced or withheld if an individual fails to perform adequately.

Suitable cooking utensils should be provided and the men detailed for work at daylight should not have to cook their own breakfast.

Breakfast should be prepared by colored cooks or by a detail of men not required for other duty.

Permanent cooks are greatly to be desired.

Those who work all day in the woods should take dinners with them and feed should always be taken for the oxen. Much time is lost driving them a distance to feed.

If the force is designed to operate at points with which there is not continuous rail communication, tools must be transported by wagons.

B
REGULATIONS OF JUNE 11, 1862
CONSTRUCTION CORPS
DEPARTMENT OF THE RAPPAHANNOCK

1. The Construction Corps of the Department of the Rappahannock will consist of such commissioned and non-commissioned officers, privates and civilians as may be detailed from the force under the orders of the Department Commander, or especially enlisted or employed for the service of the Corps.

2. The duties of the Corps will consist of the construction and reconstruction of roads and bridges, erection of buildings required for transportation purposes, preparation of materials for construction, and performance of such duties as may be assigned to them by the Chief of the Department.

3. The Corps will be organized into squads of ten men each. Each squad will be under the command of a non-commissioned officer, each two squads under a lieutenant, and the whole under an officer designated by the Department Commander.

4. The Adjutant of the Corps will keep a personnel roster of each man, including name, residence, company from which detailed, former occupation, kind of work in which best qualified, and other pertinent data.

5. The Adjutant will also function as Commissary and Quartermaster. He will be responsible for furnishing the Corps with rations and supplies. He will keep all records including time-reports furnished him by officers of the squad.

6. Acting under direction of the Adjutant, a clerk will keep records of all tools, implements, and government property belonging to or used by the Construction Corps. Each individual will be charged with the tool furnished him. Each squad will be responsible for certain categories of supplies.

7. When on active duty, when every hour of daylight must be used, breakfast will be at the dawn of day, and will be pre-

ceded by reveille and roll-call, at which all who are late or absent will be reported. Immediately after breakfast the Corps will assemble by bugle call, squads called out by their numbers, and marched to their work. Although periods of excessive exertion will generally be of short duration, men who are not willing to work, even for 16 hours continuously, when required, are not wanted in the Construction Corps of the Rappahannock and are requested to leave it and return to their regiments at once.

8.   Extra pay will be given for all time actually engaged in Construction, or other work. Officers in charge of squads will keep time by the hour and return the same weekly to the Adjutant of the Corps.

9.   Officers will observe their men with respect to work, deportment, and habits. All who habitually use profane or obscene language, who are immoral, vicious, indolent, or insubordinate, and especially those who commit depredations upon the property of citizens will be sent to their regiments with a statement of the offense committed. The members of the Construction Corps are not authorized to investigate and decide upon the loyalty of the inhabitants of the country, much less to condemn them as rebels and appropriate their property to themselves. All who are not in arms against the Government are entitled to protection against injury or insult.

10.   Each squad will occupy its own tent and will be responsible for the tent, tool-box, cooking utensils and other property assigned to the squad.

11.   No member of the Corps shall discharge firearms without the orders of a commissioned officer, except where imperative necessity requires it.

12.   Civilians, employed as superintendents in charge of construction will be considered to have the equivalent rank of captain; and foremen the rank of lieutenant, and will be obeyed and respected accordingly.

13.   Civilians, employed as ordinary mechanics and laborers, will be entitled to the same pay and rations as enlisted men de-

tailed for service in the Construction Corps, and must conform to the rules, regulations and discipline of the Corps in every particular. In case of dismissal for improper conduct, neglect of duty, or other cause, the officer in command may require the forfeiture of any back pay that may be due, which may be given to others as premiums for good conduct, or extra services or otherwise appropriated at the discretion of the officer in command.

14.   A diary shall be kept by the Adjutant. From the diary will be compiled quarterly reports to be submitted to the Department Commander. In these reports will be cited those individuals who have been distinguished by efficient services, and also those who have been sent to their regiments for misconduct or inefficiency.

15.   It is expected that all who have volunteered in defense of their country in the present eventful crisis are, and will show themselves to be gentlemen as well as soldiers. No one whose deportment and conversation prove that he is not such, can remain a member of the Construction Corps of the Rappahannock for a longer time than may be necessary to procure a substitute.

C

PHOTOGRAPHS OF NEW AND EXPERIMENTAL ELEMENTS IN MILITARY RAILROADS

The operations photographed included:

Plans of transporting loaded cars on floats, so as to connect the water termini of different railroads, and transfer cars from one road to another without break of bulk or loss of time.

Plans for constructing floating docks, wharves, warehouses, and bridges, so as to avoid delay in establishing landings and river depots, or loss of stores or improvements if an evacuation becomes necessary.

Plans for destroying bridges with apparatus so portable that it could be carried in the pocket, and in a period of time not exceeding five minutes.

Plans for destroying track at the rate of five miles in an hour with apparatus that could be carried in saddlebags, and which twists and bends rails so effectually that they could not be again used.

Plans for straightening rails and reconstructing roads that had been destroyed by the enemy.

Plans for various new kinds of truss, trestle, and suspension bridges, designed to permit the use of rough sticks and other material that would not require transportation.

Plans and expedients for crossing streams with boats that two men could construct, of rough sticks, in four hours, requiring transportation of only about 8 pounds of ropes, cards and material to each man. By means of these boats, rafts, ferries, and bridges could be formed capable of crossing infantry at the rate of 10,000 to 20,000 men per hour; also artillery and wagon trains. They could make possible operations which had been considered impossible by the best military engineers.

D
ORDER

1. That a bureau be established in connection with the War Department to be designated the "Bureau of United States Military Railroads."

2. The chief of the Bureau shall organize and direct the operations of the various military railroads and regulate government transportation on other roads in the United States. He shall prescribe rules, regulations, modes of operations and forms of reports, and make such arrangements with the approval of the general in command of each department, as will promote the efficiency and economy of public service.

3. He shall be authorized personally or otherwise to inspect, supervise and direct all operations in military construction or transportation in each department, to correct abuses, remedy difficulties, and with the approval of the general in command to

appoint and remove all officers connected with the construction and operation of military railroads, prescribe their duties and fix their compensation.

4.   He may at his discretion be absent from Washington whenever the public interests do not require his presence for the purpose of inspecting the condition of military railroads or to attend to such other public or private business, as may be necessary.

5.   No interference will be permitted by officers of any grade with the orders of the superintendent, or with the running of the trains or any military railroad, except by the general in command of the department in person, or through a written order signed by himself.

Brigadier General Herman Haupt is appointed chief of the Bureau of Military Railroads with authority to do whatever may appear to him expedient and not inconsistent with the railroads of the service to promote economy and increase the efficiency of the military railroad organization.

E
BRIDGE-DESTROYING TORPEDO

"A simple and expeditious mode of destroying bridges and rendering locomotive engines useless to an enemy, is often a desideratum. Cavalry may penetrate far into an enemy's country, may reach bridges forming viaducts on which important lines of communication which it may be desirable to break effectively or in retreat, the destruction of a bridge may be essential to the safety of an army, and yet time may not be sufficient to gather combustibles or they may not be accessible, or the fire may be extinguished, or the damage may be so slight as to be easily repaired.

What is required is a means of certainly and effectually throwing down a bridge in a period of time not exceeding five minutes, and with apparatus so simple and portable that it can be carried in the pocket or a saddlebag.

These requirements are fulfilled by a torpedo which consists simply of a short bolt of seven-eighths inch iron, eight inches long, with head and nut—the head to be two inches in diameter, and about one inch thick. A washer of the same size as the head must be placed under the nut at the other end, with a fuse-hole in it. Between the washer and the head is a tin cylinder one and three-quarters inches in diameter open at both ends, which is filled with powder, and, when the washer and nut are put on, forms a case which encloses it.

In using this torpedo, a hole is bored in a timber; the torpedo (head downwards) is driven in by a stone or billet of wood, and the fuse ignited. The explosion blows the timber in pieces and if a main support, brings down the whole structure.

The time required is only that which is necessary to bore a hole with an auger. Ordinary cigar lighters, which burn without flame, and cannot be blown out, are best for igniting the fuse, which should be about two feet long.

For portability, the auger should be short, say thirteen inches, and the handle movable and of the same length.

The proper place at which to insert the torpedo is of much consequence. Most of the Virginia bridges are Howe trusses without arches. In this kind of bridge, the destruction of the main braces at one end, and on only one side of the span, will be sufficient to bring down the whole structure. There are usually but two main braces in each panel, and two torpedoes will suffice to throw down a span. Two men can bore the two holes at the same time without interfering with each other.

Cartridges containing a fulminite would be more portable, but they are not always conveniently procurable, and their use is attended with risk of explosion.

It is only necessary to operate at one side and on one end of a bridge. If one side falls, the other side is pulled down with it. If the structure contains an arch, two additional torpedoes will be required; but in this case it may be equally advantageous to operate upon the lower chord.

Experiments made at Alexandria proved that a timber placed in the position of a main brace, and similarly loaded, was shattered

into many pieces, some of which were projected by the force of
the explosion more than a hundred feet.

The superintendent of the Orange and Alexandria Military
Railroads has instructions to furnish sample torpedoes to officers
who may order them. Address J. H. DEVEREUX, Superintend-
ant Orange and Alexandria Railroad, Alexandria, Virginia.

H. Haupt in Charge of U.S. Military Railroads."

F*

Railroads in Virginia, Maryland, and Pennsylvania Used at One Time or Another as Military Lines by the U.S. M. R.R.

| Name of Lines | Terminal Stations | | Length In Miles |
	From	To	
Alexandria & Washington	Alexandria	Washington	7
Alexandria, Loudon & Hampshire	Alexandria	Vienna	15
Orange & Alexandria	Alexandria	Mitchell's Station	68
Warrenton Branch	Warrenton Junction	Warrenton	9
Manassas Gap	Manassas	Strasburg	62
Richmond, Fredericksburg & Potomac	Aquia Creek	Fredericksburg	15
Richmond & York River	White House	Fair Oaks	20
Richmond & Petersburg	Manchester	Petersburg	22
Clover Hill Branch	Clover Hill	Coal Mines	18
Richmond & Danville	Manchester	Danville	140
South Side	City Point	Burkesville	62
Army Line & Branches	Pitkin, etc.	Humphrey, etc.	18
Norfolk & Petersburg	Norfolk	Blackwater	44
Seaboard & Roanoke	Portsmouth	Suffolk	17
Winchester & Potomac	Harper's Ferry	Stevenson	28
Western Maryland	Baltimore	Westminster	36
Hanover Branch & Gettysburg	Hanover Junction	Gettysburg	30
			611

* McCallum's report of May 26, 1866

G

CHRONOLOGY OF HAUPT'S SERVICE WITH THE ARMY OF THE POTOMAC

DATES	CAMPAIGN	ARMY COMMANDER	RAIL LINES	STATUS OF THE "CONSTRUCTION CORPS"
April 20, 1862 to June 26, 1862	Shenandoah Valley	McClellan (McDowell was Haupt's immediate army commander)	Aquia Creek and Fredericksburg; Richmond, Fredricksburg and Potomac; Manassas Gap; Orange and Alexandria	On May 28, 1862, Haupt organized a construction corps composed mainly of soldiers detailed from line regiments
June 26, 1862 to Sept. 2, 1862	Second Bull Run	Pope	Orange and Alexandria	Construction Corps temporarily abolished by Pope, but later reactivated
Sept. 2, 1862 to Nov. 5, 1862	Antietam	McClellan (Haupt active only in Virginia)	Cumberland Valley; Baltimore and Ohio; York and Cumberland; Loudoun and Hampshire; Franklin; Manassas Gap; Orange and Alexandria	Construction Corps active only in Harper's Ferry area, but not employed in battle area
Nov. 5, 1862 Jan. 26, 1863	Fredericksburg	Burnside	Manassas Gap; Orange and Alexandria; Aquia Creek; Richmond, Fredericksburg and Potomac	Corps abolished by order of Burnside. Haupt used an unwilling group of 200 soldiers during Battle of Fredericksburg
Jan. 26, 1863 June 27, 1863	Chancellorsville	Hooker	Baltimore and Ohio; Orange and Alexandria; Aquia Creek	An independent corps of civilians organized—numbering about 300 men
June 27, 1863 to Sept. 12, 1863	Gettysburg (and later)	Meade	Baltimore and Ohio; Western Maryland; Cumberland Valley; Franklin; Hanover Branch; Northern Central; Gettysburg; Manassas Gap; Orange and Alexandria	The newly-organized construction corps, consisting entirely of Negro "contrabands," under white leadership, performed brilliantly at Gettysburg

H
MILITARY RAILROADING 1832-1861

The use of railroads in warfare had been publicly discussed
some thirty years before the outbreak of the Civil War. In 1832
was published *A Treatise upon Railroads Considered in Relation
to the Defence of a Country* by Lame and Clapeyron. Later, discussions on the same subject appeared in the Darmstadt *Gazette
Militaire* (1840) and in the French *Journal des Sciences Mili-
taires* (1842). But such discussions were of a theoretical nature
and it was not until a genuine war broke out that practical studies
could be made. The Crimean War presented, for the first time,
such an opportunity, or rather it enabled the French war department to elaborate a system which was in good working order in
1859 during the Italian War.* In an article entitled "The Military Use of Railways" in the *Pall Mall* Gazette, a British author
pointed out that the tramway from Balaclava to Sebastopol was of
much use to the British Army in the Crimea, but it was during the
French campaign in Italy that the uses of the railway in military
operations were first illustrated in a striking manner.

The dismayed Austrians, looking down from the heights of
Montebello, beheld train after train arriving in the plain be-
neath, each disgorging hundreds of French soldiers, and then
darting off for more.**

I
U. S. REGULATIONS FOR THE TRANSPORT OF HORSES
BY RAIL

The regulations as laid down in Roeliff Brinkerhoff's *The Volunteer Quartermaster* provided that horses should be placed in
railroad cars as compactly as possible to prevent their turning
around or lying down. Bottoms of cars were covered with a foot

* Railroads in War", *The United States Service Magazine,* Vol. 1, pp.
271–272.
** *The United States Army and Navy Journal and Gazette of the Regular and Volunteer Forces,* Vol. III, No. 9, p. 142.

of hay or straw. Shoes were removed from the hind feet but the fore feet remained shod. Horses were placed in the cars by filling up the ends of the cars first, and facing the animals in the opposite direction from that in which they were led aboard the cars. Then the four horses in the center of the car could be led straight to their places. All horses were tied short.

From thirteen and fifteen horses could be placed in each car, and a sufficient number of men accompanied each shipment to care for the horses and make sure no accidents occurred in the horse cars. These men were equipped with hatchets, saws, and nails to replace planks which became knocked off, and to extricate horses' feet which got caught between the planking.

Horses were not to stay in the cars more than twelve hours, without being taken out, watered, fed, and rested for a twelve-hour period before continuing on their journey. Stations were designated along the rail route about twelve hours apart, to insure that these essential details could be carried out.

In contrast to the lack of specific instructions for rail movement of cavalry early in the war, the artillery arm was more fortunate. In 1860, John Gibbon's *The Artillerist's Manual* was published. In this excellent manual precise instructions were laid down for the transport by rail of field artillery—horses, guns, and men.*

J
STANTON'S RELATIONSHIPS WITH FEDERAL OFFICERS

Many officers have left us their impressions of Stanton. Two examples are illustrative of many. Surgeon John H. Brinton, an officer who served with great ability, came to the notice of Stanton because of the Surgeon's friendship with Surgeon General Hammond whose military career the Secretary had successfully ruined. Brinton tells us that Stanton looked upon him as a friend of Hammond and this, in Stanton's view "was criminal, for . . . [Hammond] had differed in his opinion from the Secretary . . . In my judgment," said Brinton, "The Secretary looked upon men from his own peculiar standpoint. He was, I think, an honest man, and patriotic, but very strong in his own convictions. Believing himself to be right, he regarded all those who differed in

* Gibbon, John, *The Artillerist's Manual,* pp. 423–430, New York, 1860.

opinion from his as wrong thinkers, and wrong-doers, criminals, in fact, and that it was his duty as Secretary of War to punish them, when he conveniently could."[1]

The second incident is typical of the meanness of Stanton—and is one of several which showed his unconscious sense of inferiority and hostility towards the *combat* soldier, as well as his inexcusable tendency to jump at conclusions.

A colonel in the famous Iron Brigade had been severely wounded in battle. The Colonel bought a new uniform during his convalescence and "as soon as he could walk, he went with great difficulty, leaning on two canes, to pay his respects to the Honorable Secretary of War." The office of the Secretary was, as usual, crowded, and the Colonel patiently waited for his turn to be received. As the Colonel approached, the Secretary, with a glance at the new coat and bright brass buttons, blustered out as only Mr. Stanton could, "What in H..l and d..nation are you doing in Washington? Why don't you go to where you are needed?" Colonel Cutler answered, "If I had not been shot and a fool, I would never have come here. Good day, Mr. Secretary."[2]

Defenders of Stanton insist that his ruthless handling of importunate office seekers and inefficient officers was necessary for a vigorous prosecution of the Federal war effort. It is essential, therefore, in understanding Haupt's contribution, to be completely aware of Stanton's attitude and actions towards the new services which, potentially at least, were capable of hastening a Federal victory.

Most students of the Civil War period are fully aware of the fact that the North came up with certain innovations or improvisations in military science which, if completely and sensibly exploited, would have shortened the war by months if not years. It was Stanton's duty and moral obligation, as Secretary of War, to use those services whose value had been amply demonstrated, so far as his authority and capabilities would permit.

Let us examine, first of all, the status of Stanton's authority with respect to the new services. It is commonly conceded that Stanton possessed great power, both as an individual and as a cabinet officer, to utilize the various services which came under his control as Secretary of War.

Stanton insisted on maintaining control of two critical media in the war effort—the railroads and the telegraph lines. This control was necessary but even here Stanton's fondness for interference was constantly apparent. He often bypassed Meigs and dealt with such officers as McCallum directly. As with the military telegraph, the Military Railroads were absolutely independent of all control outside of Stanton's own will, including even that of the President. When Stanton desired to inaugurate a new program he secretly sent out a trusted agent to investigate and report. These agents were frequently sent to the front on missions not stated nor even reported upon in writing. Among such men were Anson Stager, C. A. Dana, Meigs, P. H. Watson, and even Haupt himself (while he was still in the Secretary's favor).[3] Men like Major A. E. H. Johnson, in charge of telegrams, who never opened his mouth or permitted a document to leave his hands, gave constant support to Stanton. Better known were such men as William P. Wood, the superintendent of the Old Capitol Prison, and General L. C. Baker of the Secret Service, whose role in the pursuit of Booth is illustrative of Stanton's employment of favorites and his sub rosa methods of operation.

As soon as Stanton was appointed Secretary of War, he had the entire military telegraph headquarters placed in an office next to his own. On February 25, 1862, by his order, military possession was taken of all telegraph lines, and communications not expressly authorized were forbidden. Stanton ruled the military telegraph service with an iron hand.[4] It must be emphasized that the peculiar status given by Stanton to the United States Military Telegraph prevented it from receiving full recognition as a military organization, and after the war prevented its survivors from obtaining a pensionable status. Even in the midst of an active campaign Stanton was arbitrary in his control of the telegraph lines. On the very day that Fredericksburg was fought, Haupt informed Burnside that the rail schedule must be maintained since "we can seldom get the use of the wire, even to give orders for trains."[5]

One of the most promising of the new services in the Federal Army was the Signal Corps. Grant himself pointed out that the services rendered by Colonel Albert Myer in organizing the Signal Corps of the Army was of great value to the service. Indicating that he had never heard it doubted that Myer was the originator of the whole signal service of the Federal Army, Grant added: Why he was displaced as Chief Signal Officer I never knew.[6] The idea of motion telegraphy as inaugurated in both the Federal Army and Navy originated with Myer, who was later organizer of the United States and International Storm Signal Service. On September 18, 1863, Myer was appointed Signal Officer of the Army but because of a disagreement with Stanton was relieved from his position on November 10, 1863. His successor, W. J. L. Nicodemus, on December 26, 1864, was dismissed from the service for publishing the Annual Report of the Signal Corps without "knowledge or sanction of the Secretary of War."[7]

Stanton's unfortunate inflexibility toward new ideas and inventions cost his country dear. It was Lincoln, not his Secretary, who welcomed new ideas and weapons in the Ordnance Department. An inventor had written a letter describing his invention to Stanton but suspecting that the Secretary "threw it into the fire" he appealed to Lincoln. His guess as to Stanton's disposition of his letter was a shrewd one; just a month before, Stanton had said of another inventor's letter: "It might as well be put in the fire." Still another inventor, Joseph Francis, had devised a successful lifeboat and an amphibious pontoon wagon. Francis had been knighted by Czar Alexander II and Emperor Napoleon III for his inventions and services. Francis offered his pontoons to the United States but the War Department would do nothing for him. Lincoln tried to open a way for the inventor but Stanton obstinately refused to do anything.[8]

As early as January 24, 1862, the month he took office, Stanton was authorized by Lincoln to make "some changes" in the Ordnance Department for "success of the military operations and the safety of the Country." But "the old fogy Ripley" (James W. Ripley, Chief of Ordnance), who combatted all new ideas in the fabrication of firearms, artillery and projectiles, was not removed for several months. There was disagreement between Lincoln and Stanton over Ripley's successor. Colonel Ramsay had long been *persona non grata* to Stanton. Much of this disagreement arose from Ramsay's action just after Second Bull Run, when Stanton in a panic ordered all arsenal stores to be shipped to New York immediately. Fully aware of the disastrous effect which such an order would have on Federal morale, Ramsay deliberately disobeyed it at the risk of his career. Lincoln himself thanked Ramsay warmly for taking such a risk. The weapons thus kept available were on hand for McClellan in his Antietam campaign two weeks later. Now that Lincoln favored Ramsay as Chief of Ordnance, Stanton, professing to have no confidence in the man, insisted that one of the Secretary's favorites be made Ramsay's principal assistant and the real chief in all but name. Stanton had been successful in a similar arrangement in the Adjutant General's Office. Stanton's plan worked perfectly. In February 1864, Ramsay disagreed with his "assistant" on an endorsement and the assistant tendered his resignation. Stanton now taught Ramsay his place, first by vetoing every name which Ramsay suggested as a replacement for his assistant, and then by giving Ramsay just one week in which to make up with his assistant or be relieved from command. On September 12, 1864, Ramsay was relieved of his command and transferred to an unimportant inspecting assignment.[9]

Certainly one of the services whose potentialities were great in the early years of the War was the Federal balloon service. Admittedly, much of the trouble was the traditional professional soldier's dislike or contempt for civilians serving with the Army. The chief of the balloon corps, "Colonel" Lowe, had hoped initially to organize a balloon corps as a military branch. He applied for a commission, but all that the powers that were would do was to grant him the courtesy title of Colonel without the authority of rank. Consequently, he was subject to every young and inexperienced lieutenant or captain who for the time being was placed in charge of the balloon corps. Lowe wrote the Secretary of War, urging the reorganization of the corps along military lines, but the Secretary never acted on his suggestion. Thus was a great opportunity lost. Nearly seventy years before the French had designed a system of military aeronautics that shames the Federal procedure by contrast. Federal balloons had demonstrated their value and Stanton, as war secretary, should have insisted that their employment be continued. However, shortly before Gettysburg, the balloon train was ordered to Washington, and Federal balloons were not to be used again during the war.[10]

But much more serious were Stanton's relations with the U.S. Sanitary Commission and the Medical Department of the Army. At the outbreak of hostilities the Army's medical facilities and leadership were antiquated. The newly organized civilian organization known as the U.S. Sanitary Commission was outspoken in its condemnation of the inept ambulance system and other serious flaws in the Army's medical service. Largely through the Commission's influence, the youthful William A. Hammond was appointed Surgeon General of the Army. But the Commission's influence at the War Department was nil and Stanton warned Hammond to beware of the Commission, one of whose leaders has left us with the following appraisal of the Secretary: "I am sorry to say that the impression of Stanton left on my own mind is that of a man with a brain in a very dangerous state of irritability, and one who in the use of his vast power forgets the rights and the position of his peers who chance to be in private life."[11] Some observers believed that Stanton's outbursts of rage were akin to madness.[12] Under Hammond's direction an extensive hospital building program was carried out and the Medical Department was thoroughly reorganized. A system of administration which had functioned for an army of less than twenty thousand men was expanded to meet "the requirement of a Department called upon to minister to the myriad wants of a million men."[13]

Typically enough, Stanton soon found fault with his Surgeon General. Hammond was not the type to fawn or flatter but insisted on improvement, especially in the system of evacuating wounded from the battlefield. Due to the lack of an efficient ambulance corps, hundreds of wounded men lay on the battlefield of Second Bull Run, literally dying of starvation and neglect. Just adopt *some* system pleaded Hammond. But no matter what Hammond suggested, he could not make his point since he still relied on the Commission and thereby gained Stanton's unrelenting distrust and contempt. Stanton was asked why, since the Medical Department and the whole army depended so much on the Santiary Commission, he opposed the Commission so much. "Well," said the Secretary, "the fact is the Commission wanted Hammond to be Surgeon-General, and I did not. I did my best with the President and with the Military Committee of the Senate, but the Commission beat me, and got Hammond appointed.

I'm not used to being beaten and don't like it, and therefore am hostile to the Commission."[14] His hostility also included Hammond. In July 1863, Stanton appointed a committee to investigate the Medical Department, and a month later he received the Surgeon Genral with a cordial handshake and sent him off on an "inspection tour." On January 17, 1864, Hammond was placed under arrest and two days later tried on charges of "disorders and neglects to the prejudice of order and discipline, conduct unbecoming an officer and gentleman." The trial was a travesty of justice. According to the review of the case, Hammond was involved in a "criminal spoilation of the Government treasury" and by his purchase of inferior medical supplies he compromised the health and lives of sick and wounded soldiers."[15] After some very questionable "evidence" from prejudiced witnesses, the court pronounced Hammond guilty of all charges. Although temporarily in disgrace, Hammond's fame is secure today. He did much to establish the Army Medical Museum, he recommended an army medical school as early as 1862, he organized nurses and cooks in an overall military medical system. According to the U.S. Sanitary Commission, Hammond brought to his office "vigour, courage and humanity." In 1879, Congress restored his rank.

NOTES, APPENDIX J

1. Brinton, John H., *Personal Memoirs*, p. 310.
2. Dawes, Rufus R., *Service with the Sixth Wisconsin Volunteers*, p. 77.
3. Flower, p. 358.
4. This was due both to military necessity and Stanton's character.
5. Haupt to Burnside, December 13, 1862. *Official Records*, Series I, Vol. 21, p. 850.
6. Brown, J. Willard, *The Signal Corps, U.S.A. in the War of the Rebellion*, pp. 167–168.
7. *Ibid.*, p. 164.
8. Bruce, Robert V., *Lincoln and the Tools of War*, pp. 77, 269.
9. *Ibid.*, pp. 265–266; 275–277.
10. This was unquestionably one of the blunders of the war.
11. H. S. Bellows, quoted in Maxwell, William Quentin, *Lincoln's Fifth Wheel*, pp. 142–143.
12. *Ibid.*, p. 343.

13. *Defense of Brig. Genl. Wm. A. Hammond, Surgeon General U.S. Army*, p. 6.
14. Maxwell, p. 234.
15. *Review of the Judge Advocate General of the Case of Surgeon General Hammond* (May 17, 1864), pp. 5–6.

K
HAUPT'S CONTRIBUTIONS AS REPORTED BY A CONGRESSIONAL COMMITTEE ON MILITARY AFFAIRS, MAY 9, 1912

Military and Civil Engineer

Assistant, Norristown and Valley Railroad, Pennsylvania, 1835.
Principal assistant, Pennsylvania State Works, railroad Gettysburg to Potomac, 1836.
On construction of York and Wrightsville Railroad, Pennsylvania 1840.
Professor civil engineering and mathematics, Pennsylvania College 1844–1847.
Superintendent, chief engineer and director Pennsylvania Railroad Co. 1847–1856.
Chief engineer, Southern Railroad (Georgia-Mississippi) 1852–1853.
Chief engineer, and contractor, Troy and Greenfield Railroad and Hoosac Tunnel, 1856–1862.
Director and Chief of Military Railroads, rank of brigadier general, 1862–1863.
Chief engineer, Shenandoah Valley Railroad, 1870.
General Manager, Richmond & Danville Railroad, 1872–1876.
Chief engineer, Seaboard Pipe Line (Pennsylvania-Maryland) 1876–1878.
Consulting engineer Hydrogen Co., New York, 1880–81.
General Manager of Northern Pacific Railroad 1881–1885.
President Dakota & Great Southern Railroad 1884.
President General Compressed Air and Power Co. 1892.
President National Nutrient Co. 1899–1905.

Author

Hints on Bridge Construction, 1841.

General Theory of Bridge Construction, 1846.

Report on General Systems and Policy for the Penna. RR, 1849.

Plans for the improvement of the Ohio River, 1855.

Numerous Reports on RR and Economics and State Tax.

Military Bridges & Expedients for Passing Obstacles, 1864.

Tunneling by Machinery, 1867.

Hydraulic and Mechanical Principles of Pipe Lines, 1876.

Compressed Air and Street Railways Motors, 1879.

The Holly System of Steam Heating, 1879.

Plans for the Radical Improvement of the Ohio, 1880.

Long Distance Transmission of Power, 1895.

Compressed Air for Suburban Traction, etc., 1897.

Numerous Reports on Food Products and Processes, with balanced rations for Army & Navy services and for domestic & hospital uses, etc., 1899–1905.

Reminiscences of his Civil War Records, 1901.

Numerous fiscal, scientific, economic, and social publications for improving the conditions of the working classes.

Inventor

Discovered a method of "Representing strains of geometrical solids; deflections by parabolic areas; and the variable pressures at various parts of beams by the corresponding ordinates of plane curves". 1840.

Invented the improved lattice bridge truss. 1840.

Invented the first automatic-feed, reciprocating power drill, designed for work at the Hoosac Tunnel, 1858.

Blanket boats and devices for crossing rivers, 1862.

Apparatus for the long-distance transmission of oil, 1876.

Automatic removable wickets for the improvement of streams, 1879.

Compressed air motors for municipal traffic. 1879.

Apparatus for the long-distance transmission of power at high pressure, 1895.

Numerous devices for the concentration of the waste products of the dairy, for balanced rations and for subsistence, 1899–1905.

Member of numerous learned societies.

BIBLIOGRAPHY

PRIMARY SOURCES

U. S. Congress, Committee on the Conduct of the War. *Report,* 8 volumes, Washington, D.C., 1863–1866.

U. S. Congress House *Report* No. 682 62nd Congress, 2nd Session.

U. S. War Department, Adjutant General's Department. *General Orders,* 1861–1865.

U. S. War Department, Annual Reports of Secretary of War 1861–1866.

U. S. War Department, Report of Brevet Brigadier General D. C. McCallum, May 26, 1866.

U. S. War Department, Annual Reports of Quartermaster General, 1861–1866.

U.S. Quartermaster General's Department, U. S. Army, *Instructions for Transport and Erection of Military Wire Suspension-Bridge Equipage,* Washington, D. C. 1862.

Official Records of the Union and Confederate Armies, 128 volumes 1880–1901.

Official Records of the Union and Confederate Navies in the War of the Rebellion, 26 volumes, 1894–1922.

Manuscripts (Library of Congress) Haupt order book, Lincoln papers, Stanton papers, Diary of B. F. Peterson (courtesy of Dr. Robert W. Chamberlain) 2nd Maine Battery 1864–1865.

NEWSPAPERS AND PERIODICALS

Boston Evning Transcript, November 17, 1862.
Colburn's United Service Magazine (London) 1861–1865.
Harpers Weekly 1861–1865.
Journal, Royal United Service Institution, 1861–1865.
National Intelligencer, July 12, 1861.
New York Times, 1861–1865.
New York Tribune, 1861–1865.
Railroad Gazette, December 22, 1905.
Scientific American 1861–1865.
The United States Service Magazine, 1864–1866.
Transactions, American Society of Civil Engineers, Vol. XXXIX, (1898).
United States Army and Navy Gazette, 1863–1865.

SECONDARY SOURCES

ABDILL, GEO. B., *Civil War Railroads,* Seattle, Washington, 1961.
ALLEN, RICHARD SANDERS, *Covered Bridges of the Middle Atlantic States,* Brattleboro, Vermont, 1959.
ANONYMOUS, *Defense of Brig. Genl Wm. A. Hammond, Surgeon General U. S. Army.*
Review of the Judge Advocate General of the Case of Surgeon General Hammond, May 17, 1864.
Army and Navy Official Gazette, 2 vols. Washington D. C., 1863–1865.
BARNARD, J. G. and BARRY, W. F., *Report of the Engineer and Artillery Operations of the Army of the Potomac from its Organization to the Close of the Peninsular Campaign,* New York, 1864.
BARNEY, CHESTER, *Recollections of Field Service with the Twentieth Iowa Infantry Volunteers,* Davenport, Iowa, 1865.
BATES, DAVID HOMER, *Lincoln in the Telegraph Office,* New York 1907.
BIGELOW, JOHN JR., *The Principles of Strategy,* Philadelphia, 1894.

BOYLE, JOHN R., *Soldiers True* (111th Penna. Inf.), New York 1903.

BRINKERHOFF, ROELIFF, *The Volunteer Quartermaster*, New York 1865.

BRINTON, JOHN H., Personal Memoirs, New York 1914.

BROWN, J. WILLARD, *The Signal Corps, U.S.A. in the War of the Rebellion*, Boston, 1896.

BRUCE, ROBERT V., *Lincoln and the Tools of War*, Indianapolis, 1956.

BUEL, C. C. and JOHNSON, R. U., *Battles and Leaders of the Civil War*, 4 vols., New York, 1887.

BUFFUM, FRANCIS H., *History of the 14th New Hampshire Infantry*, Boston, 1882.

BUTLER, BENJAMIN F., *Private and Official Correspondence of General Benjamin F. Butler*, 5 vols. Privately printed, 1917.

CALLAN, JOHN F., *Military Laws of the United States*, Phila. 1863.

CAMPBELL, E. G., "The United States Military Railroads 1862–1865," *Journal*, American Military History Foundation, Summer 1938, Vol. II No. 2.

CHANAL, DE V., *The American Army in the War of Secession*, Leavenworth, Kansas, 1894.

CLARK, CHARLES T., *Opdycke Tigers* (125th Ohio Infantry), Columbus, Ohio, 1895.

COLLINS, GEO. K., *Memoirs of the 149th Reg't N.Y. Vol. Inf.*, Syracuse 1891.

COX, JACOB B., *Military Reminiscences of the Civil War*, 2 vol. New York, 1900.

CROFFUT, W. A. (editor) *Fifty Years in Camp and Field* (*Diary of Major General E. A. Hitchcock*) New York 1909.

CULLUM, GEORGE W., *Description of a System of Military Bridges with India-Rubber Pontoons*, New York 1849.

———*System of Military Bridges in Use by the United States Army*, New York (first edition 1863; second edition 1869)

———*Biographical Register of the Officers and Graduates of the U. S. Military Academy*, 2 vols. New York 1868.

DAWES, RUFUS R., *Service with the Sixth Wisconsin Volunteers*, Marietta, Ohio, 1890.

DENNETT, TYLER (editor) *Lincoln and the Civil War in the Diaries and Letters of John Hay,* New York, 1939.

Dictionary of American Biography, Vol. III.

DOANE, A. A., *The Doane Family,* Boston, 1902.

DOUGLAS, SIR HOWARD, (General) *An Essay on the Principles and Construction of Military Bridges and the Passage of Rivers in Military Operations,* 3rd Edition, London, 1853.

DUANE, J. C., Captain, *Manual for Engineer Troops,* New York 1862.

FARLEY, PORTER, "Reminiscences of the 140th Regiment, New York Volunteer Infantry" *Rochester in the Civil War,* Blake McKelvey editor, Rochester, N. Y., 1944.

FISH, CARL R. "The Northern Railroads in 1861," *American Historical Review,* Vol. XXII, July 1917.

FLOWER, FRANK A., *Edwin McMasters Stanton,* Akron, Ohio, 1905.

FLOYD, FRED C., *History of the Fortieth (Mozart) Regiment, New York Volunteers,* Boston, 1909.

GIBBON, JOHN, *The Artillerist's Manual,* New York, 1860.

GRANT, U. S., *Personal Memoirs,* 2 vols., New York, 1885.

HAMERSLY, T. H. S., *Complete Regular Army Register . . . 1779–1879,* Washington, D. C., 1880.

HAUPT, HERMAN, *Reminiscences,* Limited autographed edition, Milwaukee, 1901.

————*General Theory of Bridge Construction,* New York, 1853.

————*Military Bridges,* New York, 1864.

HAYDON, F. STANSBURY, *Aeronautics in the Union and Confederate Armies,* Vol. I, Baltimore 1941.

HAYS, GILBERT ADAMS, *Under the Red Patch: Story of the Sixty Third Regiment Pennsylvania Volunteers,* Pittsburgh, 1908.

HAZEN, W. B. (Major General) *The School and the Army in Germany and France,* New York, 1872.

HINMAN, WILBUR F., Lt. Col., (65th Ohio Vol. Inf.) *Corporal Si Klegg and His "Pard,"* Cleveland, Ohio, 1887.

JONES, VIRGIL C., *The Civil War at Sea,* Vol. I, New York, 1960.

KAMM, SAMUEL RICHEY, *The Civil War Career of Thomas A. Scott,* Philadelphia, 1940.

LEECH, MARGARET, *Reveille In Washington,* New York 1941.

LIVERMORE, THOMAS L., *Numbers and Losses in the Civil War in America, 1861–1865,* Boston 1900.

LONN, ELLA, *Foreigners in the Union Army and Navy,* Baton Rouge, 1951.

MAXWELL, WILLIAM QUENTIN, *Lincoln's Fifth Wheel,* New York, 1956.

MCCLELLAN, GEORGE B., *McClellan's Own Story,* New York 1887.

MCKELVEY, BLAKE (editor) *Rochester in the Civil War,* Rochester, New York, 1944.

MEADE, GEORGE, *The Life and Letters of George Gordon Meade,* 2 vols. New York, 1913.

MENEELEY, A. HOWARD, *The War Department 1861,* New York 1928.

MILLER, FRANCIS TREVELYAN, *The Photographic History of the Civil War,* 10 vol., New York, 1911.

NICOLAY, JOHN G. and HAY, JOHN, *Abraham Lincoln,* 10 vols., New York 1890.

NORTON, OLIVER WILLCOX, *Army Letters 1861–1865,* Chicago, 1903.

O'BRIEN, JOHN EMMET, *Telegraphing In Battle,* Scranton, Pa., 1910.

OTIS, GEORGE A., *A Report on a Plan for Transporting Wounded Soldiers by Railway in Time of War,* Washington, 1875.

PARKER, DAVID B., *A Chautauqua Boy in '61 and Afterward,* Boston 1912.

PRATT, EDWIN A., *The Rise of Rail-Power in War and Conquest 1833–1914,* Phila., 1916.

PRATT, FLETCHER, *Stanton: Lincoln's Secretary of War,* New York 1953.

RAYMOND, HENRY J., *The Life and Public Services of Abraham Lincoln . . . ,* New York, 1865.

RICE, ALLEN T., *Reminiscences of Abraham Lincoln . . . ,* New York, 1888.

SANDBURG, CARL, *Abraham Lincoln: The War Years,* Vol. 1 & 2, New York 1943.

SHERIDAN, PHILIP, *Personal Memoirs,* 2 vols. New York, 1888.

SHERMAN, WILLIAM T., *Personal Memoirs,* 2 vols. New York, 1892.

SIMONS, EZRA D., *The One Hundred and Twenty-Fifth New York State Volunteers,* New York 1888.

SMITHE, GEORGE C., *Glimpses,* Ypsilanti, Michigan, 1887.

SPARKS, DAVID S. (Editor), *Inside Lincoln's Army,* New York 1964.

STACKPOLE, EDWARD J., *From Cedar Mountain to Antietam,* Harrisburg, 1959.

————*Drama on the Rappahannock: The Fredericksburg Campaign,* Harrisburg, 1957.

STEVENS, GEORGE T., *Three Years in the Sixth Corps,* Albany, 1866.

SUMMERS, FESTUS P., *The Baltimore and Ohio in the Civil War,* N.Y. 1939.

TREMAIN, HENRY EDWIN, *Two Days of War,* New York, 1905.

TYLER, MASON W., *Recollections of the Civil War,* New York, 1912.

UPTON, EMORY, *The Military Policy of the United States,* 3rd impression, Washington, 1911.

WEBER, THOMAS, *The Northern Railroads in the Civil War 1861–1865,* New York, 1952.

WEIGLEY, RUSSELL E., *Quartermaster General of the Union Army: A Biography of M. C. Meigs,* New York, 1959.

WELLES, GIDEON, *Diary of Gideon Welles,* 3 vols., Boston 1911.

WORMELEY, KATHARINE, *The Other Side of War with the Army of the Potomac,* Boston, 1889.

————*The United States Sanitary Commission,* Boston, 1863.

INDEX

DATE DUE

9/2			
GAYLORD			PRINTED IN U.S.A.